BREAST LEFT UNSAID

a true and uncensored story
of survival

JUDE CALLIRGOS

Breast Left Unsaid

by Jude Callirgos

Published by:
Green Acres Press
Redding, CT

Cover by Barbara Fisher of Levan Fisher Design
Author photo by Kristen Jensen
Interior layout by Victoria Wright, Bookmark Services

ISBN: 9781479115440
BISAC:
BIOGRAPHY.AUTOBIOGRAPHY / Personal Memoirs BIO 028000
SELF HELP/ Motivational & Inspirational SEL021000
BODY MIND & SPIRIT / Healing General OCC011000

True stories have real people in them and most of the names in the book are real. I usually indicate that I've substituted a name, but in a few cases I've simply changed or excluded names for the sake of privacy.

For more information: breastleftunsaid.com

Every heart, every heart
to love will come
but like a refugee.

Ring the bells that still can ring
Forget your perfect offering
There is a crack, a crack in everything
That's how the light gets in.

Leonard Cohen

JANUARY 9, 2006

This past summer I went for my regular mammogram. The radiologist told me I should come back in six months because "there's something in there we want to keep an eye on."

Fair enough. But now that I am in the throes of a gut-wrenching divorce, this follow-up appointment, though grossly overshadowed by the tourniquet around my heart, is a big pain in my ass. I am incredibly busy at work. I am frantic about feuding lawyers and desperately trying to keep my cool at home to keep from get sucked back into a life I don't want anymore and probably haven't wanted for years, and the mercury has plummeted below freezing. I hate the cold.

But it dawns on me today, in my forty-sixth year, that I've never truly minded going to doctors. It's just not a fear of mine—nor is it anything other than maintenance to me—although today I feel terribly alone walking into the eerily lit mammography chamber. A young radiology assistant with a hint of a Spanish accent is trying her best not to hurt me, gently coaxing my middle-aged breasts into her torture device with soothing tones, so she probably doesn't notice that there is an errant tear forming in my right eye, quickly followed by a runaway on the left, as I abruptly realize that I am going to be quite alone with this body, the one that's not looking so hot in this oversized smock get-up, for a long, long time. This is my choice of course, but a sad revelation nonetheless.

"Okay. Just hold your breath, almost there...hang on. Got it!"
"Thank god."
"Jeez, you've got dense breasts."
"I prefer perky."
"Yes, ma'am, for a forty-six-year old lady, they are very perky!" she laughs a bit and describes her own enormous breasts to me, engaging in that peculiar boob-bonding thing that women do. And then, suddenly, she is quiet.

1

"Uh-oh," I hear her whisper. For my benefit, she says louder, "Okay. Just one more for me, honey, okay? I'm so sorry, I don't think I got that last one exactly right."

"Lucky me."

"Hang in there, sweetie," she says as she mashes my left boob for the third time and I hold my breath, turning blue waiting for the all clear.

And that was the seemingly mundane verbal exchange that heralded the end of my old life and the beginning of my new life. I just didn't know it at the time. She wanted a do-over on that last slide because she had seen something she didn't like and wanted a closer look.

I had no inkling of this whatsoever. I just stared down at my stupid pink smock and my breast that now looked like a thick piece of pita bread, praying for this visit to be over so I could go home, close the door to my bedroom and drink cheap Pinot Grigio out of a beer mug while watching Comedy Central from my half-empty bed. Due to recent events, my escape-fantasy standards had been dramatically lowered.

Even when the head radiologist called me in to his office minutes later to show me the "tiny calcifications" on my milk ducts on the mammogram film and counseled me to come back immediately for a biopsy, the threat of disease still had not registered. Despite the fact that my seventy-five-year-old mother had, just one year prior, been diagnosed with ductal carcinoma in situ, i.e., breast cancer, and underwent a lumpectomy and radiation, I was busy trying to figure out which meetings I was going to have to postpone so I could have this damned biopsy. I was annoyed. It was just one more thing that I didn't have time for. Besides which, as I mentally perused my overflowing Personal Life Plate while staring at an x-ray of my left breast, there was nothing on that plate that even appealed to me anymore. Life was already hard and this is making it just that much harder. Dammit.

JANUARY 10

As a human resources executive based in Stamford, Connecticut, with my mothership in Silicon Valley, I had ample flexibility to move my schedule around for something as serious-sounding as a biopsy, although I agonized over which meetings to move. The local hospital in Danbury said they would take me any time, as long as it was today, so I just had to call and let them know I was coming. The uncharacteristic sense of urgency should have been a tip-off.

At the hospital, I sat in the waiting room with my pink Candie's slippers, gray yoga pants, and an oversized sweatshirt because I was instructed to be "comfortable" and to me this was comfort. The only thing missing was my mug of wine and an episode of *The Daily Show* with Jon Stewart. However, I didn't know I was going to be sitting in a waiting room with five other women and their concerned and attentive partners—a glaring reminder that I was the only woman in the Pepto-Bismol pink room without one. I knew I didn't want the person I was divorcing to be there. But it would have been nice to not be so, well, by myself.

Just as I had never really minded going to doctors, I've also never had any serious hang-ups about the majority of my body; in fact my self-image from the waist down is pretty darned positive. I don't diet because I've never needed to, nor do my siblings. The genes my parents handed down to us include an above-average intellect, shapely legs, thick hair, and fantastic metabolisms, so we never focused on weight-watching or body image while growing up, and we were the envy of all the kids who did.

Waist-up is another story. As a young girl I had terrible acne, to the point where dermatology visits became mandatory. Braces for four long teenage years corrected a pronounced, and some might say comical, overbite. And I watched helplessly from my 32AA Maidenform trainer as my best girlfriend's breasts grew to 36Cs and beyond. My friends used to tell me I had a body like Cher to try to make me feel better, but it didn't, and I didn't actually grow breasts that garnered any appreciable notice until my twenties—so I coveted them.

Therefore, despite the fact that I actually morphed into a fairly attractive woman with clear skin, even teeth, and long, straight thick hair that reached below my average-sized, still-perky breasts, there are, regrettably, still days when I revert back to the ugly, awkward, flat-chested girl being snickered at by all the cute boys and completely ignored at parties, until I want to lunge for the door to keep from crying. This was one of those times.

When the nurse finally called my name I was relieved. I followed her down a long hallway while she flatly instructed me where to change and how long the procedure should take. "Take off everything from the waist up and put on the smock hanging in the dressing room, opening to the front. You can leave on your pants and socks. Meet me in this room when you're done," she said as she pointed to where I could change. She disappeared behind another door. When I was done I knocked on that door before entering and saw her and two other assistants maneuvering around various work-stations; she was on a computer with a large screen, another was setting up an instrument table and the third, I guessed, was the concierge, as she was the only one smiling. The concierge greeted me and tried very hard to make idle conversation having nothing to do with this procedure and was speaking to me in the manner that I speak to my dog, Sophie, when she's been a good girl. It felt very forced and weird.

The only other object in the room is a long, metal surgical-looking table much like the one at the vet that even Sophie hates with a passion. I'm beginning to understand why. Only this table has, I kid you not, two holes cut out for my breasts to hang through. I am told to lie face down and rest my arms above my head and then my left breast is secured with something that feels just like a mammogram vise only not quite as tight. I can't see what's happening but when the doctor comes in she barely speaks as the minions actually dimmed the lights, hushed their conversation and raised the table up about two feet so the doctor, with the LED light strapped to her forehead like a miner, can sit underneath me and take tissue samples from the comfort of a three-legged stool.

Seriously, can't we do this standing up, for god's sake? Unstylish I can handle; undignified is not normally in my repertoire. This is something out of a bad movie and I am truly disturbed at how I must look from any angle in the room. I almost pass out from the sheer humiliation.

The biopsy hurts. It hurts like hell, and then the doctor admits that she, um, missed and needs to do another. Really? Where have I heard that before? I say okay, as if I have a choice, and try to go to my happy place knowing that I am in for the same dreadful procedure a second time.

Dr. Sharpshooter numbs the area again with several shots of Novocain and then sets about to dig out a portion of my inner breast tissue in rather close proximity to the hole she had just made, which was precariously close to my nipple. I'm flinching and they warn me to "hold still"—as if I didn't know that was the goal. My arms are going numb and I am freezing. After she was done, forty-five minutes later, I sit up and look down at my left breast. My whole body shakes at the sight of the blood and bruising on my breast as it finally dawns on me that they might actually find something bad. Something dangerous.

The concierge must have read my cue because she rushes to my side and holds a fresh bandage tightly to my chest as if that act of caring alone would stop not just the bleeding but the panic, and whispers, "It's all right. You're going to be fine."

"I know," I lie. "I'm just tired."

JANUARY 11

Here's the crazy thing that divorce does to you: you become completely overwhelmed by the enormity of the pain, paperwork, and pending total life change. Hearing the results of your breast biopsy becomes the news feed at the bottom of the screen instead of the top story of the day.

My interactions with my husband were so rigid and fraught with landmines by then that I didn't even tell him I was having a biopsy. It hadn't seemed important enough to bring to the table. Whenever I had health issues he could be counted on to tell me it was psychosomatic and cheerfully ask if I'd had a fight with my mother recently. The only person who knew was my colleague Kim. Kimberly Howard was about to become my best friend in the world.

So the work day passed with the usual agita from my attorney bearing news from the front. My primary goal for the day was to prepare a complex travel itinerary to our other offices. I often work later in the day than most, because the majority of my clients are in California; the time difference lends itself to going in around nine thirty a.m. and staying late.

It is six p.m. and I'm crafting some e-mails before closing shop for the day. I have actually forgotten about the biopsies. The phone rings.

I see on caller ID that it's the hospital, so I put on my headset and take the call. I feel naked and vulnerable all over again as I swiftly reel back to lying on a metal slab with my boobs swinging beneath me like udders.

"Hello, Jude? This is Doctor Sharpshooter from Danbury Hospital." I don't recall her name because she never introduced herself.

"Oh, hi." Do doctors still make their own phone calls?

She takes a breath as if it might be hard for her to say the words. "Listen Jude, we found something in your test—" and here is where my stomach starts to lurch, "—that I'm afraid is something called ductal carcinoma in situ."

"Okay…" I hesitate so that she will tell me the rest of the story.

Quite matter-of-factly she adds that I need to find a surgeon, "and I suggest that you do it quickly; within the next few days."

She continues with some medical-speak about radiation and then oddly veers off into a series of talking points about the hospital's accommodating treatment schedule that sounds more like a commercial than instructive or reassuring next steps.

"What…" I interrupt, "are you saying, exactly?"

"Unfortunately, you have breast cancer."

I do not remember closing the call or saying good-bye or even asking any further questions. I simply took my headset off and dragged a ragged breath in and tried a long, slow, yoga exhale out to see if that might help.

It didn't.

I grabbed some colored dry-erase markers off my desk, spun my chair around and hurled them across my office. Crack! They made a good sound as they struck the whiteboard, but not what I was looking for. I really needed to throw something hard. I took the eraser, which I knew would not cause damage, but I could still really wind up and whale on it before firing it at the wall. From there, I started randomly throwing whatever I could find in my office, stopping just short of glass vases.

Then I remembered that my assistant, Hideaki, was probably still in his cube outside my office. Hideaki Watanabe is probably the coolest, most levelheaded dude in the entire company. I was privileged to have him working for me, particularly because he was such a great counter-weight to my not-so-balanced persona, which at the moment was showing signs of separating entirely from its moorings. He's the guy you talk to when you need your own personal Moment of Zen.

Did he think I had sunk to a new low in the divorce proceedings? Or that I had officially lost my mind? To his eternal credit, he slipped out and went home without letting me know that he could hear his boss's grade school tantrum in the next room:

Whack.

"Are you *kidding me!*?"

Slam. Crack.

"...like I don't have *enough* going on in my life?!"

Thud. Louder thud. Big Crack.

"Jesus Christ, this is fucking UNBELIEVABLE!"

I was not crying. I was angry, hyperventilating, and not quite clever enough to be scared yet, but contrary to the classic book by Betty Rollin, I did *not* cry first. Not one tear. I broke shit.

Something about creating physical wreckage in my office was gratifying. After several minutes, I pulled myself together and sent an instant message from my computer to Kimberly, also in Human Resources, who was traveling at the time with her sales team posse. I cannot recall the exact exchange but I know that I was frantically whining about how complicated my life already was and that *it didn't seem fair* that the biopsy wasn't clean. She wrote something in her usual social-worker tone that she had expertly applied during my last three major life crises.

The most recent barnstormer, of course, was my decision to divorce. It was not an easy choice but had been the elephant in the room for years, bellowing at us, waiting for one of us to wake up and acknowledge him. My husband struggled with so many demons it was hard to keep track, but his answer to all of life's challenges was to drink Sierra Nevada Pale Ale. Essentially, we had finally worn through the last layer of kindness and civility we had for one another. Whatever love was still there was just a nice memory of people we used to be when we cared more for the other person than ourselves, and before the demons won him over and forcibly pushed me aside one last time. This was not a mutual decision, however; I was in the unenviable position of presenting it as a fait accompli because history proved that any other approach would have resulted in something loud and hateful, just extending the misery. After his initial barking and righteous indignation subsided and the idea of a new life that didn't include me started to sink in, he agreed that it had been over for years. A sixteen-year relationship and ten-year marriage had died, taking with it countless friends, beloved family, and irreplaceable memories—yet to continue on would have been madness. Once you breathe that first breath knowing for sure that the charade is over, there is no going back.

The second crisis, a little less than two years before, was the tragic death of David, my dearest friend in the world, from a pulmonary embolism at thirty-eight. He was a wonderful husband and father and the only person on the planet I had an unconditional relationship with; full stop. We loved each other like family and spent all our time together solving life's problems large and small; talking music and literature and philosophy, and by figuring out how to make each other laugh until the proverbial milk came out our noses. He was a brilliant musician, incredibly literate, a master carpenter, and excelled at just about everything he tried to do with his hands. David was average looking and fairly overweight but had a killer smile and a set of twinkles in his blue eyes that disarmed most of his opponents. David tended to engage in human interactions strategically, like a giant game of chess. This was his

Achilles heel: people. He generally didn't like them and certainly didn't trust them—only a rare few—which sadly is not uncommon for people in Human Resources. But for some reason he liked me. I hired him as a technical recruiter; we became best friends in about a week and continued to work together and make each other think, laugh, and care deeply, for the seven years he was in my life.

Our spouses were patient with us and we sometimes worried that we appeared to be blurring the lines, but we never crossed them. Nor did we want to. This was not a physical attraction; it was a purely cerebral connection. We used to joke that we must have been siblings or star-crossed lovers in another life, but whatever the bond was between us, it was as impenetrable as it was essential. The last time I saw him I was sending him home from work.

"Good morning. Jesus, what's wrong with you?"

"What do you mean?" he said, taking off his glasses and looking at me with glassy, red-rimmed eyes.

"You look like death."

"Thanks, boss. Is this your motivational speech for today?"

"No, seriously, David, what is going on? Your skin is gray."

"Not feeling my best, but I'll be okay. I have a bunch of stuff..."

"No, you don't. You need to pack up and get yourself to a doctor. You're scaring me."

"Really, Jude..."

"Pack up. *Now*."

"Yes, ma'am."

"David? Call me when you leave the doctor's office and let me know what he says."

I was incredibly worried, because he had had several bouts of walking pneumonia since I'd known him and two years earlier, just two weeks after 9/11, he'd volunteered to clean apartments for a week at Ground Zero, in a haz-mat suit. His lungs were surely compromised and his breathing sounded labored. When he called me to let me know they found something on his lung and he needed to go back the next day for another round of tests, I was on my mobile phone driving in a sketchy part of town and kept losing the signal.

"What tests? I'll go with you!"

"It's so sweet that you worry about me, but Jude, I'll be just fine." And his voice sounded very peaceful and calm, and then he said something else that was lost forever in the static.

"I'm losing you, David!" I shouted into the phone, meaning the connection, not realizing that the last thing I said to him would be so prophetic. He was dead twenty-four hours later. On that snowy afternoon in December the shock of having to suddenly navigate the world without him forced me out into a blizzard; I walked for hours without feeling the cold, screaming at god, at him, at the wind. When I returned, my husband was at a loss as to what to do, so he chose to leave me alone in the house for the rest of the day.

I went to David's funeral and was relegated to the back of the church in the colleagues-from-work section and realized then that no one in his family, his life, really, knew, or would ever know, the depth of our relationship. I felt utterly forsaken. It was like being invisible at your own brother's funeral. At the reception in the church basement afterwards, I noticed someone who looked just like him only taller and perhaps older. I moved in his direction and extended my hand to offer my condolences, introducing myself as a friend from work.

"I'm sorry. I didn't get your name?"

"It's Jude. I was his boss."

This man grabbed me and hugged me tightly and whispered, "*You're* Jude. David talked about you all the time. He adored you." At least his brother knew. And he also knew that not many other people would understand. I saw his wife and son when I returned David's personal effects from the office to them at their home on the day after Christmas. She and I had, for the first time, a surprisingly intimate talk and she gave me a photo of David, a terrible picture, really, that I keep in my office and talk to every day.

Shortly after David passed, my father, who had been showing signs of rapid short-term memory loss and increasing tremors in his hands was, after many false starts, finally diagnosed with something called Lewy body dementia. When I read the description for this monstrous disease, I couldn't fathom how someone so kind and wonderful deserved to die this way—or *anyone*, for that matter. By all accounts, it would aggressively deconstruct his cherished mind and dismantle his motor skills in one-third the time of Alzheimer's, but he would most likely be cognizant throughout, even after he lost his power of speech. It is inhumanely destructive and incurable.

Dad is in his late seventies and is still the quiet patriarch and grounding force in our family; a reluctant entrepreneur who is a talented draftsman but always ran his own business, rather than manage the absurdities of knowing more than everyone else in the room and not being the boss. Now long retired, he is a soft-spoken soul who molted off all those layers of intense worry and stress that go along with feeding and housing a family of six, but thankfully has not lost his deadpan and always well-timed sense of humor. He is still that handsome, impeccably dressed, Paul Newman-blue-eyed man from my childhood that I looked up to, feared, and fought at every turn, but I am so enjoying his company now that we're both older and calmer and I'm not trying so hard to impress him anymore. Girls need their fathers in different ways at different times in their lives. I desperately need mine to keep being my friend and trusted counselor, so there is really no way to adjust to this kind of news. It doesn't fit anywhere. It cannot be rationalized. It just waits for me in the corner of my mind until I can allow myself to stare at it and cry undisturbed.

In just two years, the three most important men in my world, the men I depended on, needed, and loved so deeply, were effectively gone. I didn't know that a heart could have so many breaks and continue to beat.

As inconceivable as it sounds, there was a secondary personal crisis-category that is no less hideous. But maybe, because there's no room left on the front burners for sadness and loss, I could, with less raw emotion and slightly more intellectual control, deal with my mom's breast cancer. Now that she had completed treatment and appeared to be doing well, it felt less like a three-alarm blaze compared to Dad's horror show.

And finally, on a warm summer evening, we received word that my husband's estranged and unwell brother shot himself in the head with a twelve gauge shotgun in his home. He was not found for days and the police then did nothing to locate his family. We heard about it a month later from a friend of his who had worried when Bill went missing. It was nightmarish and tragic but sadly not a surprise for someone living alone with untreated mental illness and an antique gun collection. But the complex set of emotions that emerges when someone takes his own life can obscure simple grief and become an unwieldy and destructive force in their own right. I can't say that this event didn't serve as the catalyst for finally ending my marriage; there is only so much pain and suffering you can squeeze into one house, one relationship. The demons had finally run amok.

Kim was beginning to resemble one of those wobbly clown punching bags that no matter how hard you slam it keeps bouncing back up with a perfect, slightly unnatural grin on its face. She can listen, distill, and deflate most of my award-winning drama in an artful way and for some reason never sounds surprised or shocked. Her stock in trade is a veil of calm and reason that she can pull from her purse at a moment's notice and drape over even the most ludicrous sounding situations. Kim is much younger than me, somewhere in her thirties, and recently divorced; she also lives less than a mile from my house. She is robust in spirit but cautious and naturally untrusting in the manner that David was; but she plays chess much more strategically than he ever could. Not surprisingly they did *not* hit it off when they first met; but once they learned more about each other through me, they started to become fast friends. Kim was your typical blonde-haired blue-eyed high school heart-breaker right out of central casting who can still create a stir with boys of any age when she walks into a room. After she read the word *cancer* she wrote back *calling* and my phone rang instantly.

"Oh Jude, this *sucks*. I'm so sorry."

"It's DCIS. This is what my mom had."

"Oh that's right. Jeez. Okay, well, you find a surgeon and get it out of there, just like she did."

"Kim, they're talking like six weeks of radiation after the surgery. *Every day*. I barely have time to feed myself between work and the divorce and...when am I supposed to...*Christ*, I'm scheduled to leave for Paris next week!"

"One thing at a time, missy; *breathe*. Just go home—get out of there and we'll catch up tomorrow. Really sorry but I have to go back to a meeting. I just jumped out when I saw it was you calling."

"Oh, like home is so much better."

"Lock yourself in your room. Call me later if you need me."

Thinking back, I know that neither one of us knew a damn thing about this disease so we were quite neatly compartmentalizing it as something entirely manageable with a few deep breaths and some organizational skills. Relax. Find a surgeon. Get it fixed.

My new boss, Steve, was of course the first person I called after I spoke to Kim. I say "of course" because I was staring at my task list and calendar, terrified of everything I needed to do before I would be able to "take some time off to deal with this" and he would have to grant clemency for a change of schedule.

Read that again: I called my boss *before* I called my family and I was worried about meetings. Very worried.

I had coordinated these business trips with my own brand of surgical precision that allowed me to be in three of my most-beloved cities for work, and then a quick break in Napa with my dearest cousin, Julie. I was to start in Manhattan for a meeting at the Algonquin for a few days, drive home, and then fly to the Paris office for a week, head straight to San Francisco from France for a conference, and then drive into the wine hills of Sonoma for some sun, wine, and relaxation. It was a perfect marriage of work and play to help me get some distance from the depressing environs of my home. The international meetings were set up, I had arranged my itinerary to include a "serenity room" in the Paris hotel, and I had even purchased the expensive black pumps from Shoe-La-La that I'd lusted over for months so I could be the stylish American in the Rueil office! Ah yes, this trip would be the perfect diversion. By the time I called Steve, I was still planning on the New York to Paris leg of the trip and thinking about whether I could squeeze in California or not.

I am not joking. This is what was going through my head: not *life-threatening illness* but *work-threatening annoyance*. Steve zeroed right in on this insanity and in his own tactful way, let me have it.

"Oh Jude, that's unbelievable. How did they find it?"

"I had a biopsy yesterday. Well, two actually. She missed the mark with the first one," I said, as if pointing out the doctor's incompetence was in any way relevant.

"Jesus. And with all the personal stuff you've got on top of this...my god. It just doesn't seem fair. Not to be flip, but who did you piss off?"

"Not sure, but they must have a bigger job than me."

And then I immediately jumped back into logistics. "Listen, I think I can still get everything done on the Paris trip and I guess I'll go to San Francisco, but they told me tonight to find a surgeon."

"Well, then that's what you do. Forget about the trips, Jude. You should just—"

"Oh, it will be okay. I'm sure I can find someone and then head to Paris after our New York conference."

"I think you need to think about the fact that your body is trying to tell you something."

"What?"

"I mean, the trips can wait, Jude. You need to see a doctor. Have you told your family?"

"No."

(Pause) "Okay, well maybe you should start there. You need to get some support around you."

"I'm *okay*. Really, Steve."

And at that precise moment, I was. My mother's lumpectomy and radiation less than a year before was successful by all accounts and she seemed to be completely back to normal. Mom lives about an hour away and my younger sister Jodi lives less than a mile from her, so she ferried Mom to radiation every day for six weeks following her surgery. I sent flowers and called. But I didn't really show up for the hard stuff. It's not like I didn't worry; I just didn't let it take up too much of my time. As much as I loved them both, Dad's dementia and Mom's cancer made driving to see them in Glastonbury, Connecticut, a struggle because I selfishly saw everything through the prism of my own sense of loss and discomfort. Besides, I told myself, Jodi knows how to handle this stuff much better than I. So I listened carefully for two phrases from her, "surgery went well" and "doing great in radiation" and didn't bother to learn a damn thing about the disease. Jodi also shared that things were getting so tough for Mom as a caregiver that she actually looked forward to getting out of the house for her treatments; got all dressed and put lipstick on like she was going out for a nice lunch instead of to a hospital for a blast of radiation. How bad could it be?

Therefore, when breast cancer was being scribbled in my medical chart, I was convinced that it could be "managed" like I micro-manage everything else in my life. The fact that I didn't want to worry anyone or, really, tell anyone else, I felt was rather smart and selfless of me. I had already burdened enough people close to me with the whole messy divorce scenario and everything that came before it. There didn't seem to be any reason why I couldn't find a surgeon, keep this from my colleagues, rearrange my schedule, squeeze in some hospital time, and then do that radiation thing when I got back; oh, and call my divorce attorney to make sure it didn't conflict with court dates. It was pure lunacy, of course, but it was making perfect sense to me at the time.

"....and Steve, I'd appreciate if you not tell the team. I'd like to keep this quiet for now. It would just be a huge distraction for them," I said, feeling ever-so-noble and proud of myself.

"Okay." (pause) "But...can I say...hmmm, how can I say this politely, that I think you're being foolish?"

"Excuse me?!"

"You just found out you have breast cancer and you're already trying to control everyone's response to it. You may want to consider their help and concern for you, Jude. I think you need to consider that, well, you might *need* it. Much as you think you're the Rock of Gibraltar and all—I don't understand this stoicism of yours—and it's certainly not going to serve you well in this situation."

I was stunned; speechless. It wasn't an attack per se, but it was a direct hit to my missile defense shield and I needed time to assess the damage. My face flushed and my heart starting racing like child who's been caught in a serious lie. And perhaps I was.

"Uh-huh. Can I think about it?"

"Of course."

This was how I first learned that my boss thought I was too controlling and lacked perspective. *And* that I could be a huge idiot. Steve was a great person to have in my life at the time and he'll always be in my heart as a gentle reminder to allow other people to care about me. I still get chills when I reflect on how I behaved—as if I should be able to arrange *how* everyone responds to me and *when.*

"Do what you want, Jude," he said "I'm just telling you that I've been through this before with someone a lot like you and I can see it coming. You should tell your family, cancel your damn trips because we *can* and *will* survive without you, and find yourself a surgeon and a way to take care of yourself. Just my opinion; you can choose to do whatever you want. You know I'll support you."

Over the next few days, I heard Steve's sentiments echoing through my friends and family when I told them of my diagnosis first, and then tested the idea that I still could to go to Paris and wear my new shoes. I deserved Paris! I earned those shoes. Within days a rather surprising group of people openly calling me on my bullshit was already forming and it started with unanimous votes for me to stay grounded indefinitely. This group grew into the indefatigable Inner Circle I still have today.

Here are some excerpts from those conversations, when I was still in Classic, Super-Deluxe Phase-One Cancer Denial:

"Who gives a shit, Jude? Paris will always be there. Jesus, just cancel it."

"Are you completely insane?"

"Please tell me you're kidding. Oh, my god. You did just say you have breast cancer, right? Oh, my god."

"Fucking wear the new shoes to bed. You're not going."

It took me a few days to realize that everyone was right and I was not only wrong, but completely out of sync with reality. Horribly, woefully, out of my mind and inhabiting some parallel universe. I am humiliated in hindsight that I couldn't see the gravity of the situation for what it was, yet everyone else around me could.

JANUARY 17

By this time, a mere six days later, I had called several area surgeons and found only one that could see me "before sometime in February."

I couldn't believe that I was begging to be seen by breast cancer surgeons and this one, let's call her Dr. Coldhands, came recommended by my gynecologist so I figured I was safe until I was actually examined by her. I felt as if the Grim Reaper's older sister was touching me and breathing on my warm, exposed body. She was in her late sixties or early seventies, which at first I thought would mean "grandmotherly type" but in reality meant "cynical, tired, insensitive type."

All right, I'm sure she is a good doctor. I don't want to disparage her based on my biased and admittedly emotional visit. Reflecting on her complete lack of bedside manner, I assumed she must be so jaded by all the boobs she has removed or cut into over her long career that one more set was pretty meaningless to her. At this point in my diagnosis, I had not yet put the words "cancer" and "incurable" together yet, so I never even considered how many patients she might have actually lost.

I waited a ridiculously long time, freezing in her examining room, and then an empathetic but slightly prying nurse came in to ask me no fewer than 500,000 questions about my heath history, family history, diet, love life, and mental stability, which I handled well and really didn't mind except for the fact that when Dr. Coldhands came in for her star turn forty-five minutes later, I had to answer almost every single question again, as if Inquisitive Nurse didn't actually work there and was just wandering around doing a random survey of women in pink open-front gowns for her own enjoyment. As I curtly answered this repeat battery of personal questions—which also sounded vaguely like the last round of questions my attorney asked me—I feared that my mental stability was now beginning to show signs of dangerous wear.

After feeling me up with her freezing cold, bony old-woman-doctor hands that have me wincing and shivering, and looking at the films sent over by the hospital, she says unceremoniously, as only the Grim Reaper's creepy older sister can, that I am indeed doomed for the surgical table. "Well, it's DCIS and it's got to come out, so we'll try to do a lumpectomy and you'll probably need radiation but we need to do it soon. Get on my calendar for next week. The girls at the front desk will set it up for you."

And with that, she is washing her hands and preparing to leave. "I do surgeries on Tuesdays and Thursdays at the hospital. The nurses will tell you how to prepare."

"Whoa, hang on. I have a few questions, is that okay?"

"Shoot." Although there's a touch of can't you see I'm busy here in her tone.

"What do you mean by try to do a lumpectomy and probably need radiation?"

"Well…"

She does try to reply, but I just keep talking because despite the fact that I hate her and what she's saying, I do not want her to leave me alone in that room with that silly smock on without making it better; saying something that I could hang on to — something hopeful.

"What are the options or next steps after surgery? Why wouldn't the lumpectomy be enough? How will you know whether I will need radiation (why aren't you looking at me when I'm speaking, you old crone)? How many of these have you done recently? I think I'm supposed to ask you how often you do these lumpectomies…and what will I LOOK LIKE WHEN THIS IS ALL OVER, DAMMIT??!!" I am fraying.

If it's possible to offend an evil spirit, I have done it. She looks at me with those watery, beady blue eyes and says, through pursed lips, "I don't think you need to be worrying about what you'll look like, Jude. You have a very serious illness and your first order of business is to remove the tumor and surrounding tissue. If the lumpectomy doesn't get it all, we'll do a mastectomy on that side. If the radiation is not enough, well, we'll cross that bridge. But your breast will look different from the lumpectomy for sure, because we're taking a good amount of tissue out. It will be dented and you won't be symmetrical anymore. That's all. Some women with your diagnosis do bilateral mastectomies just to be safe. If we can conserve your breast, we'll be lucky."

It was the first time I had heard that word and she just casually uttered it twice — that horrific word that gives most women nightmares just by the sound of it: *mastectomy*.

I remember seeing a photograph several years ago in a magazine; a black and white self-portrait by a model turned photographer named Matuschka who had a mastectomy and did not have reconstructive surgery. She was nude from the waist up with just the shadow of one hand reflected on her torso reaching up longingly toward the flat, almost concave area where her breast used to be, now branded with a long, winding scar that reached off the page and curled around my neck and chest until I couldn't breathe. It was so stark and sad in contrast to her beautiful breast on the other side that the healthy breast looked tragic and almost freakish all by itself. This was similar to the reaction I have to other photos of amputations but this one masterfully created a horrifying two-way mirror. I stared at the picture for no more than twenty seconds and in that short amount of time felt a dizzying, suffocating fear. I lurched from the couch, picked up the magazine and threw it away. I shoved it to the bottom of the waste can with both hands so that there would be no chance that I would ever have to see that picture again. I was shaking. That was three years ago.

Mastectomy, she said. Oh. My god.
"What do you mean?" I stammer as my eyes instantly brimmed over with little girl tears.
"Jude, we will do the lumpectomy, but you've got a decent-sized tumor. Let's get it out and we'll take it from there. Listen, most women just get used to the way they look after surgery. I am sure you will, too." On that cheery note, Dr. Coldhands left me sitting in the refrigerated examining room looking down my pink smock at the breast that was now suddenly in grave danger and I reached up to touch it softly; then I hugged myself tightly so that I could squeeze all the tears out before I had to talk to the women at

the front desk, feeling as isolated as any woman has ever felt;
lonely, sick, abandoned, and so very cold.

I arrived home and looked briefly at my husband.
He stared back at me and said, "Where were you?"
"At the doctor. Another test."
"What's up?"
I thought about lying and I thought about pushing it aside to deal with it alone in my room. But I wanted him to feel pain. I wanted someone else to feel something awful and he was the only one there. Poor bastard.
"I have breast cancer. I need surgery. I could lose my breast entirely. And no, I don't want to talk about it."
I was saying this to the person who under other circumstances would have been the one to try to comfort me but we both knew we were way past that point. After so many years together, he knew I was serious and was shocked by the sound of the words I just spat at him. He looked at me sort of helplessly and as he started to speak I shut him down again with some callous comment relating to the latest in the divorce proceedings and went storming in to my bedroom with the stack of pink-ribboned pamphlets I was just awarded, to absorb all the self-pity and self-hatred I could muster. How did I let myself spend so much time with someone I no longer loved? How did I allow myself to get so sick? And why doesn't crying make it feel any better? God *dammit.*

JANUARY 19

I promised Steve that I would attend the end of our meeting at the Algonquin, in New York City. By this time I was researching this disease like a woman possessed, arming myself with as much information as I possibly could so that I never had another doctor visit like the one with Coldhands. I envisioned myself knowing more than my physicians and this was somewhat of a comfort to my competitive nature and my desperate need to take control of this mess.
The initial outcome of all the Internet research and chat rooms and blogs is that I now understood how insidious and dangerous

this disease is, but in truth I still hadn't accepted most of it. A thin, albeit peeling, layer of denial was still cloaking my heart, protecting me from pondering my own death. I was reading one thing but thinking another:

> *Sure, in "some cases" a mastectomy is advised, but "most early stage" cancers can be removed with a lumpectomy and radiation.*
> *Unless there is a metastasis, which I doubt, so it most likely will not be invasive and try to kill me.*
> *See how simple this is? Just like Mom's. And she's fine now, right?*
> *Right. Pack for New York. Really need a good distraction now.*

I had finally accepted the fact that I would need a few weeks off very soon and since all of my California colleagues were going to be together in New York, I wanted to go and tell them in person. I had driven down the day before, happy to spend a night away from my sad house and be in the company of work-friends.

When I got to the first meeting of the day I was asked to present an update on my project. My mind was immersed in the search for another surgeon and awash in Internet pictures of dented and reconstructed breasts, and the PowerPoint flashing before my eyes looked cartoonish and just plain silly to me. I cannot even remember what it was about, frankly, but it was important at the time and so I rambled on about something having to do with corporate goals, god help me.

I took a few colleagues aside one by one and told them about my latest predicament and that I was going in for surgery sometime soon but that I was going to be working until then. Their reactions were astounding. I had no idea that people would be so worried. I had no inkling that they would piece it together with my mother's diagnosis, my divorce, and the other recent tragedies of my life as a long, continuous streak of bad things happening to me. I had no idea that they were silently thinking, "Holy shit, she could die from this." I just thought they were nice people, being nice.

JANUARY 20

Researching doctors and finding one I would let touch me who also had appointments available before next Christmas was becoming more difficult. Sometimes, I would call an office and if their receptionist was snotty or they took too long to answer the phone, I would cross them off the list. It was foolish of course, but this was part of the control game.

I received an instant message from Kimberly saying she was going to get the name of a surgeon who "saved her mother's friend's life" at Memorial Sloan-Kettering in New York City. I was sure that my medical insurance would not cover me in the state of New York and, while I appreciated her effort, I didn't think it would amount to much. Her mother's friends have lots of disposable income and treatment at Sloan has a hefty price tag. Isn't that where all the stars go for treatment? Later, there was an encouraging yet directive e-mail from Kimberly to call this number, *today*. He was the Chief of Surgery for Breast Cancer at Sloan and was reputed to have an actual bedside manner. This, of course, sounded too good to be true, so I continued making my calls and then finally decided to call my insurance company to see if they could make a decent local referral. After entering ID codes and every conceivable number associated with my life into the phone system, I finally heard what sounded like a friendly human voice.

"Listen, I need some help."

"Of course, how can I help you today, ma'am?"

"I was just diagnosed with DCIS and I need to find a surgeon—quickly—and it seems everyone is completely booked up or it isn't their specialty. Is this normal?"

"Oh. I'm so sorry. How did they find it?"

"Excuse me?"

"I'm sorry about your diagnosis. Are you okay?"

And this was the first time that an outsider, a complete and total stranger, weighed in on my diagnosis and was clearly concerned, which freaked me out entirely, so I switched to Teflon mode.

"Well, yes, I'm fine! I would be better if I could find someone who would deign to see me before spring, though." I immediately realized that my attempt at humor fell flat and sounded a bit childish. This customer service person actually sounded upset that I was ill but I couldn't shake the fact that I *felt perfectly okay*. I was still on a task mission with zero insight into what those tasks represented. Find a surgeon; get it fixed. Breathe.

"Ma'am, let me see what I can do. What company do you work for?"

"Hyperion."

"Hmm. Okay. Oh, look at this. Did you know that they subscribed to something called Cancer Resource Services?"

"No. What's that?"

"It's a service provided by your insurance company that allows you to go to a recognized Cancer Center of Excellence anywhere in the country and will cover you in-network, regardless of whether it is in-plan or not. Also if it's more than fifty miles from your home, you can get reimbursed for gas, tolls, meals, and hotels for all your visits. It's a very nice rider on the policy, ma'am."

"So, even though I live in Redding, Connecticut, if I wanted to go to Memorial Sloan-Kettering...."

"You are covered in-network 100%. Yes, ma'am, that's right."

"I am in the HR department of my company and knew nothing about this."

"I hear that a lot. I'll connect you with one of the nurses so you can get registered. They can help you even before you find your doctor. And good luck."

Good luck. This felt like the first piece of good luck I had to lay my hands on in quite a while. I could get the very best treatment. I was entitled to something other than another pounding of bad news. *And* I had the name of the chief surgeon with a personal referral. Now all I had to do was get in. I poured another cup of tea and called Sloan. It was Friday and I had several other new surgeon tryout appointments on the calendar for the next few weeks and was also in the process of shuffling medical records, pathology reports, MRI appointments, divorce papers, shrink appointments, and travel arrangements. It was a busy day.

I should mention that I had a wonderful therapist who had been a tremendous support over the last six months, but I am afraid I may have broken her. The staid and frightfully composed, Spocklike rational, impeccably dressed counselor who listened to all of my recent tribulations without flinching while doling out brilliant advice unfettered by emotion, came very close to losing it during our last session when I told her about the cancer. This news struck a chord with her that unraveled all of her wonderful objectivity in one fell swoop and to her credit, returned her to humanoid status; she cried. I felt terrible but also instinctively knew I might as well do this on my own or find an on-line support group if I felt I needed one. I had no tolerance for emotions that could be interpreted as pity. And I didn't like the responsibility I felt for having possibly pushed this woman to the brink. So I just kept cancelling appointments until she stopped calling.

After hanging on hold for what felt like an eternity, I practically threw up on the receptionist telling her that I was recommended by blah, blah, dropping names and rambling desperately about how hard it's been to find a good breast surgeon.

She stopped me by saying something outrageous in its simplicity: "Ma'am, I know its short notice but we have a cancellation on Monday. If you can get me your pathology reports faxed from your hospital today and access your films so you can bring them with you, we can see you Monday morning."

I felt like I won the lottery.

JANUARY 23

Monday morning in New York City, draped in yet another pink gown on the exam table and surrounded by several earnest interns from Ecuador and my cancer-savvy sister Jodi, Dr. Graham (I so dubbed him for the graham crackers piled in his waiting room) holds court. He apparently likes to start with the most optimistic outcome possible in his patient conversations. So the initial possibilities on this first visit with him run from the sunny and well-reasoned: "The pathologists may look at your slides and disagree completely with your hometown hospital so it could be just some dense breast tissue and nothing to worry about" to a slightly dimmer view: "If there *are* abnormalities that we're concerned about, we'll just remove them surgically with a lumpectomy and most likely prescribe a round of radiation just to be safe" to the game changer: "not that I even remotely expect this, but if the area is large enough we could be looking at a possible mastectomy, but no reason for us to go there just yet, so just relax and let's see what *our* tests say."

Jodi and I were instantly elated that there was even a possibility that it could all be a silly mistake on the part of some overworked pathologists in our "hometown" lab that he adeptly made sound like Hooterville Hospital. We were convinced that Dr. Graham was indeed the God of Breast Cancer Treatment and that I would be *fine*. That was until he shuttled us downstairs for my first round of magnified mammograms in their radiology department and another, much less magnanimous doctor came out to read them, confirming that it was indeed carcinoma on the new pictures, which is when I realized that the God of Breast Cancer Treatment may indeed be the best at what he does, but he doesn't like to lead with his best punch; he leaves that to the guys in radiology. So, I went home that first day from Sloan with a nice little depressing note on their best embossed stationary confirming the carcinoma in my left breast and an MRI appointment for later that week, but relatively convinced that I was in the right hands. Finally.

Jodi and I had a solemn trip home on the train on this cold and rainy January afternoon. My sister, I realized, having been to this movie so recently with Mom, was the perfect person to have on this inaugural visit, not just for her knowledge of the disease but for her even-tempered and resilient manner, laced with a tireless sense of humor. I remember telling her I was glad we'd be reimbursed for all this. What I meant was I wish there were a way to pay her back, but it was the best I had at the moment. My gratitude muscles were stiff from lack of exercise.

JANUARY 24

I cancelled my "hometown" MRI with Coldhand's cohorts, blew off my back-up breast surgeon appointments, called my attorney for a divorce update, found an appraiser to look at the house, perused more pictures of deformed breasts after surgery, and made tea. It's my mother's seventy-fifth birthday today. I called her and made sure she knew I was thinking about her, and then we both put forth our best efforts to directly avoid sad topics that have become the quiet subtext for all our conversations. We laughed and joked and had a few exchanges that were cut short by our mutual ability to never discuss that which will force pressure behind our eyes and lodge tennis balls in our throats.

My mood before the phone call was bleak and I admit I was truly expecting that it might get worse afterwards. Mom wasn't doing cheerful look-backs in those days. But oddly enough, her surprisingly chipper attitude blew a breeze of optimism my way that propelled me to try and do something nice for myself. I hung up the phone and thought, "With all she's got going on, damn, she's still got it going on!"

I decided to apply some make-up to conceal my puffy eyes, and go browsing, as Mom would call it. I call it shopping for stuff I can't afford with zero intention of buying anything. After hours of viewing pictures of horribly disfigured women and reconstructed boobs trying to picture what I might look like by next year, a spontaneous trip to the Lillian August Storewide Furniture Blow-Out Showroom Sale made perfect sense; it was *not* clothes shopping, it still required a sense of style, and all the beautiful room displays represented scenes of comfort to me. I just avoided all the big, fancy mirrors because I was recently rendered incapable of looking at my own reflection.

In two weeks of living with the preliminary diagnosis of DCIS, I was learning that the coping comes in waves, much like any grief process. But it is easier to take when you think about what *others* might be going through and stop the incessant doting on yourself, your mashed self-image, and the myriad uncertainties that cancer dances into your previously ordered life. So when I reflected on Mom and Dad's situation and others like them who have so much everyday loss to bear, I did manage moments of clear perspective. Likewise when I could focus on things in *my* life that are abundant and good, it created a momentary clearing in the minefield, however fleeting.

But there was no escaping the fact that Mom and I both had breast cancer and were both losing our husbands. Dad was slowly waltzing away, leaving behind for my mother a needy patient who still bore a striking resemblance to the love of her life for the past fifty-four years. And in my case, I made the decision to end my marriage, but the pain of saying good-bye to your life partner via ruthless attorneys while you're still living under the same roof is truly heartbreaking. There is no other word for it.

In the first two weeks I read a great deal on websites devoted to alternative cancer treatments. Eastern medicine suggested that breast cancer is the outcome of a broken chakra. That is to say, theoretically, if the chakra of the heart is broken, or there is anger and resentment toward a love in your life, the pain can manifest itself in this insidious disease. I thought about that yesterday when I looked around the waiting room at Memorial Sloan-Kettering. I tried to see behind the eyes of all the women in various stages of coping. When they were diagnosed, had they been angry at someone? Had their hearts been broken? Had they been in mourning? And then I thought maybe I was just seeking something more tangible or romantic to blame than risk factors, statistical odds, and incredibly bad luck.

Anyway, there I was in the Lillian August showroom, walking around, looking purposeful and pretending that I could afford everything and it suddenly dawned on me, right there next to the antique Tibetan sideboards, that my life was, indeed, starting over. A chain reaction began on that fateful day in the mammography chamber and was mutating daily to the point where this life I inhabit was no longer recognizable to me. And there was no going back. That's a hard message to absorb when an energetic saleswoman is handing you fabric swatches and price lists. It landed like a well-placed punch.

I took a deep breath and began moving ever so slowly towards understanding the randomness of it all while browsing, avoiding mirrors, and seemingly going on with a normal life.

Happy birthday to both of us, Mom.

JANUARY 26

I find it fascinating that there can be such a clear delineation between those who are sick and those who are well, because moving from one category to the other can be so subtle, private, or in my case, just plain invisible. It's only fifteen days and despite feeling

27

completely well, I can now admit to being moved, against my will and better judgment, into the *sick* category.

For example, tonight I was lying in bed channel-surfing, looking for a distraction from the stack of How-to-Get-Healthy books on my bedside table and the treacherous risk of letting my mind wander on its own. The books are inspiring but, after ingesting about five of them, the only through-line I can find is advice to drink water, eat broccoli, and do yoga. I am not a big fan of television, mind you; however, it does have its advantages when you need a quick, mindless brain-drain so you can fall asleep. But it suddenly seems that every image depicts a young woman with masses of healthy cleavage and not-so-subtle allusions to having or desiring sex. This is not true, of course, but it's what my mind is reading back to me because today's events have convinced me that not only am I officially "old," but I will forever be disfigured and no one will ever want to sleep with me again. My sex life, my comfort with my body, my feminine mystique—all history, along with any hope of future desirability; full stop. So "Top 100 Hottest Celebrity Bodies" feels like a bit of a slap in the face, considering how I'd spent the earlier part of my day.

Today was my MRI at Sloan. I went alone. I am still a week away from hearing their recommendation for treatment, making it my third opinion—and I am banking on it being my final—before making a decision about what to do with these tiny tumors invading my milk ducts. It's the kind of limbo that should be reserved for really bad people who steal food from blind orphans.

A not-so-subtle shift from well to sick came to me in a new form of denial in the waiting area. I was in a room full of cancer patients who traveled from all over the country, and probably the world, to be there. Sloan was the holy cancer shrine and they were all hoping to drink from the healing waters and be zapped with the magic health rays. Not to mention, I appeared 15–20 years younger than everyone else, clearly way too young and hip for this depressing scene. How did I get here? But deep in my heart, I knew better. It was going to be another crappy test and more bad news.

I refused to sit down. Everyone else had settled in with their *New York Times*, Starbucks coffees, and crossword puzzles. I stood on the opposite side of the room so I would not be confused with the old, sick people. I looked stylish and above it all in my designer coat and beret, imagining I was waiting for one of the handsome oncologists to take me to a power breakfast. But when they called my name, mispronouncing it, I snapped out of my reverie and became like all the other lemmings, dutifully following the somber nurse down the hall to once again put my boobs in the hands of total strangers.

In short, I became a sick person. I gave up my modesty and identity to a disease that I couldn't even see; to something abnormal that grew silently in my left breast in the space of just six months. How did I go from being a healthy, independent woman embarking on a new phase of life with hope in my heart and a clear shot at happiness, to a sick woman who was going to lose a portion of, or possibly *all* of, one of her most prized body parts? I was learning that cancer coughs up a lot more questions than answers.

So here I am in the prep room for the MRI with a nurse who doesn't like pesky patients who ask a lot of questions. She was large and soft and wore a just-too-tight uniform and a tad too much make-up and *eau de parfum* for the cancer ward. Almost as if she were trying to jazz it up a bit for the folks in the hideous pink, open-front gowns. When she was tying off my arm to jab in the intravenous needle, I made the mistake of asking what was in the solution they were going to pump into my arm while I lounged in the magnetic resonance tube.

She looked at me as if I had asked how many bowel movements she'd had that day, and said, "It's just some solution that will help us see what's going on in there," and smiled sweetly as she jammed the needle into the front of my wrist, missing the vein completely.

"Ow! Okay, I hear that. I just want to know what's *in* it. Like, what are the properties of this solution? Do you know? Because it's going to be in *my* bloodstream for twenty minutes and that's a pretty important place in my book..."

She sighed heavily and looked down at the mess she made of my wrist as if to imply that my stupid question had thrown off her aim, and said, "Oh, I'm really sorry about that. I never do that...we'll have to try the other arm." And then she said with the most subtle breeze of sarcasm, "I'll have to check on those *ingredients* for you when we're done here."

Finally, I looked at her name tag quickly and said, "Jennifer, have *you* ever had this test done?" As she shook her head no and was about to answer me, I offered, "If you were having this done, and didn't work here every day, wouldn't you be curious? Wouldn't you want to know what was going into your body before you made the decision to allow it? I mean, this test is not mandatory. I am making the decisions about my treatment, not you, and one of them is to know exactly what is going into my body at all times (pause), Jen."

Well, that did it. I had clearly crossed the nice cancer patient line and she left the room to get the list of "ingredients" while I sat in the chair with my breasts tumbling out of the too large gown, my wrist throbbing, and true fear in my heart.

Don't get me wrong. There are millions of wonderful and selfless healthcare workers practicing all kinds of medicine— Eastern, Western, alternative, shamanism, but the ones who scare me the most are the ones who say in essence, "Just do what the doctor tells you." And Jen didn't say that exactly, but she did want me to fall in line and not question a test that millions of women have on a weekly basis, not to mention where did I come off making her job more difficult today?

She came back into the room with a piece of paper with all the ingredients in the MRI cocktail and read them off, looking at me like I was an idiot for wasting her time. She struggled to pronounce several of the words on the list; I didn't recognize a single one. But it didn't matter. I smiled and said, "Thank you, Jennifer. I can't tell you how important it is for me to know what's going into my body. It's the only thing currently in my control." And I suddenly, embarrassingly, burst into tears at the sound of this Lifetime channel revelation.

Yes, millions of people get breast MRIs and no, it doesn't actually hurt. The most disturbing aspect of the procedure is a repeat of the shame I felt during the biopsies because once again, I am lying face down with my boobs hanging into two holes on a cold metal slab; only this time, the slab slides back and forth into a long, scary tube like a dispenser on a giant coin-operated, front loading washing machine. While in the tube, I had my arms stretched over my head for over forty-five minutes, wearing earplugs to help with the noise, and an IV in my arm pumping in that mystery solution while an *entire team* of people watched the pictures it was taking from safely behind a glass wall. They talked to me through a small speaker in the claustrophobic cylinder robotically instructing me when to breathe. I was really disappointed that no one had said anything nice, or even mildly amusing, to break the tension. I guess Jen warned them about me.

Since you can't move or even breathe normally while it's doing its thing, it's best to try to meditate with your eyes closed and go somewhere far away. I chose to tune in to the incredibly loud noises and try to match them with the percussive backdrop of popular rock anthems, and then pretend I was at a concert instead of being abused by a big-ass superconducting magnet. My favorite was one particular series of pictures that sounded as if Pink Floyd and The Who had a love child, and had the MRI people been a tad friendlier, I would have shared that musical discovery with them as well. Their loss.

Now, on a normal day, a typical Thursday in my old life, I would have been sitting at my desk answering e-mails, attending seemingly important meetings, and generally keeping my clothes on at all times. That is something else I've had to get accustomed to—the whole "keep the gown open in the front so everyone and their assistants can feel you up" thing. At work I would have asked rational questions much in the same manner I asked Jen a question, and expected replies but without having to open a vein to get an answer. On the bright side, work sounded more and more like paradise lost and less like a job to me every day.

The test was over and no fewer than six people shuttled into the room to undo me from the machine and the IV. I think a few others came in just for the fun of it (Have I mentioned I have great breasts?) and got the room ready for the next patient. I was shaky and feeling a little lightheaded, so when someone named Raul came over and tried to help me off the table, I told him I wasn't ready. "Take your time," he said, and then exactly four seconds later said, "You ready now?" I'm guessing he's the guy who keeps everything humming in the MRI chamber so people like Jen can get to lunch on time. I decided not to make a big deal out of it and stumbled out of there humbled by the experience, awfully curious about the science of it all, and humming Pink Floyd tunes. However, it was not my favorite way to spend a morning.

Losing my privacy, ability to watch TV or movies without mourning my sex life, and surrendering my identity and daily rhythm as a well person is an interesting life lesson. I guess because I feel rather healthy, these endless doctor visits feel a bit surreal, like I'm stuck on an episode of post-Clooney ER that just won't go to commercial. I have no symptoms now other than fear of living out my life in the shadow of this mess of a disease. So I'm sick with fear, but I'm drinking water, eating broccoli, and doing yoga, waiting for the results of those pictures they took of me today and hoping that they will give me a ticket back to the well camp. I liked it better there.

JANUARY 27

How on earth had I gotten through my life thus far without recognizing how incredibly stubborn I am about asking for help?

After the last round of tests I went back to work for a few days, because there really is nothing to do while you wait around for destiny to cast its ballot on your life. Being a Virgo, I am quite adept at compartmentalizing and work is like a religion, so I got dressed and put on my best face, eager to be back with my Connecticut-based HR teammates who, despite long hours of dealing with the corporate crazies, can still make each other howl with laughter. Yep, this was exactly what I needed.

I had been intentionally less than forthright with most of these people. Cancer has roots embedded deep into most families and psyches and, despite what my boss advised, I still wanted to avoid emotional complications with most people at work, if possible. After a week of researching things like radio-frequency ablation, sentinel lymph node biopsies, and the side effects of Tamoxifen on pre-menopausal women, I thought a good dose of "So, what did you and the kids do this weekend?" was in order. Actually, I wanted several helpings and found myself truly interested in hearing their answers in excruciating detail.

Kim, however, being "in the know," bounced into my office that afternoon and cheerfully inquired, "Who is going to Sloan with you next week?" She was referring to the appointment when I was to hear the results from yesterday's MRI, the new mammograms, and the slides from last month's biopsies (that their pathologists needed to weigh in on) and, of course, the verdict from Dr. Graham and his international squad of minions, better known as fellows.

"Um, no one...just going in alone, I guess. Not a big deal." And as the words left my mouth I realized that I had just assigned this meeting no more value than a dentist appointment.

I hope that everyone has a friend like Kim, the person who takes on everything in your life as if it was her very own and never flinches or gets tired of listening to you talk. I was beginning to worry that due to my world-class dramas of late, I was dangerously close to tipping the scales of friendship so far out of balance that I would lose Kim forever and she would run screaming down the hall with her hands clasped to her ears yelling, "No more of your goddamned misery, please!" I was legitimately afraid of such a scenario because as I was trying to convince her that I could put my big-girl panties on and go it alone, I was terrified that she might actually buy my false bravado and leave my office, satisfied that she *tried.*

Kim and I became closer friends after David died. He was her colleague, too, and his passing forced us both to examine the cruel randomness of life and love while carefully unearthing whatever absurd humor we could possibly find to salve the wounds. I was lucky to have attracted a friend like Kim and while I didn't realize it at the time she had started the process of being that unconditional friend that David had been for so many years. Recently though, I was feeling as if I might be taking advantage of her good nature and resilience, risking losing her and the critical thinking she applied to my daily doctor-lawyer status updates. My baggage was getting heavier by the day and I imagined it was weighing her down as well.

"I don't think you should go alone, Jude," she said matter-of-factly. "I'll go with you," and then she deftly changed the subject to logistics, "just let me know what time and I'll let my boss know I'm taking the day. She won't care. Wanna go to lunch? I'm starving."

And there it was. No games, no earthly reason to refuse, and once again I was saved from myself because for some reason, *asking* her or anyone else to accompany me, would have pained me to my very core. It would have meant I needed someone for something as simple as a visit with a doctor and that sounded awfully weak and victim-like, not to mention patently un-Virgo. We are *independent*. Aside from the reality that I was going to learn the extent of my cancer and what treatment, if any, would be required, I still could not believe that people around me might be as concerned as I was about the outcome.

What the fuck was wrong with me anyway?

FEBRUARY 1

Going into Manhattan, or *schlepping*, as we like to call it, from Connecticut is always a bit of an adventure. It starts with making three very important decisions: who will drive; what side we are going in on, meaning are we taking the West Side Highway or the FDR; and where we are parking. Luckily, Kim is a veteran of the neighborhood on the Upper East Side where Sloan Kettering takes up several city blocks so we slipped into the labyrinth with no difficulty whatsoever.

I had been there several times by now, but the weight of this trip started to dawn on me around the Willis Avenue Bridge, which was a bit dangerous since I was driving. The thought crossed my mind that it might be not such great news, for no other reason than the way my luck had been going recently; I saw no reason for a break in the clouds. Although I'm not prone to them as a rule, I had a strong premonition after my first biopsy that I was in this for the long haul.

Kim and I sat in the waiting room for, I kid you not, three and a half hours waiting for Dr. Graham to see us. I'm not exactly the most patient of patients to begin with, but the agony of sitting in that room with dozens of other women who were all in various stages of treatment and testing was more than just a little unsettling. Plus, the magazines were full of pre-Oscar celebrity photo-spreads replete with every beautiful starlet in LA encased in breast enhancing garb, staring at me and reminding me again that I was not young, and one of my breasts is now imperfect and diseased and would probably look like shit in one of those Vera Wangs by the time this is all over.

There is also something very unnerving about being in proximity to so many people who have cancer. It's not like sitting in your doctor's office where some are sniffling and others are just there for their yearly exam, or wrestling their kids to sit still and be quiet. This is the all-cancer-all-the-time channel. Everyone is unnerved and no one is smiling. I was popping crystallized ginger like...well, it *is* candy, but most people retch when they eat it.

Kim was doing her best to get me focused on the travel magazines and trips that will surely be in our future, like Croatia and Mexico, reminding me once again of her bottomless capacity for optimism. When we finally got in to see Dr. Graham, I had my questions all ready to go, but whatever positive energy I had started the day with was gone. I was tired, and so it appeared, was he. Considering what he did for a living, if he was three and a half hours behind schedule, I ventured a guess that he must be having a pretty crappy day, too.

He reads the results from the pathologist with as empathetic a demeanor as he can muster but essentially says that the left breast has an area that needed to come out, which I fully expect, but that the MRI identified another "mass" or area that looks suspicious. "Nothing to get worried about yet Jude, but I'd like to do some biopsies of that area as well when we go in for the area we know is DCIS, okay?"

"Okay...I guess."

"Do you have any questions?"

"What... will I look like? Am I going to be all, like, deflated?" Here I go again, caring more about my appearance than the diagnosis, confirming my suspicion that I may still be harboring a wee bit of denial.

"No, the area of DCIS is about the size of a walnut, and then we'll do what's called a needle localization to identify the other areas I want to biopsy and those will be miniscule. I'm trying to conserve as much of the breast as possible. And then we'll also take a few lymph nodes out just to be sure."

"Sure of what?"

"That there's no invasion of those cells; that the cancer is contained in the breast. We detected what's called a micro-invasion on the left meaning the tumors that usually stay in the duct are starting to break it open; it's early stage, but important that we check the lymph nodes right away." I'm starting not to trust his early-stage disclaimers.

"Right. Okay. Thanks." My face collapses into a mask of disappointment and soundless tears.

"The nurse will bring in the consent forms for the surgery; we can do this pretty quickly Jude, within the next week or two."

"K."

At this point, Kim asks a reasonable question or two. Then Dr. Graham hands me the pathology report as he leaves with his practiced "I'm really sorry" face, exiting quickly to find his nurse to do clean-up detail with his now weeping patient. Unfortunately, the poor woman he sends in to talk me through the surgery process receives the brunt of my anger, frustration, and snide comments.

I look through the pathology reports as she drones on about the pre-surgical precautions and I notice something that makes the hair on the back of my neck stand up. "What does this mean?"

"What?"

"It says right here, 'Right breast suspicious area, recommends biopsy?'"

"Oh, I...don't really...it's probably just a typo."

Now, call me crazy, but I'm in the best cancer treatment center in the world looking at an eight-page pathology report that I've got to believe is the culmination of several very smart people's input, so a "typo" seems not only unlikely, but a horrifying oversight, if it's true.

"Uh, I don't think so. This says very clearly that there's something on the right breast. Please ask Dr. Graham to come back in here."

"Well, I can't, he's with another patient, and I'm sure..."

"Now. I want to talk to him NOW."

She grudgingly leaves to retrieve the good doctor for his encore performance. Kim looks at my soggy and swollen face as if to say something but thinks better of it and goes back to her notes. I must look a mess. In about three agonizing minutes, Dr. Graham returns with the pathology report in his hand and his tail between his legs. He confirms that yes, the right breast will also need to be biopsied, but "honestly, it's probably nothing. We'll just take a small section to be sure."

I am too annoyed and freaked out to ask how this had been overlooked in our first conversation, but after waiting as long as we did, I assume that he was completely overbooked, tired, and capable of missing stuff. It is another loud reminder that I am in

*the driver's seat with this disease and have to push hard and pay
close attention because all these medical experts are just human
beings. Getting mad at the man who is going to dissect my chest in
a few days is about as big a waste of energy as I can think of.*

His nurse, however, was another story. I know it's mean, but I
just couldn't stop. After Graham left the room again and I was
signing the new improved consent forms to slice into both breasts
and my armpit, the poor nurse had to endure my condescending
bullshit for the remainder of the appointment. I'm sure she's used
to idiots like me because she didn't ruffle, but Kim was looking at
me with an expression that read, *Jesus, Jude, it's not her fault you have
cancer.*

Then the nurse asked a final clarifying question that sent me
over the edge that I thought I had already fallen off. "You didn't
complete this part of the form. Who is going to be your health care
advocate the day of the surgery? We'll need a name..."

There was no way for her to know about the divorce and that
the person who should be sitting with me and comforting me, who
should be present for the surgery and taking care of me afterward—
and telling me I'm still beautiful despite my disfigurement—was
actually suing me and breaking what's left of my heart on a daily
basis. So I barked, "I don't know!"

"Well, it's a rule that we have to have someone..." and I could
hear in her tone she had had just about enough of me for one day.

"I *said*, I don't know. I'll figure it out by the time I have surgery,
okay? It's not something I planned for today. Please don't ask me
again." I honestly didn't know who would be, or who would want to
be. Again, Kim was sitting right in front of me and I didn't even
make that connection. I just crawled into the self-pity penalty box
and went completely blank.

We stopped at the front desk to schedule pre-op and surgery
dates. The adorable receptionist, who must be used to engaging
with women who can no longer breathe through their bright red
stuffed noses, checked the doctor's schedule and said, "His next
available date is February 14, does that work for you?"

My first attempt at humor in over an hour was to answer, "Sure,
not doing much else on Valentine's Day this year. Let's make it a

date." I now know how bombing comics feel when the only person laughing in the audience is their agent. I have to work on my delivery.

We walked a few blocks to get something to eat and during that chilly stroll I got my first dose of "whisper talk." Kim had thoughtfully planned ahead for us to have a nice afternoon getting facials at Georgette Klinger to forget about our troubles, never imagining that my one-hour appointment would turn into five. As she was chatting with the receptionist to explain why we missed the appointment, it sounded as if they were trying to see if we could head over right away and fill another slot. Kim asked me what I thought, but I don't remember answering her—I think I was still hyperventilating—so she commenced to "whisper talk" into the phone. I suspect the folks at Georgette Klinger could not fathom that there were two women in New York City who would not jump at the chance to fill a cancellation for a facial, so Kim most likely dropped the Sloan-bomb to substantiate our decision and keep our reputations intact. There would be more whisper-talk in the coming months, but I was taken aback because although I couldn't actually hear every word, I knew it was about me and that was just plain weird since I was walking right next to her. *I have cancer, I'm not deaf.*

Eventually I got some of my bearings back but as we sat down to dinner I could feel myself struggling with how I was going to orchestrate my life around the surgery over the next month.

Kim read my mind. "Okay, where are you? What are you thinking about?"

As I sputtered about everything from the divorce proceedings to the surgery to who was going to watch the dogs, she calmly smiled and said, "Breathe. Just breathe. It will all take care of itself, Jude. Whatever you need, we'll figure it out. Eat your dinner."

Which is when I realized that I would probably never learn to ask for help or stop dwelling on the insignificant things, but if I surrounded myself with people who could read my mind and call me on my bullshit, I would probably be okay.

I went back to my salmon and tasted it this time.

FEBRUARY 9

Today was pre-op appointment day and I honestly could not think of a single person who might be free to join me for a round of blood tests, EKGs, and chest x-rays. Besides which, I knew damn well I was going to need to call in a few favors after the surgery in a few days—dog walkers and such—so I schlepped in alone.

I moved from examining room to examining room in a strangely serene stupor just waiting to be told when to undress and when to put my clothes back on. My heart was fine; my blood was still pumping red; and there didn't seem to be any immediate cause for alarm. I guess once you know you already have cancer, what the hell else is there to worry about when you're in a hospital, germs?

FEBRUARY 13

Once I had my surgery date in hand, I let my Inner Circle know what was going on. This group includes my immediate family, a few close friends, my cousin Julie, and my boss Steve. The circle formed over the course of a few weeks and I had little to do with framing it; it just evolved.

I read somewhere that the personal support group that develops on its own is the one you should pay attention to. If I had used my own stupid instincts, I probably would have formed a different group entirely or none at all. But thankfully, I had read in one of my depressing Oh-Shit-You-Have-Cancer books to watch for those who come forward and pay attention to how much comfort it gives you. For instance, if your annoying neighbor keeps showing up on your doorstep with bad casseroles, causing you anxiety, thank her and then politely ask her for privacy. But if friends, co-workers, or family members are relentless in their support and it actually does make you feel better or safer, grab it and hang on! Don't even think about it, just accept it for what it is and tell them what you need without hesitation. Easier said than done, of course.

I reached out to family first and immediately my sisters jumped into the fray and offered to come to New York with me as they had with Mom in Hartford just last year. They both have husbands and families and tons of obligations, so I was grateful but concerned about what a logistical challenge it would be for them. I called around and got a great hotel that provides discounts for Sloan patients and their families, reserved it for two nights and splurged on a swanky suite with all the trimmings because the Cancer Resource Services angels were paying $100 per person per night for lodging near the hospital and I picked up the rest. I was totally pumped that the sisters would be in a luxurious hotel to make up for the ugly nature of the trip. I figured we could kind of make it a grown-up pajama party the night before, at least until midnight when I had to stop eating and drinking fluids.

I was told I needed to have some radioactive material injected into my breast the day before the surgery so that the surgeon could inject a dye into me the following day that would lead him to the lymph nodes most likely to be the problem children. This was Step One in the sentinel lymph node biopsy procedure that I was undergoing in addition to the multiple lumpectomies and biopsies. It didn't really sound like a big deal, so we three amigas drove into New York in a pretty decent mood and were only about ten minutes late for the appointment due to the twenty-six inches of snow that had fallen the day before. New York was buried under a thick blanket of winter's best and even though driving was a bit treacherous, it was quite beautiful.

"Jude, do you want some of your trail mix?" Jodi asked as we were heading out of the MSK parking garage. In addition to the crystallized ginger I was eating to settle my stomach, I had taken to mixing it with raw walnuts. The combination was awesome, particularly on days when my appetite was non-existent. I kept baggies full of this trail mix ready to go at all times.

"Yes, please, my stomach is not happy."

Jodi's question was innocent enough but I felt a pang of guilt that I had put my sisters in a position where they felt they had to take care of me; *look out for me.* Why this bothered me, I don't know. I know I would have done the same for them but her comment rang in my ears as a harbinger of things to come.

After parking the car we walked down First Avenue with Jodi and me in the lead and Jayne trailing behind us. It was a positively brilliant day in New York, and being the day before Valentine's

Day, the stores were festooned with hearts and flowers and provided a colorful, albeit bittersweet, backdrop for our stroll. My sisters would be without their husbands and kids, and I... well, let's just say that Valentine's Day felt outrageously trivial.

As we rounded the corner of the building where I was supposed to have my procedure, I guess I should have been more put off by the sign screaming "Nuclear Medicine" but I was so focused on getting through the next day's surgery I honestly didn't give it much thought. I had so many injections lately that one more didn't strike me as particularly ominous.

The sidewalks were an obstacle course of snow, sand, and ice so we were taking our time and being cautious. All of a sudden Jodi and I, and most of the Upper East Side, heard a loud, guttural scream behind us. We spun around, terrified of what we might find, only to see Jayne completely covered with snow from head to toe and even (get this) jammed in behind her glasses so she was unable to see. She was awkwardly flailing her arms trying to balance. And she was still screaming. Apparently the awning Jayne was walking under decided to relieve itself of all twenty-six inches of snow that had fallen on it the previous day, and landed like a bull's eye on my sister's head like a mammoth slush ball from space. Everyone who saw what happened was either staring or pointing and the three of us just dissolved into hysterics — tears, doubled-over, screaming laughing — during which Jayne announced to anyone who would listen that she had also wet her pants.

We were still laughing in the waiting room when they called my name. I was in a pretty light mood when I followed the nurse down the hall and she asked me if I had ever had this done before. I said no but I was somewhat annoyed, thinking, "Shouldn't she have known that?" I put on the obligatory open-front tunic that I'm tempted to purchase for myself when this is all safely behind me, just because they're so *practical and stylish*, and waited for her to finish her ministrations with what looked like something out of an Ed Wood horror movie replete with dry ice and skull and crossbones. She was preparing a fat hypodermic needle that came out of what appeared to be a smoking, round steel garbage can, with the precision of someone dismantling a ticking bomb. Apparently, nuclear medicine is tricky radioactive stuff that is so dangerous that the nurse cannot handle any part of it directly, but I'm just sick enough to have it injected into my body.

She was swabbing the area just above my left nipple and dangerously close to the hematoma from my last unhealed biopsies. "This will burn a bit," she said, "and it might sting for a few minutes afterward, okay?"

There was really no going back if it wasn't okay, so I snapped, "I guess it will have to be!"

As she injected me, she actually looked me in the eye and whispered, "I'm sorry."

Two seconds later, what felt like a firecracker going off in my breast tissue exploded and my entire body broke out into a full, heaving sweat. It was the most pain I can remember feeling in a long time and I just couldn't help but let out a horrible noise as I tried to just inhale and breathe through it. I grabbed her arm waiting for it to subside.

And she said again, "Really sorry. Just a few more minutes of a slight burning sensation."

"How long?" I sputtered.

"About ten or fifteen. You okay?"

"Jesus, that hurt."

"I know, hang in there. Just put your clothes back on when you're ready and be back here in two hours so we can take the pictures."

"K."

I realized that my sisters were waiting for me in the waiting room and somehow that helped me pull it together. I didn't want to cry, not now; this was just the pre-game show. I just breathed deeply and carefully put my clothes back on. It was now just a slow burn and not excruciating, and I tried to rally by thinking that if this is what I had to go through to save my breast and my health, I could deal with it. My sisters were another story; they looked at me like I was a ghost when I walked back out into the waiting room. Maybe I was glowing from the radioactivity now coursing through my system but I could feel the presence of kid gloves as they greeted me.

"How'd it go? You all right?"

"Fine. Gotta be back in two hours so they can take pictures of it. Let's get *out* of here."

I caught them looking at each other with that almost imperceptible oh-shit expression they do so well, and then we silently and simultaneously decided not to address the fact that I was in some pain. We felt it better to push through it and get to our next stop on the agenda.

We walked tentatively to the hotel and checked in. This was not going to be the have-fun-in-the-city-the-day-before-surgery day that I had hoped, although the fact that Dick Cheney shot his friend in the face while quail hunting two days prior provided a fail-safe comic diversion. I was shaky and a bit unnerved by the fact that no one warned me, at any point in the "preparations" for today, that this was going to hurt. Not even the flimsy "discomfort" warning; nothing. Let's face it, I knew to expect the addition of physical pain into the equation from the *surgery*, augmenting the mental anguish of having cancer, but not from a test the day before. If the girls had not been not with me I would have gotten in my car, never to return.

We discovered as we unpacked our belongings back at the hotel that, without planning it, each of us had brought something from home that made us feel better; Jodi brought one of her son's Beanie Babies, Jayne brought cookies her son baked and a lavender eye pillow, and I brought a bag of ginger snaps and the scented candle from my bedroom and the ever-present trail mix. We settled in and found our spaces as if we had been doing it together for years and started making plans for after my next visit to the York Avenue clinic in two hours, but we kept coming back to "just a nice dinner close by" because I must have looked like someone who was not really up for snagging tickets to a show or going clubbing. Ultimately, we bought two bottles of wine, put our sweats on, and ordered room service that evening, despite the fact that we were in the restaurant capital of the planet.

On the walk back to the clinic a couple of hours later, I was hoping that the picture-taking would not involve any hypodermic needles or skin punctures and, being a former actress, I was reasonably sure that I could get through a photo session without trauma or incident. I was escorted into a large room with a long, very narrow, and slightly concave bench, for lack of a better word, with a miniature pillow on one end that I surmised was the target I was supposed to hit with my head. I couldn't help thinking that this had to be a god-awful humiliating nightmare for fat people. How would they do it?

I got into position and the assistant began giving me instructions on what to do with my body and head to rehearse what I needed to do once the camera was on. I couldn't understand why I needed to work so hard on my right and left head turns which, in most circumstances, come pretty darn naturally, until I looked up and saw a series of enormous boxes suspended from the ceiling forming a large T. It was as if someone strung together a bunch of refrigerators. It was huge. And it was starting to move ever so slowly down from the ceiling towards my helplessly prone body. I was beginning to have an irrational fear of being crushed to death and suddenly understood why we had a dress rehearsal for the head-turning business. The camera was now precariously suspended literally millimeters from my nose, running the length of my body. Did I mention it was *huge*? Panic sweat exploded through every article of clothing I had on for the second time in one day.

Then, the woman and man who were administering the test made the unfortunate choice of holding a banal personal conversation during the test as if I wasn't in the room.

"Oh, this is good."

"Whatcha get?"

"The caramel with some extra cinnamon. Yum. Ma'am, can you turn your head to the right, now? Oh yeah, this was worth the walk. Want some?"

"How many of these are we doing for her?"

"Whole series. Hold it for another twenty seconds please. Why didn't you go last night? It was awesome..."

And so on. I was a piece of meat on a slab and they were young upstart medical professionals more interested in their lattes and personal lives than their now wildly claustrophobic patient trying to balance mentally and physically into a happy place that would not cause her to scream or vomit, while she imagined being crushed to dust by a fucking camera. By the time I could get up, I was so relieved to get out of there, I actually thanked them.

They gave me the "pictures" and told me I needed to bring them back the next day for my surgery. "Don't freak out when you look at them. You won't understand what it means so just better not to look and speculate."

"No, I won't, I promise." So of course, I promptly opened the large gray envelope and looked at the photo of my breast where the nuclear blast took place. I kid you not, it looked to me exactly as it felt: like a small bomb had been detonated. I didn't speculate. I just took a deep breath, put the pictures back, and headed back into the waiting room with a sad feeling about everything I was going to put my poor breasts through tomorrow. The girls were there to greet me, of course.

"How'd it go?"

"Fine. Can we *drink now*?"

"Hell, yes. Let's get out of here."

"I spotted a liquor store over on Second Avenue. Let's pick up some extra vino for the room."

"It is Valentine's Day so I vote for red."

"There was never a question."

I finally realized that both of my sisters, who are moms and wives, were on some base level relishing the quiet, the freedom, and the just-us-girls atmosphere as if it were a gift that they never asked for but reluctantly accepted anyway, trying to find something useful to do with it. Believe me, I understand the underlying panic that we were all feeling. But I could also sense that being forced into this situation was presenting us with something I never thought we would have again: time alone with each other uninterrupted by children, husbands, and the endless list of things they do for their families' welfare. Suddenly we were vying for the prime real estate on the vanity for our make-up and toiletries and for space in front of the small hotel mirror like we were teenagers. Oh, and the ritual Borrowing-of-the-Clothes. Do we ever grow out of the need to do that? But something was different. And it wasn't just that thirty-something years had passed since we were younger women with smaller waistlines. We knew, this time, not to take it for granted. I started taking mental pictures of the random and wonderfully ordinary activity in that hotel room.

Then suddenly Jayne said something that was so wildly out of character that I was not quite sure what to make of it. "So, did I tell you I signed up to walk in the 3-Day for the Susan B. Komen Foundation?"

Not knowing what "the 3-Day" was didn't much matter. Jayne is not a *joiner*. Nor has she ever been anything remotely close to athletic. She is an observer. She is the super-brainy kid whose only high school friends were the nerds and social misfits from band who all went on to be doctors, lawyers, or other professionals requiring many initials after their names. The initials after hers are numerous and intimidating. Jayne graduated from university fourth in her class with a 4.0. She never played a sport in her life unless you count marching band, and I certainly don't. Jayne went ice-skating with me once at my insistence when we were in our twenties so I could introduce her to some of *my* friends and she gamely went out onto the frozen lake but promptly lost control of both ankles, hit the ice, and gave herself a concussion, ending all hopes of an Olympic career. She typically uses that day as a glaring example of her non-athletic prowess anytime someone foolishly suggests another opportunity for her to become engaged in a sporting activity. But to her credit she did recently begin practicing yoga, which considering its general proximity to the ground, I think is a good choice. Jayne is classically pretty with very dark brown hair and eyes; one of those women who appears much younger than the calendar would have you believe but doesn't really have to work at it. She doesn't do make-up unless it's a special occasion and hates to shop for clothes (this fact alone makes me question our genetic link). We are three years apart and everyone assumes she is the younger one. Which is really annoying.

"I know what Komen is but what is the 3-Day? And where are you walking?!" I ask.

"Jodi and I are going to do it, right Jo? In Boston. July." Jayne was happily perusing the aromatherapy amenities menu trying to decide between the lavender and rice pillows.

"Yep. Still have to sign up, though," said Jodi without a hint of hesitation in her voice.

"Oh, let me bring up the website so you can register!" said Jayne as she excitedly fired up the 3-Day site and navigated Jodi to the online registration page. "Jodi and I decided we're doing this and we have to raise $2,200 each by July and then we're walking sixty miles over three days. It's very cool."

Apparently Jayne had reached the bottom of the helplessness and worry pit and decided to do something meaningful. Something absolutely insane.

"You're walking *how far?*"

"Sixty. Miles."

"Holy crap, you do know how far that is, right?"

"I'm putting a team together. I'm the captain; we're calling ourselves The Sole Sisters."

Who *were* these people? Didn't they know how far that is?

I certainly wouldn't have guessed it at the time, but my sister's act of lunacy was actually a brilliant and brave leap into the unknown that would, in time, have a profound impact on our entire family. Jodi sat at the computer registering and the two of them casually talked about the upcoming Double Marathon of Walking like it was an extended shopping jaunt. Jodi, though a considerably more coordinated and social being—and just as striking as Jayne— is still a bit of a delicate flower when it comes to sports where actual sweat is involved. Back in the day, she was a gymnast and baton twirler, and growing up she did her share of Jazzercise, but I don't think I've seen her in a pair of sneakers since junior high. I'm not even sure she uses deodorant. This is the woman who does not leave her house unless her entire outfit is perfectly coordinated. Think Ann Taylor meets Garanimals. Wicking shirts and sweatpants have no place in her public life. She is a perfect size four, mascara-only, perfect hair-styled mom who also looks much younger than me because she is. By about six years. Which is also annoying.

So after the shock wore off, the knowledge that my decidedly non-athletic sisters were undertaking this humongous physical and fundraising commitment on behalf of me and my mother and others in their lives was nothing less than humbling. It also scared me a little bit when I realized that I'm now one of the people who will benefit from organizations like Komen; I'm not just someone who sends them money anymore. I'm on the other side of the charitable donation equation.

Sleep was easy to come by after two glasses of red and a long day of fighting the specter of more pain and general worry, but the best part about it was that the girls were in the next bed, ready to do and be whatever I needed and I cannot remember another time in our lives when that might have been true. Not that we are neglectful or bad people, but we just never had a situation when we needed to let all our guards down simultaneously and methodically plug away at the activities and emotions surrounding the fact that one of us was in mortal danger. This was new territory for all of us. And to their credit, their instincts and talents as good mothers were probably even more important than the sisterly bond. I needed, for the first time I could remember in a long time, to be mothered. I faulted myself for not recognizing sooner the channel of strength and security that my sisters could provide and were probably always ready to provide, sick or not.

FEBRUARY 14

The next morning was an interesting test of will for me because I was not allowed to eat, drink anything including water, or use deodorant, makeup, body lotion, perfume, or any other product that might make me feel female or human. I did, however, insist that I apply my eyebrows.

"What are you doing?" Jodi asked when she saw my makeup kit in the bathroom.

"Brows."

"Why?"

"Because I need them."

"No, you don't."

"I am completely monochromatic without them. Plus, if I can't talk they will have no way of reading my expression unless they can see my eyebrows. And I'm kind of hoping I'll see some hot doctors."

"All right. Down, girl. Just no other makeup or anything."

"I know. Just brows. I don't go anywhere without them."

Then Jayne piped in. "I don't think the paparazzi will be in the OR today, Jude."

The girls were getting themselves together and trying to avoid eating in front of me, which was nice, but entirely unnecessary and I told them so. "Let's get out of here so you two can grab a bite. This is going to be a long day...you need to eat something."

"We can get something at the hospital."

"You're opting for hospital food when we're walking right past a New York bagel shop? Who's the sick one here?"

I had taken a Xanax with no water before we left so that I could be a bit more relaxed for the series of procedures leading up to surgery later. It did the trick, because I remember not even flinching at the fact that not only couldn't I eat, but it was really cold outside and it was a six-block walk to the hospital; I didn't feel a thing.

I was called by a nurse to put on the standard-issue surgical gown and slipper socks. Then I was sent back to the waiting room until I was needed for the MRI. Let me tell you—once you've donned the gown and the robe, which only hangs to your knees, and you're in the hospital dispose-o-panties, the last thing you want to do is display yourself in the waiting room in front of all those families. There were other women suffering the same fashion indignity as I, but I couldn't see them through my own self-consciousness. Luckily, there was an oddly comic diversion of a man—we guessed waiting for his wife or partner in surgery—who did not wish to be slowed down one iota by this sad turn of events and set about creating a makeshift office in a waiting room full of anxious cancer patients. He had his cell phone on loud, his laptop fired up, and his briefcase sprawled over two chairs, and was selling commercial toilet paper holders to companies in New Jersey like a hearing-impaired Willie Loman on crack.

"Hey, howarya? Yeah, yeah, still hangin' in. You? Greeeaat. I hear you guys are doin' some business, right? Hah? *Sure*. You get my e-mails? Are we good, then? Those three shipments...hah? No, I *told* you guys they were on their way. Two days, tops. *Awe*some!!" He was screaming into his cell phone like it was a Dixie cup with a string. It was hilarious, rude, psychotic, and completely objectionable to everyone within earshot but honestly, we couldn't help but marvel at his insensitivity and plain old audacity and had to hide our laughter behind magazines. Only in New York.

The MRI was next on the menu and we were escorted to another part of the massive building by a lovely volunteer who tried valiantly to make us laugh. Jayne, who has RD, LD, and CNSD after her name on her medical center business card, is an expert nutritionist, and was now my legal healthcare agent and general interpreter of hospital protocol and jargon, came into the holding tank with me. A nurse came in and asked me if I wanted to be part of a clinical trial that would leave me in the MRI machine an extra ten minutes. Of course I wanted to help and as she explained it to us, it seemed like the only positive thing I could do in this place to help other women not have to follow me down the hall someday.

Our next visitor was a doctor to explain the procedure to me, which heretofore I thought was just an MRI. He looked *exactly* like Geoffrey Rush, the wonderful actor, so let's call him Dr. Rush. Still feeling the effects of the Xanax but wanting to be as thorough as possible in my understanding of what was about to happen, we engaged in a short conversation that ended with me feeling like I had stepped over the line. Again.

"So Jude, just so you understand how this works, I'm going to be inserting tiny needles into your breasts for each one of the areas that Dr. Graham is going to be removing later today. It will help him conserve as much breast tissue as possible. And then we'll take pictures of it in the MRI."

"Needles? Okay."

"Any questions?"

I started with a stupid one, but I was temporarily at a loss. "How long will it take?"

"Well, unless I miss my marks on the first try, expect about thirty minutes or so."

"How big are the needles?"

"Oh, pretty long. About the size of a kebab skewer, but very thin, like a guitar string."

"How often do you miss?"

"Excuse me?"

"How often do you miss your marks? I mean, what percentage of the time are you off?"

Well, this totally pissed off Dr. Rush, who didn't realize that I was half-joking and just trying to understand what my chances were of having those needles puncturing my breast tissue more than necessary this morning, since I needed five of them inserted for Dr. Graham to do his magic and this was the first I was hearing about it.

"I am usually pretty good at this, Jude; I've been doing this for quite some time." Then he paused and looked at me with a wicked look in his eye and said, "But let's just say I'll keep doing it till I hit my mark." This was his way of saying, *Don't even go there.* Jayne started to squirm and laughed nervously, sending me the vibe that I should probably not get into a verbal sparring match with Dr. Rush minutes before he was going to use me as a human pincushion. So I joined her with a weak giggle and looked at them both as if to say, *Touché. Let's roll.*

"Okay, then, we'll see you in just a few minutes. Your sister can wait in the front lobby."

"Can't she come in with me?

"No, she can wait in the front."

"But the nurse said she could…"

"It's really not…something we *advise*. She can come in when we're done, alrighty?" And with that he was already walking away because the conversation had ended.

Jayne looked at me and said, "I can't believe you said that to him! 'How many times do you miss your mark?'"

"Well, wouldn't you want to know?" And off I went into the MRI room again.

Can I tell you that I was not expecting what happened next? The MRI was chugging away and I lay face down with my breasts in the two holes in the center of the slab. Suddenly about five nurses came in and surrounded Dr. Rush like worker bees to their queen. I was completely invisible to them until he turned to me with a small needle and said, "This should deaden the area for us this morning" and injected something into my left breast.

However, I don't believe he waited the requisite time before beginning "our" procedure because when the first needle went into my breast tissue, I thought I might die. Right there, on the MRI slab. And my back flinched up from the pain but there was a hand firmly on my upper back to hold me in place. From behind me, a nurse said something soothing, but she was also pinning me down so she couldn't have really cared very much. I suddenly felt very,

very nervous as I realized I had four more of these to go, and then I still had to be rolled back into the MRI so they could take pictures of his arrangement, which is unpleasant even when you don't have five needles sticking out of your chest. Then I remembered my commitment to the clinical trial to stay in there ten minutes longer. This was turning into such a nice morning for me.

I tried to go to the happy place, but by the time he moved to the right breast I had been rolled into the MRI several times and my neck was in spasm. I was crying. It was horrible. And Dr. Rush, who was clearly a perfectionist when it came to playing darts, was trying to be sympathetic but had a hard time assembling meaningful phrases. "Okay. Okay....okay. Okay, all right now" was pretty much the extent of his bedside patter while his patient was lying panicked and weeping under the forceful hands of his nurses. Someone needs to get this man a thesaurus.

When it was over, forty-five minutes later, I was a mess. He looked at me and said I did great and then escaped like a bat out of hell. I looked down and had five guitar strings protruding from my breasts (four in the left, one in the right) and was bleeding and sore. The worker bees were wrapping me in gauze and tape, but none of them had the presence of mind to address me. They spoke amongst themselves as if I weren't even there until I asked with some authority, "Where is my sister?!" which broke the ice and clearly their rhythm, so they were forced to remember I was actually still alive and could speak and hear.

I was escorted by a young nurse to find Jayne and on the way, she told me that I needed to go to radiology next to have some mammograms taken.

"What?!"

"We just need to get really good pictures of the needle localizations to make sure Dr. Rush hit his marks."

In the elevator, dazed and slightly freaked out, but completely elated to be out of that room and on my way to a procedure I understood, I must have looked like mental patient in my ugly gown, slipper socks, and being held up by a hospital escort. Jayne asked, "How was it?"

"Not fun."

"You okay, Jude?"

"Not really. No. I'll be fine."

Then I remembered that a mammogram consists of squeezing your breasts until you think they might explode; and I had needles in mine now. *Dammit.*

The radiologist at least had a sense of humor and was very accustomed to meeting up with Dr. Rush's women. Since it was Valentine's Day, when she applied the little stickers to my nipples so they could help with alignment on the films, they had little red hearts on them. I'm not making this up. I'm bleeding, crying, and in horrible fear of what this mammogram is going to feel like now that I was part porcupine and she's cheerfully applying holiday pasties. I had to laugh. It forced me to see the absurdity of the situation and I was grateful for her silly attempt at humor. And for the day god invented Xanax.

It didn't feel as bad as it looked because the anesthetic was finally starting to kick in; I can compare it to when you have to squeeze your own finger to remove a splinter. So after we managed to get all the appropriate angles in the machine and squeezed my poor mangled breasts about seven times, she left me alone in the room because apparently Dr. Rush had to approve the films before I moved on to the next event in the Breast Horror Triathlon.

He came in looking rather smug and approving of his own work and I was just letting out my first sigh of relief when I heard him mutter, "No...we need more here."

I turned to him and demanded, "More what!?"

He must have realized I was on the brink so in his sweetest voice he cooed, "Jude, I'm afraid we're going to have to do one more needle insertion to give Dr. Graham what he needs for your surgery. But don't worry, we don't need another MRI, we can do it right here."

And before I could protest or even ask another question, he had whipped a guitar string out, had Nurse Ratched sterilize it, and was plunging it into my breast with absolutely no additional anesthetic. Nada. Nothing. His marksmanship was astounding and thankfully he had finally "hit his marks" and we were done with the breast darts, but they were to remain in my breasts for the rest of the day until surgery. It was about eleven a.m. at this point and my surgery was scheduled for four. Dr. Graham later joked that with one more, he could have strummed a song on me. He thought it was very funny and probably killed with it in the OR.

Again, a Sloan escort took me and Jayne back to the holding tank. She was saying something to me in the elevator but I didn't really hear it. I was officially, and completely, freaked out. No other way to describe it.

Now typically, when we experience stress in our lives, really high levels of stress or pain or even sadness, we can reach for something that takes the edge off. Chocolate, wine, or assorted painkillers come to mind. But I was stuck in that horrible limbo of being in pain, unable to even drink water, and wildly depressed about what was happening to me. When I think back on those awful hours in that waiting room (a preposterously long day, since I was the last person called in to walk down the surgery hallway at six thirty that evening; I guess it was assumed I was young and strong and could stand the wait) I keep coming back to the fact that there were people with me who kept looking at me and after me, and were waiting on me hand and foot who, I realized, were the reason to not dissolve into puddles of self-pity. Oh yes, there were magazines and idle chat and borrowing of iPods to pass the time. But in my heart, I was hanging on to the notion that my kind and wonderful sisters did not deserve to lose their sister at forty-six.

I later discovered that both Jayne and Jodi had packed granola bars and various Jayne-approved snacks and were taking turns sneaking around the corner to the elevator to eat. There must have been a whole system of sign-language to facilitate this because I had absolutely no idea. By the time Kim arrived I felt a small twinge of guilt that these three busy women were taking big chunks out of their week to work through this mess with me. But it was a small enough twinge that I could easily let it go and replace it with gratitude, learning in spite of myself to flex that muscle, and no one was the wiser.

Dr. Graham stopped in the waiting room throughout the day to speak to each family waiting patiently to hear that their loved one was okay. We have two basic fears in a hospital waiting room: Complications and Death. Everything else is really just happy noise when surgeons are talking. I was glad that this was his protocol so that Jayne and Jodi would have word that I was indeed alive and sans complications after the cancer was cut out of me. Let's face it, it had been a pretty dreadful Valentine's Day all around and they deserved a nice big hug and some ebullient happy noise from my doctor. Not to mention a bottle of wine the size of the Chrysler building and a joint.

When my name was finally called, *seven hours* after the wires were inserted, I was so wiped out—exhausted, inconsolably hungry, uncomfortable, sad, and anxious—that even though the Xanax had worn off hours before, my body had mercifully and instinctively started to anesthetize itself. It was as if I was watching and listening from another part of the room, having effectively separated myself from the jagged, stinging waves of pain and the inexorable reality of what was to come.

"Judy Callirgos? Ms. Callirgos?" And I looked up to see a stout and pretty Hispanic nurse with round cushiony arms and faded lipstick but the robust smile she reserved for her end-of-the-day patients. I had requested to speak to Dr. Graham before the surgery because I needed to look him in the eye and ask a few questions. In hindsight, I cannot even remember what those questions were, but damn, they were important at the time.

She put her arm around me and started to walk me down the hall and I stopped and reminded her that I was supposed to talk with good Dr. Graham before he cut me open this evening. She said, "Oh, yes. Sure, sure. Take a seat in here and I will ask him to chat with you and your sisters for a few minutes."

So Jodi, Jayne, and I went into another sterile-looking tiled room with jail-break lighting and I felt so weak I thought I was going to pass out. I knew I looked bad. But I was not prepared for what I saw when the formerly quasi-attractive Dr. Graham walked in wearing his blood-stained scrubs and a face that said, "I'm *exhausted*! I've been slicing and dicing breasts since eight a.m. and it's now six thirty and I've still got *you* to talk to before surgery, plus, it's Valentine's Day and my wife is waiting for me to take her to dinner." I am probably exaggerating just a little bit but bottom line: he looked like shit and he was nowhere to be found on the happy-noise meter.

I can't recall the specifics, but we must have been chatting about boobs, needles, or Dick Cheney, but my guess is all I wanted him to do was to look me in the eye and tell me that it would all be over soon and that I would be all right. But at the end of our pre-surgical tête-à-tête, the wilted Dr. Graham asked if I had any other questions. At this point my brain had left the building and my heart was in some form of hibernation but my stomach was apparently still awake and now squarely in the driver's seat, "Yes, when can I eat pizza?" At which point I'm sure the good doctor was *so* glad he made a special stop to talk to his patient.

The moment he left us his nurse came in with a surgical bonnet and sterile foot condoms for me so I could finish accessorizing for surgery. She asked me to "say good-bye to my sisters" which I thought showed poor judgment considering the circumstances, nevertheless, I put on my blue hat and booties and hugged the girls before shuffling down a long, empty hallway with her.

By the time I reach the operating room I am elated at the prospect of being put into a deep and wondrous sleep, completely eclipsing my fear of the surgery itself. There are about ten people all milling around with purposeful energy and brightly colored scrubs when I walk in and take my place on the operating table. They immediately circle around me, albeit in a much more maternal and less threatening way than the human yellow jackets in the MRI chamber, and proceed to put a warm blanket over me and line up my legs in the vibrating leg warmers; all while saying soothing, almost sing-song unintelligible things, at which point I probably could have just passed out into a week-long coma without any drugs at all. But the nice lady with robin's egg-blue eye shadow and the lovely hypodermic needle comes from out of nowhere; truly, she just materializes like a Jedi-doctor; ties me off, introduces herself, smiles a very sweet smile and says, "You're going to feel a little pinch and then I want you to count backwards from a hundred, Jude, okay?"

"Bring it on," I say in a slurred almost otherworldly voice. I hear some slow-motion tittering echo and fade into the ceiling tiles and before a single number passes my lips, I am suspended in pure narcotic bliss, thank god.

Waking up in recovery, I was wrapped up in bandages held in place by a bloody tourniquet around my chest, and completely unable to create moisture in my mouth. It was fruitless. My sisters were right there with moistened swabs and jokes and I understand I was saying some pretty funny things but I can't remember much about it other than Jodi was still giggling over the earlier pizza comment. I do remember being asked to get up to see if I could walk and then floating down several long hallways as I got some of my cognitive abilities back, and heading for the exit with my hospital all-chick-entourage. Kim, Jayne, Jodi, and some lesser version of me.

I vaguely recall getting into a cab after leaving Sloan, a New York taxicab, mind you, and going the longest, most pothole-filled six blocks of my life. I was starting to feel sore and feeling like I should have been allowed to sleep for a few more days instead of being hastily excused from the hospital at almost eleven p.m. after it was clear that I could drink water and, ironically, eat a graham cracker without yakking.

But when we all got back to the hotel, I made myself comfortable in one of the two lovely, pillow-covered beds and felt about as relieved as any human could possibly be. I was safe. My sisters were with me. Kim was bearing silly and thoughtful presents like cheesy Valentine's Day jammies and a unique brand of optimism that should someday be made available at retail stores. I had a bottle full of painkillers, and my candle from home was burning a familiar scent into the hotel air. Life could resume and aside from the fact that it would take a full forty-eight hours before I had the nerve to look at my mangled breasts and armpit under the tight Velcro boob-vest and bandages, I was already feeling like I was on the other side of this torturous journey; the cancer was gone, I had both my breasts, albeit in a less attractive form, but the worst was behind me and life could only get better.

And that's what I believed that night. With all my crazy Valentine's Day heart.

FEBRUARY 17

About a week before surgery I had received a call from my hands-down-favorite cousin Julie in California who was concerned about what was happening with my soon to be ex-husband, and the latest on the surgery. She listened patiently and then asked, "So, who's going with you to the hospital, kiddo?"

"Jayne and Jodi are coming; I got a terrific room for the three of us in a totally swank, super-modern hotel on the Upper East Side."

"Nice! Will they be staying with you when you get home?"

"Oh, no, they've got to get back. I'm sure my friends will look in on me," I said, even though I had not made any arrangements of the kind yet, except for the first night, when an old friend said she would come by after work and stay over if I needed company. I honestly didn't think I was going to be requiring live-in support after the surgery.

"But who's staying with you, Jude?"

"Absolutely no one, Jule; the husband finally agreed that he can't stay here while I'm recuperating, so I will be gloriously, wonderfully alone."

"I don't think that's such a great idea. Do you want company?"

"Julie, you live in California and last time I checked you had a *job*. Don't worry about me. I will be fine."

"I have a ton of vacation time and honestly, I would feel better if you weren't all by yourself *out there*...."

Part of the panic that people in my life feel for me being alone is actually born out of where I live. My very small mid-century home is on a gorgeous plot of land, which I affectionately dubbed Green Acres, along the Saugatuck River and is, truly, in the middle of nowhere, which is just the way I like it. I cannot see a house from mine until the leaves fall in autumn and at that, those houses are a good distance away. There are large parcels of preserved land in almost every direction with acres and acres of densely wooded, glorious hiking trails. I don't need curtains. My town doesn't even have its own gas station, although we do have a train station. Mark Twain built his final home here and named it Stormfield. Helen Keller, after visiting him here, referred to it as Eden, which is apt and not overly generous or romantic. Horses from one of the local farms walk down my street on a regular basis, much to the consternation of my dogs. Deer, turkeys, herons, hawks, and the occasional bear traverse the land. Julie has been here and though not exactly a city kid herself, having grown up in rural upstate New York, she thinks that Green Acres was most likely originally built for someone in the Witness Protection Program.

"I'd love to see you, but I won't be much—"

"I'm calling Jet Blue today."

That's how Jules decided that, instead of spending her well-deserved vacation in sunny Mexico at the swim-up bar, she was coming to New England, in February, to take care of me. She rearranged her life with Tasmanian-devil speed, got on a plane, and took a red-eye out of Sacramento, arriving in Redding, Connecticut, at ten a.m. with a Starbucks in her hand exactly forty-eight hours after I arrived home from the hospital.

The very first night an old theater friend named Susy stopped by and decided after she saw my bandage get-up that she would stay the night and make sure I was okay. The following night I was alone but getting texts from Julie that she was on her white horse and heading this way.

I know many women have had lumpectomies and been up and about in no time. I was not. I endured those crazy needle insertions, what finally amounted to two lumpectomies, four more biopsies and an armpit lymph-node removal. Make no mistake, all you pink ribbon twirlers—it really, really *hurt*. I had sutures and bruises on both my breasts. I couldn't move my left arm for the pain and stitches in my armpit, nor could I look at myself in the mirror without shaking. The hideously tight Velcro-boob vest that I was strapped into 24/7 was impossible to part with because when I tried to loosen it or take it off, the pain just got worse because my breasts would fall and the wounds would stretch. The pain pills I didn't think I would need were going down every four hours like clockwork. I really didn't think I was out of the woods so every time a well-wisher would say, *Aren't you relieved the cancer is gone?* I would agree, of course, and then say a silent prayer that it was so. Now that I had actual physical pain to contend with I started tuning in to this disease on a more visceral level and it was a formidable foe. Every day that passed without word from Dr. Graham about "getting clean margins" made me more and more anxious. He should have called by now. *Dammit.*

Julie, a/k/a Jules, is a soon-to-be-retired researcher at the local university in Sacramento, but she could have been a nurse, a comedienne, a psychologist, or a time management guru in some other parallel universe. She executed all four jobs here with practiced precision. Jules is about ten years older than me, looks about three years younger, and could pass for my sister. I believe we extracted the exact same social and style genes from our mothers, who are sisters, because we are so alike in our thinking and tastes that over the years we have actually purchased the same clothing, artwork and furniture without discussing it with each other first. It's uncanny.

When we were children, before her family moved out West, my family would visit Julie and her sisters, Beth and Debbie, and her parents, Aunt Clara and Uncle "Jukebox" Joe in their very small and neatly decorated farmhouse in Marlboro, New York. I grew up on Long Island so when I would hear that we were going "upstate to the country" it was very exciting to me because I loved that they didn't have ugly curbs and sidewalks; they had rolling hills with a split-rail fence and a gravel driveway. On the ride up I would press my face to the car window staring at acre after acre of apple orchards hoping to catch a glimpse of a horse or a cow, and marveling at wildflowers that had sprung up, not in a garden, but wherever they darn well felt like it, which at the time was terribly exotic to me. I loved and looked up to my cousin Julie because she was always unfailingly kind to me; we connected. She taught me how to do the Mashed Potato and how to make my hair go in a flip. I remember trying to copy her laugh when I was very little because whenever she laughed it would make my dad smile.

Today, Julie has an authentic West Coast, laid back, hand-me-my-flip-flops approach to life, and a surprising talent for taking control and nurturing in the same breath. She was the only one in her family not only to complete college but go on to graduate school, which required a good deal of personal fortitude on her part, having funded it entirely herself. But Jules has spent most of her life burying bad memories from that house on the hill in

Marlboro, so what she sees reflected back in her mirror is not the Julie everyone else sees and adores. Trying to convince her of what a great human being she is like trying to teach a dog to meow. Still, I believe she would have been an incredible mother, although when I say that to her she swipes her hand through the air as if to erase the very thought and says, "*Nooo*, thank you."

I am not an easy person to take care of, exhausting most mortals in just a few hours, on average. Probably in response to life's calamities, I developed a need to dissect everything in a quest for a deeper or hidden meaning, which is tedious even for me. I also decided that my already poultry-free diet is now going to be full-on vegetarian and organic *only*—because all my Oh-Shit-You-Have-Cancer books recommend eating pretty much nothing but what comes out of the ground or falls off a tree and washing it down with water and a lemon slice.

Julie stayed for over a week and dealt with blood, bandages, medications, legal proceedings, organic oatmeal, my cooking, visits from friends and neighbors, two dogs, and frigid temperatures. She also convinced me that wine would be a perfectly natural and organic substitute for those painkillers I was taking. But she went above and beyond the call of duty when she accompanied me to the courthouse, when my husband's misogynist lawyer decided that a week after my surgery would be a terrific time to drag me into family court to argue their case for alimony. *Alimony*. Don't get me started.

FEBRUARY 19

I still had no word on whether the margins were clear; five days and nothing.

"Jude, just call the doctor. He should have called by now; maybe they're just busy."

"I know."

"Then call."

"I should."

"You want me to call?"

"It must *mean* something…"

"I'm calling. Where's his number?"

"They won't release any information to you."

"Then how about I dial and hand you the phone?"

I finally got through to Dr. Graham's assistant's assistant who called me back hours later to say that he had some results but they were preliminary and could I make it in to see him on February 27. "Really? I had my surgery on the fourteenth. You're one of the largest cancer labs in the world and can't turn this around any faster? Am I okay or not?"

"I'm sorry ma'am. I don't know what to tell you."

"You can start by telling me that Dr. Graham will call me back and tell me what's going on. This is my life we're talking about here. Thank you." A few hours later, Dr. Graham called back and Julie raced to answer it, handing me the phone like it was a precious, sought-after jewel.

"Hey, Jude, sorry this is taking so long. How'd you like that nifty incision I gave you on the left side—bet you're wondering why it was so big?"

"Yeah, kinda."

"Well, just in case we need to go back in there...."

"What did you find?"

"Not sure, still doing cuts of the tissue samples, but one of the lymph nodes did look a little funky. Could be nothing, could be something. We'll know in a few days. I'll see you on the twenty-seventh." Click.

"Jules. If it were good news, he would have told me."

"Don't read too much into it."

Too late.

FEBRUARY 24

My lawyer is aghast. My Inner Circle wants to throw a blanket party, which entails throwing a blanket over someone's head and beating the crap out of him, and I am just plain angry. I am pale, still sore as hell, in clothes too big for me, gingerly making my way into family court arm in arm with Julie at ten on a frigid, ice-crusted February morning. At this point she must really be questioning the wisdom of choosing this scenario over the

Tiki bar in Cancun and back massages from hot Latin cabana boys.

The sterile courtroom has a center aisle and two sections on either side to sit behind the opposing, correction, combative lawyers. To add to the absurdity of the drama, these two legal eagles really cannot stand each other. It's a primal and seething hate that's making the scene that lies before us that much more unsettling. It was a grade school boys-against-the-girls brawl.

"Well, this is cozy," I whisper to Julie.

"I'll sit behind you on the bride's side," she whispers back.

It's a circus. Opposing counsel is trying to argue that, because my husband decided he didn't really feel like earning a living for the last five years, I should pay him alimony for the next six years at a ridiculous rate so he can maintain his lifestyle. My lawyer is cracking legal eggs on his head and it's getting very heated indeed. I slump in the chair next to her, convinced that my husband had in no way thought up the scheme being presented by his insane, delusional, woman-hating attorney because it bears no resemblance whatsoever to our original conversations prior to securing lawyers. I've never known him to be malicious. But I'm exasperated that he is sitting there and going along with it.

I start to feel faint. The guard rushes over to offer me some water. The judge asks my lawyer what's wrong with me.

"Your honor," she replies, "my client is recovering from very recent surgery."

"I'm sorry to hear that. For what, may I ask?"

"Breast cancer, your honor."

The good and wise Judge Frankel is a middle-aged woman with commanding judicial presence whose demeanor seems balanced, but I suspect she has the testicles of several bad men floating in formaldehyde locked in her chambers somewhere. She was not amused. She turned to opposing counsel and delivered an icy-cold scolding for wasting the court's time with this ridiculous motion and shows the Boy's Team the exit door. I turn around to glance at Julie and she looks like she does when she's watching *Law & Order*: absolutely mesmerized. As we walk arm in arm to the elevator she whispers, "Well, that was an interesting way to spend a morning. It was just like TV. I don't know why I thought it would be different. We love her. The judge."

"Yes, we do love her."

"She should have her own show."

We giggle all the way to the car in the freezing rain, holding on to each other for dear life and feeling just a little bit less cold. I do not know what I would have done this week without her.

FEBRUARY 27

I'm sitting on the end of the cold papered exam table literally unable to see. Tears have formed in my eyes but I don't dare blink for fear of starting an unstoppable flow of embarrassing waterworks so I'm just sitting there as if looking through balls of crumpled up cellophane.

After all I've been through in the past few weeks — the nuclear blast in my chest, the MRIs, the needle localizations, the incisions across both breasts and under my arm, the incessant stinging of severed nerves as they died off, and being completely unable to use my left arm for anything more strenuous than zipping my jeans — I am, once again, out of luck. They didn't get clean margins and there is a microscopic metastasis in that funky-looking sentinel lymph node: decidedly not good news.

Dr. Graham is trying to explain to me and Kim why a mastectomy is our only logical course of action.

I've stopped listening because what is coming out of his mouth now is just an over-rehearsed rationalization — the opposite of happy noise — because it's not for my benefit; it sounds like it was crafted for people in the room who might still be listening as he drops the M-bomb. Kim is taking notes.

"Honestly Jude, if you were my sister..."

Which I'm not.

"....I would recommend the same course of action. Believe me, I know how hard this is."

How is that, because you have a breast about to be amputated? Or is it because you give this lame reassurance speech every day? I have an idea, Doctor: Why don't I try explaining to you why it's

*necessary for me to surgically remove one of your balls and then
tell you I know exactly how you feel!*

It wasn't until he started talking about recommendations for
reconstructive surgery that I re-engaged with the activity in the
room on a more cerebral, less grade-school hair-pulling, I'd like to
kick him in the knees, sort of level. I left his office with the long
Middle-Eastern name of a plastic surgeon, a date for my
mastectomy, another pre-op appointment including a heart scan
and lung x-rays, and my head on the shoulder of my best friend.
The Big-M appointment was set for March 16, the day before St.
Patrick's Day. With the recent St. Valentine's Day massacre behind
me I realized I now had a new holiday I could forever brand with
my illness. Hallmark would have been a tad challenged to find the
right words for this one, but Erin Go Bra-less comes to mind.

When Kim and I left Sloan that night, she thought it best to
take me back to her house instead of to mine so I could react in
peace to the news that I was now indeed facing a modified radical
mastectomy on the left with more lymph nodes to be removed,
hoping to avoid chemotherapy—if they could get clean margins *this*
time. One would think that removal of the entire breast should do
it, but those pesky lymph nodes were really starting to piss me off.
They hurt the most and were completely destroying any hope of a
non-disfiguring, full recovery. Damn, damn, *damn.*

The first day I had spent adjusting to my preliminary diagnosis,
I read the pink-ribbon-festooned pamphlets they give you to
prepare you for the absolute worst. I cried like a two-year-old after
reading about the horror of having a mastectomy but was relieved to
learn that it was an "extremely slim possibility" in my case and that I
would most likely need a lumpectomy and radiation. Not that this
was good news either, but it wasn't the wholesale removal of my
breast, thank you very much. Now here I am two months later with
visions of those hideous pictures in my head, trying to connect with
the reality that I will look just like that in a few weeks time.

"Kim, can I have some more wine?"

"Help yourself, girlfriend; that bottle is for you. And there's
another waiting behind it when you kill that one."

Kim's house is a lovely old New England vintage home that she's meticulously decorated in French country colors and fabrics that seem to personally invite you to lounge and relax the moment you walk in. It became the place I would go for refuge when I first began divorce proceedings a few months ago, and had become a safe haven for me now that I was in the throes of yet another epic crisis. I vaguely remember Kim telling me, as we pulled into her driveway, that she would start dinner while I "made my calls." And that's when I knew for sure that it wasn't just some awful mistake that I could take back. I had to now tell other people and she was going to wine and dine me until it was done.

It's interesting how I found myself tailoring the message depending on whom I was talking to that night. Jayne got the CliffsNotes, short and to the point. Someone who works in a hospital every day cannot be schmoozed with any great efficiency.

"How'd it go?"

"Yeah, it's uh, not good news. Not what I had hoped...so I need to have the mastectomy."

"Oh, Jude. Oh, no. All right. When?"

"As soon as possible, Jayne. The only good news was that the right breast showed something called lobular neoplasia; more like a global marker for cancer, and not immediately dangerous but needs to be watched. But in the left I've got two entirely different types of cancer growing just millimeters apart, and one tumor is rather large and invasive."

"Shit."

"So, we can't leave it there. It's all got to go." And then I took a very deep breath because, of all the people I needed to call tonight, she would immediately understand the implications of my next declaration. "And there's a small metastasis in the sentinel lymph node, so we're going back for a few more of those."

"*Really?* (Pause) Okay."

"It's...just...NOT...what...uh...we wanted, right? But, there you have it."

The word metastasis connected to the words lymph and node means, in essence, that the horse is out of the barn. The cancer took a detour from the breast and was seeking something else it could destroy, and Jayne would know this was very bad news, indeed.

"I'm so sorry. Just let me know what I can do, and I'll be there. I'll come with you again. I'll call Jodi to see if she can, too. It will be okay." I could hear my stoic and rock solid sister begin to falter a bit and that was all I needed to hear to want to immediately hang up the phone before she slipped down that scary emotional slope taking me along with her. Instinctively, I needed her, of all people, to be strong and unbending.

"Yeah. Thanks. I appreciate it. Listen, Kim's making dinner, so I'm going to..."

"Yeah, okay. (Pause) Hang in there. Are you going to call Jo or you want me to?"

"I'll do it."

Jodi, who is famously sensitive and socially correct in all matters concerning the human condition, received a slightly veiled version of my previous conversation that excluded the word *metastasis*, which for some reason my internal censors deemed too shocking for her. My mother was matter-of-factly told, "Don't worry, Ma, I'll be fine! It sucks, you know, but honestly I'm glad to finally have an answer," which was *total and complete bullshit*, but what's the sense of driving your mom crazy with worry? "So, how's Dad?" was my ridiculous segue and subtle hint that I was not up for a long distance weep-fest and was calling just so she would move away from waiting, literally, by the phone and go back to her routine of watching TV, sipping chardonnay, and intermittently snacking until she goes to bed. That is what I really wanted. Oh yes, and I also wanted to go back in time to when my life was not a Category Five hurricane.

My boss on the other hand, came out of the blue with the most honest and normal phone call I had all night. We actually talked. And I didn't rush him off the phone. He is one of those people who jumped into the fray from my first diagnosis with exactly the right tone and appropriate questions, and quickly became a sharpshooter when taking aim at my childish, counterproductive defense mechanisms, all from three thousand miles away.

"Hey, Steve. It's me."

"Oh, hi. I didn't know if I would hear from you tonight."

"Yes, well, it's not good news."

"Oh Jude, that's awful. Jeez. Will you need chemo? Do they know?"

"They're not sure yet; won't know until after this next round of surgery."

"God, you've got to be disappointed. You can't seem to catch a break."

"Yeah, I've thought about that." And then trying to dig my way out of a potentially emotional corner with my boss, I tried some humor. "You know, between the divorce and the cancer, I can't decide if my life should be an episode of *Law & Order* or *ER*."

To which he countered, "I'd vote for *CSI: Special Victim's Unit*."

We laughed as if we hadn't used those muscles in weeks, and on the waning curve of that laughter he asked, "So, you think you will you be needing a nipple reconstruction?"

Okay. I'm relatively sure that I'm one of the most progressive people I know. But when my sixty-something male boss inquired about my need for nipple reconstruction, and actually knew that the procedure entailed getting a tattoo, it took my day to a whole new level of surrealism.

I think I responded by saying, *"What?!"*

"Well, I remember when a friend went through this," he explained, "that it can be kind of time consuming, all that reconstruction. But hey, it's worth it, right? And you're in the best place, Jude." He was, of course, referring to Sloan and the good doctors who, in my opinion, range from godlike to insensitive jerks. But when he said it, I immediately related it to being at Kim's house and thought, *Yeah, I am in the best place right now.* It was incredibly sad and isolating to feel as if I no longer had a home of my own and that my sense of personal place was completely in limbo, but it wasn't the top story today, so I moved it to the back burner.

"On the bright side," I said, "there's always the boob job at the end of the tunnel. And if I'm a candidate for the microsurgery, I can get a tummy tuck at the same time."

We laughed again, although with less enthusiasm this time. It was starting to hit home that I was having my breast amputated and was in for some nasty surgery and recovery time, to say nothing of the spreading cancer, and here I was talking openly about it with my family and my boss. This was not a play or a TV show, and nothing in my trick bag was going to take the sting out of reaching this point of no return. My reality had just surpassed standard life drama and I was ill-equipped to handle it. As it turns out, Steve had been the VP of Human Resources for a Silicon Valley CEO when she was undergoing treatment for breast cancer that almost exactly mirrored my own, except for the fact that she is a big, important executive and I am, well, *not*. Steve was in her Inner Circle and made a subtle effort to let me know that when it came to these matters, he not only wasn't a stranger, but he could be depended on to actually know what the hell to talk about when it came down to discussing hard choices and next steps, both personal and professional.

So now, learning that the first attempt at surgically removing the cancer proved unsuccessful, I could feel myself inching headlong into a dark tunnel of fear and utter helplessness as I lobbed these dreadful calls from Kim's kitchen, clinging to whatever solace I could find in the carefully chosen words coming back at me. She was calmly cooking us dinner and refilling my wine glass, reminding me to breathe and, in her inimitable way, being the exact right person to have in the room when coming to terms with the sudden tenuousness of my life and the earth shifting beneath my feet. Again.

Before we said good-bye, Steve said, "Your life is never going to be the same, kiddo. It's not a bad thing, and it could be really great down the line, but you need to get used to it; everything changes after today."

I didn't know yet whether that was good news or not but I knew, deep down in the pit of my churning stomach, that he was right.

MARCH 6

Kim accompanied me to the plastic surgeon today because I think she knew that I should not be left alone in an examining room with another new doctor and his coterie of starched-white Mini-Me's. One false move and I would take them all down with my raging rudeness or pathetic hysteria, depending on which way the mood pendulum was swinging.

When we met with the doctor in his office on Fifty-Third Street, I immediately realized that some beneficent force, most likely my late friend David, had arranged for me to have the most stunningly handsome doctor in the universe—seriously, drop-dead gorgeous. I just stared when he came in the room. Kim did the flirty eyelash flutter thing without even realizing she was doing it. It was shameless. He was over six feet tall with a perfectly lean, broad-shouldered body that was covered in mocha latte-colored skin and a pale blue short-sleeved tunic; very dark hair around his angular face and the whitest smile I've ever seen housed right next to a subtle dimple on one side of a very sexy mouth; he looked like he even smelled good. We instantly dubbed him McDreamy.

I was quite prepared for this meeting, intellectually anyway, in that I had been doggedly researching breast reconstruction options since I got my first pink ribbon pamphlet. I had already decided exactly what I wanted and was laser-focused on it: the DIEP flap surgery with the skin and nipple-sparing procedure, an exciting new micro-surgery. They would take tissue from my abdomen and move it up through my core to lump it around where my breast used to be, form a new one under my real skin and preserve or re-attach the blood vessels so it will be warm and my own actual tissue, not some fake lump of Hollywood silicone or a cold bag of saline. Plus, it would have my very own precious nipple on top. Voila! Okay, so the nipple wouldn't actually work anymore but at least it would still *be there*. Not some hideous 3-D tattooed version or worse, the creepy Barbie-boob look of women who don't bother (not that I can even begin to understand why) to replace their missing nipple. I mean really. What are they thinking?

I told all this to McDreamy and he directed me, in essence, to put on the pink smock and assume the position. So I was faced with the sad humiliation of showing this beyond-handsome man my mangled, bruised, recently sutured, middle-aged breasts. Pink gown was on open in the front; McDreamy looked pensively at my chest and then asked me to unzip my jeans, which under other circumstances on some far off-planet that I used to inhabit, would have been thrilling. So I unzipped. He felt around my stomach, looked at me, and said, "I thought so."

"What?"

"You're pretty thin."

"Well, not as thin as I'd like to be..."

A charming sort of TV-doctor smile crossed his face before he cleared his throat and said rather callously, "You're not a candidate, Jude. You just don't have enough fat. We're going to have to go for either the silicone or saline implant and the chest expander."

I was devastated. "*What*!?"

"No can do; if you were about twenty pounds heavier, maybe...but even then."

"Wait, they never mentioned anything about having to be fat to have it done!"

"Who else did you talk to?"

"I read it on the Internet. They said..."

"Well, don't believe everything you read. And you don't have to be fat, you just need to have a certain percentage of extra fat in a particular area. You don't."

"What if I start eating Häagen-Dazs every day until the surgery!?"

"Jude, look," he intoned as he casually displayed an implant in his hand and began rolling it around so I could just imagine how fabulous it will look lodged in my chest, "*this* is the way to go. I highly recommend the silicone over the saline. What I'll do after Dr. Graham finishes his surgery is come in while you're still under and insert a chest expander so you'll have a small lump there when you wake up."

The expander is a fairly recent revolution in plastic surgery, if you think the 1980s were recent, which I certainly do. I'm not sure I want to know how they figured this out, but it was determined that human skin, when subjected to a steady stretching force, will not only expand but actually grow. So plastic surgeons were suddenly given a whole new playing field and reconstructing parts of the body were taken to dizzying new heights. In breast reconstruction, tissue expansion is an option post-mastectomy after the breast tissue and any skin deemed to be at risk is removed. An expander can be placed in the chest immediately, as in right after the breast surgeon is done with you on the operating table, or sometime after the fact; I think you can guess my preference.

"We continue to fill up the expander with saline until we have the size we want over a few weeks and then we put in this little beauty. Are you having chemo?"

"Don't know yet. Why?"

"Because we can't do the exchange surgery until afterwards, which could be like six months, but we'll cross that bridge in a few weeks." *Great.*

"What about my nipple?" I was totally fixated on the nipple-sparing procedure because I honestly didn't know how I would get through life without one.

"Dr. Graham is in charge of that; as long as he doesn't think there's any risk leaving it behind. If not, we'll fix you up with something down the road," he chirped, making it sound like an after-dealer options package on my new Lexus.

"But I don't want one of those things!" I whined from behind a tsunami of tears and then heard him rattle off something barely intelligible as he was backing out of the room about his assistant who was going to come in next and show me implant pictures, yadda, yadda, sign consent forms, yadda, yadda, your friend can come in now, *yadda.*

I lost another round.

MARCH 8

I'm in my lawyer's office listening to her take my husband's deposition. Pass the trail mix.

MARCH 9

I'm in his lawyer's office giving my deposition. Pass the Xanax. I've got pre-op tomorrow and no one's available to come with me.

MARCH 10

These past few weeks, Jill, my attorney, shifted gears from fastidious, thorough counselor of crumbling marriages to Shirley MacLaine at the end of *Terms of Endearment*. She became a force to be reckoned with after she learned that I had to go back for the Big-M. The boys on the groom's side were ratcheting up the heat, not backing down one iota from trying any angle to have me part with as much of my hard-earned money as possible. But she advised me that she was going to try to get a court date for a family court judge to hear the case in open court so we could hopefully get some sort of agreement on paper before my surgery. Considering the back-up on the docket, I wasn't holding my breath.

Then she says something that gives me real pause. "Do you have a DNR?"

"Well, yeah, as part of my will."

"Change all your paperwork as soon as possible. The DNR, the power of attorney, and the health-care agent, everything, in case of …well, you know."

"Uh...yeah."

"You are having major surgery and going through a contentious divorce. Just play it safe."

So, today on my agenda is my pre-op appointment at Sloan, an EKG, heart scan, chest x-ray, a complete re-do of all the blood work they did last month, calls to find a reputable cleaning service to help me with the house after surgery, and a cheery meeting to update my end-of-life documents with the officious estate attorney down the hall from Jill. How much fun, really, can one girl have in a day?

MARCH 14

Jill worked her lawyerly magic and secured an appointment for an open hearing of the divorce case at eight thirty this morning, in none other than Judge Frankel's court. Apparently there was some talk in chambers that considering my health situation a new approach was needed. I had no idea what to expect but this hearing was geared to convince the other side to drop the alimony case and get back to negotiating based on facts and figures, not grudges.

I met Jill at the courthouse and was asked to sit in the antechamber of the courtroom; my husband was sitting in an identical one on the other side of the hall. The seating arrangement felt contrived and very awkward to me. Only the attorneys were allowed in the courtroom to argue their cases before the judge while their clients, the people whose actual finances were at stake, sat in the equivalent of game-show soundproof booths. After the first round, Jill came back into the room and told me things were going okay but that she needed to ask me a few more questions. I couldn't imagine what she didn't already know about me by now, but I understood her reason for wanting to get all her financial facts completely correct. It felt like an eternity went by before she came back again.

She popped the all-important bonus-round question: "If I can get them to drop the alimony suit they will want something in return. Can you live with paying him this number?"

I was doing all the paying in this equation because aside from some joint equity in the house, I earned all the cash and prizes in this marriage. I looked at the number and shivered then cringed. "Can I think about it?"

"No. We need to come up with something today. If we can settle, Judge Frankel said she'll meet us back here tomorrow and you'll be divorced by ten a.m. She's making a special arrangement because of your health. What do you think, Jude? I know it's sudden but I think it's what we want."

"Do it."

"Really? You're a hundred percent okay with this?"

"I'm not a hundred percent okay with any of this but I want it *over*. Just take the ball and run."

"I'm on it."

So I left the courthouse with a gigantic sum of money I had to figure out how I was going to pay, but the key to long-awaited personal freedom would by mine in about twenty-four hours. The grim fact that my mastectomy was forty-eight hours away sort of put a damper on my celebratory mood, but I tried to carve out something like relief that the end of this hideous road to dissolve my marriage was in sight. One nightmare at a time, I thought.

MARCH 15

After I left the courthouse, I summoned something akin to joyfulness, if not victory. This was happening quickly and I would still need to get a few things in order—primarily finances. How the hell I was going to pay my soon-to-be-ex a gigantic sum of money in the next thirty days?—as well as preparations for my second stay at Memorial Sloan-Kettering Hospital in as many months. I also needed to make some phone calls and let the Inner Circle know the latest in the nonstop psychodrama that is my life. I received a good many hoots and hollers about this "great news" and while I knew that to be true, in my heart of hearts I was also sad that it had come to all this childish nonsense; sad that I was going to be legally and officially alone at a time when I needed someone most, very sad that I agreed that he could take one of the dogs even though it was the right thing to do. My conversations were positive and upbeat and I needed to keep that spirit to get me through.

I realized that I was going to have to apply for another mortgage and re-buy my house from the bank to free up some cash to pay him; the other funds would come from my savings. I was not going to be bankrupt, but it wasn't going to be pretty by any means. Oh yes, and my full pay stops today; I'm now on disability which is seventy percent of my salary.

I sat in the courthouse today for the Big-D with a bag of trail mix in my lap, watching Judge Frankel hear testimony about a marriage that had circled the drain for the last time. Then I signed a ream or two of legal-sized papers with my name on them. I walked out of the building, without so much as a good-bye or good luck from my now ex-husband, despite the fact that he would return to the house — which I just agreed to buy him out of — after I leave for the city today. During one of our more civil exchanges last week, he volunteered to look after the house and dogs while I was in the hospital, which was either an attempt at kindness or a desire to get back into the house for a few days. His motivation was never clear. All that mattered was that I had just legally become the invisible non-entity I always suspected I was to him all these years. He was going to get a pile of my hard-earned money and get on with his life, and that really was all there was to that. I thanked Jill profusely for all her counsel and support and drove home with a to-do list that read as follows: apply for mortgage, pack for hospital, make sure there's enough dog food, disability calls and paperwork, download directions to the Affinia Hotel, drive to the city. Jayne and Jodi were coming to pick me up this afternoon so we could drive to our now-favorite hotel, have a nice dinner, and get ready for round two of please-get-this-cancer-out-of-me surgery.

The people at the bank did not understand my general sense of urgency this morning regarding the mortgage application so when they couldn't find anyone available to help me on the phone, they sent a link and I applied online. I needed to focus so I could get the process started *today* and lock in a good rate but my brain was not cooperating so I got kicked out of the system about three times before I got it right. I left a mortgage broker my mobile number so she could call me with questions but asked that she please wait a day or two because I had "something to take care of" making the gross understatement of the week.

I love my dogs and I feel for them because they know that things are very, very wrong in this house. I don't think there is any way to escape the truth of what your dogs know about you, and forgive you for, on a daily basis. It's a helpful reminder when you think you have the rest of the world fooled. I hated leaving them *again* but I had a conversation with both of them, Louis and Sophie, and told them that I would be back very soon. They seemed to understand but gave me the solemn stare-of-shame when they saw my suitcase come out of the closet as if they just forgot everything I said. I packed for the hospital in a flash because I had already decided generally what to bring and I knew my sisters would pick up the slack for anything I forgot. I was literally waiting at the door with my bags when they arrived.

I had a ridiculous amount of nervous energy which I'm guessing was a natural by-product of my divorce three hours earlier, so I offered to drive us to the city. My nephew Kevin and his girlfriend live there and said they would like to join us for dinner at Il Vagabondo, the only restaurant in New York that offers dinner *and* bocce, to celebrate the final dissolution and whatever else it is you're supposed to celebrate when your aunt has the Big C. They met us at the hotel at about six thirty where we promptly started drinking wine and didn't really stop until dinner was over somewhere around eleven.

I won't pretend; this was very stupid. But it was necessary. We were each experiencing our own personal weirdness about what was going on, not just with me but the rest of the family that in such a short period of time was bequeathed four incurable diagnoses; Kevin's stepmother, my brother's wife, Daryl, was also just recently informed, after actually losing weight on a trip to Italy, that she had Type I diabetes. We were moving en masse into the sick camp in the space of just three years and were ill-prepared for the emotional backdraft. So drinking copious amounts of wine seemed like the best if not the only logical thing to *do*; hangovers were the least of our worries. Knowing I couldn't drink liquids, take Advil, or eat anything after midnight rightfully should have excluded me from the Pinot Grigios and Chiantis being cheerfully passed around the table, but I kept telling myself I deserved it. What *for*, I'm not really sure.

MARCH 16

The last time we attended the morning-of-surgery movie, the streets of New York were awash in pink and red hearts, cupids, and cupcakes for Valentine's Day. Today we've got shamrocks, leprechauns, and a lot of sidewalk sandwich signs inviting us in for corned beef, green beer, and lively fiddle music. Jodi thanked me for planning my surgeries around such festive holidays.

Dinner had been a tremendous amount of fun and silliness, all things considered. When we laughed it was not restaurant-appropriate laughter. Oh, no. We howled, slammed our hands on the table rattling glasses and plates, and generally made a ruckus in our back corner until all other diners went home with their hands over their ears and we had the place to ourselves. Thank you, good people of Il Vagabondo, for not tossing us out or cutting off our wine supply.

Back home there were all sorts of logistical machinations going on behind the scenes so that I would have someone staying with me while I recovered from what was threatening to be one really lousy week followed by three slightly less crappy weeks of recovery. My mom had volunteered for the first week tour of duty, which to her must have sounded like a vacation compared to her usual caregiver responsibilities. My brother Vic and his wife volunteered to take Dad for the week, so they would drive down from Vermont on the day I'm released to pick up Mom and Dad in Glastonbury, take them to my house in Redding, and take Dad home with them.

My brother has been regularly present by phone and e-mails, but I have only seen him once, when he came down during Julie's visit to take us to a wonderful dinner. We're close, but this diagnosis had created a thin layer of carefulness between us that I had trouble defining. His wife, Daryl, described it as *his inability to fix any of it*. "Boys need to fix things," she said. Victor was suddenly surrounded by incurably sick people whom he couldn't fix and struggling to find the right way to engage. Having Dad for a week was not only a huge help for everyone but unavoidably pulled him neck deep into waters he respectfully waded in from time to time but had been cautious not to swim.

I don't sleep much past 3:00 am. I stare at the ceiling from my spinning hotel bed trying to meditate my throbbing headache into abeyance and searching my heart for a reason to actually do this; to get up out of bed in a few hours so I can voluntarily have my left breast amputated. A quiet little voice in my pounding head starts to get louder as the sun began its slow and steady ascent over the city, suggesting that maybe, just maybe I should just take my chances, roll the dice, swipe the car keys, walk down to the garage, and drive away from here leaving Jayne and Jodi with a much nicer pre-St. Patrick's Day itinerary than setting up camp in a cancer hospital. I want the clock to stop relentlessly counting the minutes for me. I want to go back in time to before this diagnosis. No, before my marriage. No, no, how about just to last night when I idiotically put away two bottles of Pinot Grigio by myself. I want to go back in time and be that crazy twenty-year-old girl with two healthy boobs and dreams of whatever the hell I was dreaming back then. I desperately need to pee but I don't want to wake them, my illustrious bodyguards in the next bed over who should have done a better job of policing me last night. My mouth is a veritable desert and my teeth have little sweaters on them. The room is brightening through the slats of the blinds and I want it to stop. The perfect slices of light look like bars on a jail cell. I feel like John Proctor waiting for dawn on the day of his execution. I want to jump out the window and fly for five stories before valiantly decorating the sidewalk to make this easier on everyone, especially me and my gigantic throbbing head. And I really, really, want a glass of fucking orange juice.

"Jude? You up?" comes a croaky whisper from across the room.

"Yeah."

"Oh. My god. What were we thinking?"

"We weren't. We were drinking heavily and eating pasta. Really, really good pasta."

"It was good, wasn't it?"

"Legendary."

"Kevin is a scream."

"Yes, he is. That's why we love him."

"You okay?"

"I don't even know how to begin to answer that."

"Okay. I'm going to use the bathroom unless you need it."

This, of course, is Jodi speaking because Jayne could sleep through a space shuttle launch and is snoring as we speak. But now, we're in it. The day has begun. No going back.

It was a rough morning getting ourselves to the hospital in time for check-in, what with the three of us clumsily banging into each other while we packed up suitcases and backpacks scouring the room for items that may have mysteriously gone missing during last night's debauchery, using only the tiny sections of our brains that were not covered in fog.

"Anyone seen my iPod?"

"Got it."

"Tweezer?"

"Over near my makeup bag."

"Mr. Tool?" This would be Jayne's hair curling device that is an endless source of bad jokes.

"In the bathroom where you left him."

"Xanax?"

"They're in your hand, Jude."

"Yes, I know that, anybody else want one?" I said as I jammed one down the back of my throat with no water and spent ten minutes trying to work up enough saliva to swallow it. It was the one luxury I was allowed before leaving for the Big House and I was not going to pass it up, drool or no drool.

At the hospital it was the same drill—no make-up or deodorant or anything remotely feminine other than my finely lined Scarlett O'Hara brows—ugly cotton smock and robe, paper panties, slipper-socks, warm blanket. At least they're consistent. Kim came into town so my three amigas and I were back where we started a month ago, making fun of my outfit, sharing magazines and pictures of George Clooney, and passing the all-girl support baton like an expert relay team. I was terrified and tried with all my being not to give it away. But they knew. At one point during our hours and hours of waiting to be called, Kim starting massaging my feet and legs and I almost started to cry. No one had touched me other than to examine me or poke me with a needle in a very, very long time.

I knew ahead of time that the recovery and rebound from this one was going to be tough. For the last few months, right up until my first surgery, I have been practicing Bikram yoga, which is that insane "hot" yoga that people you generally don't invite to parties do on a regular basis. It's a ninety-minute yoga class in a room heated to 105°, complete torture for some; I am the girl who is always cold, so I'm in heaven. I could do it every day. And the good news is that it gets you in serious shape. As Bikram himself says, "Bengal tiger strength." My abs, while not rock hard, are probably the consistency of an under-ripe avocado. I am a legit size 5/6 and getting reacquainted with my muscle tone that has been hibernating since my thirties.

McDreamy made an appearance during the day and told me he needed me for a few minutes so I followed him into an examining room. He opened my gown and started to—I kid you not— draw on my breasts with a black magic marker. He was envisioning a lift on my right side and starting drawing lines where he would cut and where my breast would now sit on my chest. Then he drew similar scooping lines on the left and put a big "x" on it. My poor breast was just sentenced to death by a Sharpie. Not a great visual by any stretch of the imagination. He thanked me and said, way too cheerfully, "See you soon, Jude!"

By the time I was called to go down the hall again, I was too anxious to be sad. I remember glancing at Jayne, who looked very tired and worried and saying to her, "See you on the other side" or something equally lame as we hugged just before following a nurse into the operating room. I did not want to do this. Part of me wanted to surrender my current molecular structure under anesthesia and just disappear from this life to see if I could re-connect with David in a celestial place where having breasts or cancer didn't matter. But another part of me was still *wanting*; desirous of a life. I wanted *another chapter*. Lying on the operating table, the usual blue and green clad medical assistants were zipping around with cartoon-like speed to get me all squared away and prep the theater for Drs. Graham and McDreamy. This was going to be several long hours of surgery and the room had much more of a sense of gravitas than last month's lumpectomy out-patient adventure. One of the PAs was wearing a do-rag instead of the poufy bonnets everyone else was wearing and he came to the side of the operating table when he caught me staring and said, "What is your dream today, Jude?" It always takes me by surprise when total strangers call me by my first name before being introduced, but I guess if there's any place in the world you really want that to be true it's in the operating room. Good to know they've not only got *your* medical chart but that they actually read it.

"Sorry?"

"What do you hope for when this is all over? What do you dream?"

"You mean other than for the cancer to be gone? Oh...a lot of things..." He could never have known what a profound question he just asked.

"Pick one and visualize it. Think hard on it before we put you into a nice long sleep today. It will be there waiting for you when you wake up and someday come true." So I used Spain, a place I have always wanted to see for myself and had gorgeous pictures in my mind to draw upon. When they were tying me off, Mr. Do-Rag yelled to me from across the OR so everyone could hear, "So, what is it you dream today, Jude?"

I smiled and yelled back, "Spain! España!" Then I immediately felt a hard pinch in my arm and the voices of everyone in the room echoing slower and slower, *Spain, Ah yes, Si, si! Spaainn!* as I turned my eyes up at the big round light directly over my head and imagined that the sheet draped over me was a long white linen dress and I was staring into the wild Mediterranean sun.

Late that night, about eleven, I woke up in my hospital room still on the gurney and sort of stuck just inside the doorway; the orderlies had left me there until I woke up and the nurses could move me to the bed. Jayne and Jodi and Kim were all standing around me and I had an overwhelming sense of relief when I saw them. It hurt to talk so I didn't except to inquire if anyone knew if I still had a nipple. Everything was still in slow motion. The room was dark except for the light coming from the hallway and I had a roommate so everyone whispered. Kim was directly to my left on the side asking if I was hungry.

"Whatcha got?" I croaked.

"Mmm. Clear broth."

"Yum."

She was spoon-feeding me little sips of something warm and vaguely tasting of chicken while carefully avoiding all the tubes and machines I was attached to, and it was pure heaven on my tongue and throat. I was starving. It just kept tasting better and better with every spoonful. And for dessert: a lemon Italian ice! The enormity of what had just happened to me was somewhere far, far away and all I could concentrate on was right in front of me: Jayne, Jodi, Kim, and food. I looked down just once and saw a slight bump formed under the sheet where my breast used to be, and said, "At least there is *something* there" with all the nonchalance of having brought home the wrong brand of mayo from the grocery store. Morphine is a wonderful thing. I wanted to sleep but was uneasy about being left alone so Kim stayed and let the girls, my very tired sisters, get back to the hotel. And I don't remember a damn thing after that before falling into a very deep sleep other than holding her hand and telling her she was my very best friend. Ever.

MARCH 17

The day before I went in for surgery I had received a call from an old friend, Alex. He was inspiring to talk to, because he was refreshingly matter-of-fact about the cancer and empathetic at the same time. He said he was going to come and visit me in the hospital. I told him he didn't have to, but he was insistent. I still didn't believe he'd show up but if he did it would be a treat.

The girls arrived in the late morning bearing gifts and smiles and stories about their dinner and the hotel the night before. They were pretty hilarious because once again they were enjoying the sanctity of time off and making the best of things. They even squeezed in time for a training walk! The menu at Sloan looks like a fine restaurant and includes a full breakfast, lunch, and dinner menu for you and your "guests." Cancer hospitals apparently don't send your loved ones downstairs for bad burgers and greasy fries when they're hungry, nor do they believe in serving you, the patient, Jello; they believe in feeding everyone well, and in the comfort of their own rooms because let's face it, for most of us here the hourglass has already been upended. So we were choosing among yummy salads, veggie burgers and other healthful, tasty-looking fare. I was sort of upright. My head still felt like a pumpkin on a Popsicle stick so it was resting between several pillows.

However, when the nurse came in before dawn this morning to check my vitals she wanted me to sit up so she could empty my hideous drain for me and show me what she was doing so I could do it myself at home, so she started to grab me around the shoulder and I stopped her and told her I didn't need help; I just tightened up my avocado abs and promptly did a little sit-up. She said, "Wow, that's impressive."

"Yoga," I said with a dollop of pride that something hiding under this hospital gown still worked.

My roommate is horribly sick. She is in constant pain. She is miserable and has no visitors. I am grateful beyond measure that the girls are quietly chatting away about the hotel stay last night and other family news. Then all of a sudden we hear LOUD voices in the hallway and I could recognize not only Alex but my friend Ravi as well. Oh boy. Alex was born in Spain and is devilishly handsome and much younger than me, as is Ravi, who was born in India, raised in Mexico and now lives in New York. We all used to work together at Priceline and stayed friends on and off but honestly, I didn't think we were visit-each-other-in-the-hospital friends, I thought we were send-a-card-or-some-flowers friends; so as much as I am excited to see them I also feel that I might be sicker than I think.

"Oh, my god, there you are! Look at you sitting up and looking great, let me give you a hug! Ravi, look at her, isn't she amazing? Holy crap."

"Fantastic! Hey, Jude, so great to see you, how are you doing, did you eat? You're probably starving. I betcha the food in this place *sucks* so I brought you something from the guy around the corner."

"Well, I..."

"Here you go. The best!" Ravi pulled a large aromatic item wrapped in tin foil from his winter coat and proudly announced, "A nice chipotle taco! Delish."

"What's wrong with you dude? A taco—that's what you bring her? She's just had major surgery, for Chrissake."

"What? She can't eat?" Ravi asked Alex as if I weren't three inches from them.

"No, she can eat, but like oatmeal or something like that, right, Jude?"

"I'll save it for later," I tried to helpfully interject, "we were just ordering..."

"Oh, hi, who's this?" said Ravi who just noticed my sisters and is always looking to score, probably even when sleeping.

"Ravi, Alex, these are my sisters Jayne and Jodi, and my friend Kimberly," and then the boys immediately starting stealing chairs from my poor, suffering roommate's side of the room so we could all sit together and talk and nosh and laugh like we got together like this every day. They were like a made-to-order cancer-comedy team. We immediately demonstrated the same lack of couth we had at Il Vagabondo and got loud and very silly. It felt wonderful. I don't know if they actually plan to be so funny sometimes, but they totally tickle my funny bone and every time I glanced over at Jodi she had this look on her face like, *Who are these guys?*

Later in the afternoon, after the Taco Kings left, Kevin and his girlfriend came for a visit as well and brought St. Patrick's muffins or something else green that really shouldn't be. I felt so supported, and even though I could see the thin mask of worry on everyone's faces, we all happily ignored the hard topics. I managed to as well, at least until the doctor came in and took off the bandages and I looked down at what was left of me. God, I tried to be upbeat and not crash into the self-pity barriers that I knew were out there waiting to trip me up.

"It looks great, Jude," said McDreamy.

"Really? Seriously?" It looked to me like a bloody lump in the shape of a Little League pitchers mound.

"Do I have a nipple?" At least I'm consistent.

"Yep, so far so good."

"Great."

"We got the expander in there fine; we'll get you fixed up as soon as you heal a bit. We did do a lift on the other side like we talked about so that when the implant goes in your other breast will be more symmetrical. Don't look so worried, my friend. We'll take care of you. You just get better."

"Okay." Damn, he's handsome. And he was gone in a flash.

The nurse came back in and cheerfully asked, "So was that your husband who was in here earlier today? It sounded like a lively visit from the nurse's station," which I think is code for, *We could hear you in the next zip code.*

"No."

"Oh, will he be coming to visit today?" I now realized that my chart still had me listed as married.

"Doubtful, we just got divorced."

"Oh. Oh, dear. I am so *sorry.* When?"

"Wednesday."

I felt bad saying it but it was the truth. She looked like she just accidentally ran over her neighbor's kitten.

MARCH 18

During surgery, a drain was placed next to the wound inside my chest, emerging just below my armpit through a long tube connected to a clear rubber bulb, shaped and sized exactly like a hand grenade. I don't know if I blocked it out, but I don't remember a *warning* from any of the myriad medical experts I'd been in contact with. This brilliant invention is called the Jackson-Pratt drain and is actually more disturbing and painful than you can imagine. Ask anyone who has had one or two of these bad boys protruding from their recently traumatized body and they will tell you in unambiguous terms that, although they serve a purpose — helping your body rid itself of unwanted fluid and indicating possible infections — they *totally suck.*

Your body fills the little hand grenade with fluid that is a mixture of your own blood and god knows what else, so you need to keep emptying the thing or the weight of the bulb hanging from the hole in your body starts to add a new dimension to the term discomfort. You walk around with a warm bag of repugnant bodily fluid hanging from your body, requiring you to find a place for it at all times, including when you sleep. As if those indignities weren't enough, you also *cannot shower* until it's removed, which can only happen when you are leaking less than a certain volume of personal ick in a twenty-four-hour period, which can take up to a week. So not only do you have to empty the gory thing several times a day, you have to pour it into a measuring cup and keep a running log of the volume and—I am not making this up—the color of the ick, which on my spectrum ranged anywhere from Hunt's Ketchup to orange Kool-Aid. It is revolting. Jackson and Pratt should be forced to wear several of their own drains in perpetuity.

The next morning, the nurse woke me up to show me how to empty the drain, taking care not to dislodge the sutures holding it in place, and then re-plug it so it had enough suction to do its job. I undid all the respect she had for me after my fantastic yoga sit-up by snapping, "You're kidding me, right? That's disgusting. I can't do that. Seriously, that is just gross."

Jayne went with me to physical therapy class. Once again, she probably wished she hadn't. It was populated with women much older than me sitting around a table with their husbands or partners, learning about what kind of exercises we should be doing when we get home *if we ever want to have range of motion in our arms again*, which was the opposite of helpful and encouraging and sounded more like a threat to me.

The exercise drills were simple enough but then the instructor, in pure valley-speak, asked us to demonstrate the arm rolls and shoulder shrugs individually as we sat in our depressing circle of wheelchairs like cast-offs from a nursing home. *I'm a yoga freak, for Pete's sake, and you're asking me if I can please shrug my shoulders for the group?!* I was furious.

But it wasn't over. We had a more in-depth instruction on the Jackson-Pratt drains, which I was already pissed off about; I could feel my back get stiffer and stiffer as she spoke. Finally, she lectured us about what we should and should not be doing to avoid the hideous and greatly feared lymphedema, an incurable side-effect some people experience after lymph node removal, which is in essence a blockage of the lymph passages that causes incredible discomfort and disfigurement. It is a progressive disease and there is no telling who or when it will strike, but mastectomy patients who have had lymph nodes removed are immediately awarded Powerball tickets to this lottery. "So, as I'm sure you know, you will need to make sure your arm or arms are suspended above your head several times a day and massaged like this regularly, and when I say regularly, I mean daily for the rest of your life, so I suggest you do it in the shower so you'll remember. You cannot ever have your blood pressure taken on the side where you had the lymph nodes removed and you should never have an injection of any kind in that arm, going forward. You should also not fly in an airplane—"

"Excuse me, did you just say 'fly an airplane'?"

"No ma'am, fly *in* an airplane. Your risk of lymphedema is very high, because of the changes in pressure and altitude; you're at much greater risk if you fly."

"I fly for my job. I have to fly. I also love to travel. Why is this the first time I'm hearing about this?"

"Uh-huh, okay, can we talk after class?" she said continuing her Valley-Girl drone in which everything she stated sounded like a question.

"Has anyone *else* ever heard this!?" I snapped, looking around the room at the tired and sick women shackled to their IV trees, feeling a bit of a Norma Rae moment coming on. "*Anyone?*"

I could see Jayne starting to turn an unnatural shade of green to match her St. Paddy's Day shirt. "Jude, maybe we should just..." she tried helpfully.

"*No*, this is bullshit."

"Ma'am, if you need to fly, I mean if you really need to be somewhere, you can purchase a tight arm-sleeve to wear on the plane which should help keep your risk down, but there are no guarantees."

"An arm-sleeve. Like Supp-Hose for my arm? Great. That's convenient *and* attractive."

It was appalling. I acted as if I was the only person in the room experiencing these lifelong post-mastectomy adjustments. The other women, some of whom had bilateral surgery and much more advanced diagnoses than mine, paid me no mind, thank goodness. But I'm sure I made it just that much harder for them and I really do feel bad about that. Not so much for the therapist who, aside from speaking down to us in that annoying singsong manner, shared only the worst and scariest statistics rather than balancing her message and offering a tone of support so that her battered and fearful audience could leave this session with hard facts, helpful next steps, *and* a glimmer of hope. We did not. We felt worse. I can't imagine that was her intention.

As she was wheeling me back to my room, Jayne, who I fear more closely identified with the hospital therapist than her snotty sister, looked at me and sighed, "Nice going, Ace."

"What? C'mon, she was awful."

"She was just doing her job, Jude."

I was instantly ashamed that I'd embarrassed my sister but still too mad to admit it.

So, I packed up to leave with my new Memorial Sloan Kettering T-shirt, a baby-blue mastectomy jacket that my sisters bought for me, which is a cape-like garment with lots of helpful room for your Velcro boob-vest, bandages, and drain; some flowers, a plant, and instruction books on lymphedema, JP drains, physical therapy and adjuvant therapy (read: *chemo*) which I was given *just in case*, and a permanent reminder to try to be nicer to hospital staff. I was happy to be going home. It was the only thing I was happy about other than the pain-killers in my purse and the promise of decent pizza.

Jayne, Jodi, and Kevin were my escorts home. When we arrived at Green Acres my ex was just leaving. He had actually bought me flowers. It was kind of him and an emotional sucker punch I didn't expect. They were beautiful. I thanked him for the flowers and for watching the dogs and settled into the couch, letting him make his way out on his own because I honestly didn't have space in my head for him today. Vic and Daryl arrived with Mom and Dad shortly thereafter and the long-sought-after pizza was finally ordered. Daryl was the first to volunteer to help me with my drain and was as grossed-out as I was which was validating coming from someone who gives herself shots of insulin in the gut every day.

When the troops finally dispersed, it was just me and Mom. She cleaned and puttered. I took pain meds and tried with all my might to call forth my virtual organizational buckets to try and make sense of the last seventy-two hours, but the drugs took over and kept me from doing anything more intellectually strenuous than petting my dogs and fixating on my drain. Our time together that week passed fairly uneventfully aside from a few visits from friends and colleagues who were surprised that I was up and around—Thank you again, yoga. I am strong as an ox from the waist down. The discomfort was omnipresent but had more to do with the emptiness and unease I felt about my new circumstances than the pain of doing upper-body exercises to keep my chest, arm, and shoulder muscles from seizing up, the jolts as the nerves in my chest died off, and the pressure from the expander. I had almost no range of motion on the left so every time I did my arm twirls it reminded me of how far I had to go. I felt absolutely ancient in my blue mastectomy cape struggling to do something as simple as extend my arm out to the height of my shoulder, and as the days went by my inability to shower added to my despair until Mom finally took pity on me and washed my hair in the sink.

On my first night home, which was also the first time I was sleeping in my own bed as a single person, my beloved meds betrayed me. I was taking Darvocet, which is a bad-ass drug all by itself and provided a rather smooth segue from the post-op morphine. When I was released from the hospital they also recommended that I take Ambien at night so that I could be assured of the uninterrupted sleep I needed. I thought it might be overkill but I didn't really see a huge risk, so after Mom and I said good-night, I popped my new little pill and started to read.

The next thing I knew I was hearing voices in the hallway outside my bedroom door, voices that were slowly oscillating louder and softer as if someone were opening and closing the door of a crowded room filled with malevolent souls. I began to panic and realized that I couldn't move my body at all; just my head. I began to shake my head to see if I could make it stop but the strange chorus got louder and was now accompanied by *footsteps* going up and down the hall, Jesus Christ! I turned my head towards the windows of my room and there at the foot of the bed as plain as day, was an alien—a *Close Encounters of the Third Kind*, Spielberg-worthy alien about five feet tall—staring right at me with black, shiny, softball-sized eyes. The shriek that came out of me was fully supported by all my yogic diaphragmatic strength. It probably could have awakened the dead, but it definitely woke my mother.

Mom, or Big Syl as we like to call her, is a teeny, tiny person with a very large, no-nonsense, second-generation Italian presence. Although now she could be mistaken for a shorter Olympia Dukakis, as a young woman she was quite beautiful and more than

closely resembled the petite actress and comedienne, Claudette
Colbert. She and my father both grew up in Harlem during the
Great Depression. Sylvia was the second-to-youngest in a family of
eight children born to Carmine and Julia Sacchittello of somewhere
equally poor in Italy. She grew up very underprivileged, in an
environment where she had to learn a wide range of survival
techniques just to stay clothed and fed which vanquished her
childhood and hardened her sentimentality like a tortoise shell
before she reached the age of ten. While it kept her from being
crushed under the weight of most of life's disappointments, she can
also be brutally honest and unapologetically tough. This is not the
mom who baked you cookies or sang you to sleep; she baked
lasagna and blasted Frank Sinatra and the Beatles while obsessing
about keeping the house clean. Big Syl is under five feet tall and
due to her Olympic-sized stress levels now a shadow of her former
self, weighing in somewhere around a hundred pounds.

She came dashing into my room with her little hair bonnet and
jammies on and a look of true fear in those big brown eyes when I
described what I just saw. I must have been in a semi-conscious
nightmare state so when I screamed myself awake, the creepy alien
and voices immediately retreated back into my drug-addled psyche
like a colony of vampires vaporizing before a crucifix. I asked Mom
for the paperwork from the hospital and with shaking hands reread
the Ambien side effects, which were numerous, but hiding in the
fine print were the words, *in rare cases might cause auditory or visual
hallucinations*. Guess who is a rare case. Mom made me tea and tried
to calm me down but I was truly afraid to go back to sleep. I had no
idea what else was waiting for me, hiding in the shadows of my
battered subconscious waiting to lunge out and terrify me.
Mercifully, pure exhaustion took over at about two a.m. and I slept
through the night with all the lights on.

The next morning over tea, Mom opened with, "So, any more
aliens visit you last night after I went to bed?"

MARCH 22

Kim, Big Syl, and I sat in the Sloan waiting room before my first
post-op session with McDreamy. The nasty drain still hung from my

side and I was hoping I was going to hear how wonderfully I was healing and that this horrible nuisance would be removed once and for all. I brought with me my carefully organized log to prove that less than 20 ccs of ick came out of me in a 24-hour period. I also still sported my Velcro boob-vest because I had to. I was told I could not take it off until McDreamy gave me the all clear.

McDreamy's adorable intern/sidekick Kelly came into the exam room with us and asked me to lie back so she could extract the drain from my side. Just then it hit me: dear god, how is she going to get it out of there? As I let my shoulders hit the exam table, I just kept thinking about how badly I wanted to be rid of it and tried not to dwell on the fact I was probably going to get a shot of something to numb the pain in what is a pretty sore area.

"Okay Jude, just open up your gown and turn your head to the side, because this is kinda gross."

"What are you going to do?"

"Yank it out."

"Just pull until it comes out? Won't that cause me, oh, I don't know, agony?"

"I'll do it quick. Hold your breath and I'll count to three."

Was she kidding? So I pulled in a big yoga breath and looked back at her on *three* because I couldn't help myself, and grimaced as she pulled this incredibly long tube out of my chest in one long motion. Not only did I feel the thing uncoiling in my ribcage like a boa constrictor as it exited the tender hole in my side, I saw more internal goo than I ever want to see again in my life. Kelly was right. It was gross. But it was GONE. A small bandage was placed over my partial stigmata and I felt like a weight about the size and shape of a hand grenade had been lifted.

McDreamy came in to tell me that I was healing up nicely and that he was anxious to get me put back together. "Did you hear from Dr. Graham yet about your lab results?"

"Not yet, but I'm meeting with him in five days."

As soon as he heard the word *meeting* his face registered something. He knew something now. And he wasn't telling me. And it wasn't good. "Good luck, Jude."

"Thanks." Don't ever play poker with me, Doc; you will lose.

MARCH 27

Jodi and I are sitting in Dr. Graham's office, yet again, waiting for a verdict. The concept of having to wait for weeks or days for critical answers about my health is in sharp contrast to a world where I have access to all the information I could ever need at my fingertips. I have learned to spend the time vacillating between preparing for the worst and focusing on more immediate distractions, which in my case range from finances to family drama to pain management. And while I do enjoy the occasional moment of grateful clarity when I can appreciate a lull in the action, I have yet to hear positive results in this journey so sometimes a waiting period feels more like a "time out."

After Graham walked in sans entourage, I tried to read his face but he had already gone into presentation mode, "So a few things to talk about today, Jude. I think you look terrific by the way and are healing up very nicely."

"So I hear, thanks."

"But unfortunately—"

Oh, shit here it comes.

"—the type of cancer that you have is making it very hard for us to achieve the aesthetic result we're looking for, as well as a speedy recovery time..."

"What are you saying?"

"Well, it's not really what we were shooting for..."

"Tell me."

"The samples of breast tissue we tested over and over, just to be a hundred percent sure, leave us no choice but to go back and remove the nipple as well. We simply can't risk it; proximity to the tumors was just too close for comfort and after all you've been through it would be awful to lose this fight because of a small disc of skin; so it has to go."

"It does."

"I'm afraid so."

I looked at Jodi who was still composed. She offered, "That makes good sense, Jude...."

"So," he continued, "we can get that done for you right away. You don't need to go to the hospital. I can do it right here in the office. You won't need more than a local anesthetic because you have very few nerve endings left in that area. As Jodi said, it really does make sense," he ventured, tenuously trying to line up an ally before launching his next torpedo, "as does the addition of adjuvant therapy to our treatment plan. I am recommending eight rounds of what is called dose-dense chemotherapy, which is as powerful a cocktail as we have to go after this kind of cancer; and I think you should be strong enough in about a month to get started on it. Then I'll feel as if we've done everything possible to protect you; once the chemo is behind us we'll get you started on Tamoxifen to help reduce the risk of recurrence."

"Any other options?"

"The risk is too high, Jude."

Then Jodi asked, "Have you staged her again?"

"Yes, she is now Stage 2B based on our recent pathology reports. That large tumor and micro-invasion of the lymph node were the game-changers."

"Not early stage."

"No. Not early stage."

"*Okay* then." This is what Jodi says whenever she wants to put a button on the conversation and move on to something else as quickly as possible.

"Will I lose my hair?" Oh, sweet lord, will I ever stop?

"Yes, I'm sorry to say. This is an aggressive treatment, but you're young and strong and trust me, your hair will grow back. I can promise you that. I'm going to recommend some terrific oncologists for you to choose from; we'll put you in good hands, Jude. This is the right decision." Jodi looked at me and I noticed the very tip of her nose turning red which is a telltale sign that composure is slipping so I turned my head away and stared blankly at the Ansel Adams on his wall absorb it all: Stage 2B, losing my nipple; four months of chemo; road to recovery just careened off a cliff.

On the way home we talked logistics: How on earth am I going to take care of my house, two dogs — although I am about to lose Louis to my ex when he moves out — and almost five acres of property while I'm going through treatment? Can I afford another few months on disability or will I have to work full time while poisoning myself? What exactly does *aggressive treatment* mean? What if it doesn't work and the cancer is already on the hunt in my bones, lungs, or brain?

And what, in the name of all that is holy, will I look like bald?

APRIL 5

The Sole Sisters are now a team of four. Jayne pulled in two neighbors from where she lives in Bedford, New Hampshire, to share this odyssey, and they each have their own donation pages online with personal messages about why they are walking and a rolling display of donation amounts, supporter names, and words of encouragement. I have taken to logging in to the 3-Day site on a daily basis, although at first it was daunting to see messages from friends, family, and total strangers saying:

$200.00 – In honor of Jude

$50.00 – Go Sole Sisters! Jayne, you rock!

$75.00 – For Jodi's sister and mom

$250.00 – In support of Sylvia and Jude

Then there were the myriad donations *in memory of* someone's mother, sister, wife, aunt, daughter, or friend, who bravely battled and lost. The first time I read through their pages and my sister's fundraising notes, I collapsed in a heap of tears on the desk in my home office. I was overwhelmed with pride but still resisting being so publicly and permanently associated with this disease.

The final layer of denial was being peeled away, like it or not. Plus, it illustrated so clearly to me how very thin and tenuous the line is between *in support of* and *in memory of* — and that stinging, inescapable message resonates daily. My ability to finally internalize the fact that other women, women no different from me, have died from this disease, was an important and necessary milestone. I had only a few weeks to go before Chemo-Time.

By this time, the division of friends that naturally occurs after a divorce had been almost finalized. There were friends who moved instinctively and appropriately to his side or mine, and then there were the straddlers—the close friends who really couldn't, nor did they want to, *choose* between us, so they reached out to both of us in a very neutral and perfunctory way or ignored us entirely, which was fine and actually understandable; but the cancer had forced me to focus solely on myself for the first time in my life and I really had no use for anyone who wasn't going to be a hundred percent genuine with me. *I don't care if you still keep in touch with my ex-husband but I don't want you to be half a friend when you're with me. You're either in this mess with me or you need to go find someone else to spend your day with. Oh, I'm sure you're still a very nice person and all, keeping your conflict-averse, I'd-rather-not-stand-too-close-to-the-flames nature intact, but I need more than that; a lot more. I need real friends; fighters; people who aren't afraid of a little heat and a lot of risk; and frankly, I've got too much at stake to worry about how you feel.*

I was learning to make hard decisions about my personal associations quickly and decisively and, some might say, rudely. But I didn't care. There were plenty of friends and acquaintances who heard about my situation and would talk about it among themselves as if it were happening someplace far, far away—not a place they had any intention of ever visiting. I didn't fault them; I just had no use for them.

After checking on the latest Sole Sister stats, I drove to New York with my good friend Monica for an appointment at Sloan for my first official "fill-up". Monica is a friend from our theater days; my ex and I were both actors when we met and formed a theater company together years ago called Danbury Actors Repertory Theatre, or as we cleverly called it, D'ART. Monica was still in the college drama department when she joined our company of artists and became one of our dearest friends, even moving into our neighborhood after graduation. I loved her bold sense of humor, her passion for literature, and her relative innocence when it came to relationships. Being that she was ten years younger than me, I sometimes found myself in the role of mentor as well as friend. But over the years we became girlfriends on equal footing, providing counsel to each other, respecting each other's opinions—and capable of shoe-shopping without killing each other. I know Monica still keeps in touch with my ex, but when she reached out to me, she knew exactly what to do and say and let me know in no uncertain terms that I could call on her with whatever I needed and that she had a surplus of unused vacation time. Testing her well-intentioned statement I told her I could use someone to accompany me to my first boob-fill-up, if she was interested. She quipped, "I can't think of anything I'd rather do on a day off!"

"You'll get to see McDreamy."

"This offer just keeps getting better and better. How about we head to MOMA for some cult-cha afterwards?"

The tissue expander lodged in my chest is shaped exactly like a deflated breast. It has an integral "filling port" that is a small pocket near the top of the expander cleverly ringed with metal. In order to have an injection of saline to start the skin-stretching process, a small rare-earth magnet is gently moved over the skin at the surgical site until the internal port is located and then the fun starts. Lying down in McDreamy's office, Kelly was exuding her usual this-is-no-big-deal vibe as she piled up her instrument table with forbidding-looking objects that looked more like the *mise en place* of a sushi chef than the implements of a plastic surgeon. Monica was flipping through magazines and checking out the admission prices for the Edvard Munch installation at the museum. I was mildly disappointed because as much as I like Kelly, I was hoping my inaugural fill up would be hosted by her handsome boss.

"Okay, Jude? Here's the deal. As soon as I find the port with this little gizmo, I will insert a tube into the opening and we'll start pumping in the saline until we think you've got some decent stretch going. Probably about 100 ccs to start, okay?"

"How do you insert the ..."

"It's attached to a needle. I'll just jam it in there; it's barely a pinch. You have very little feeling there, remember?"

"Yes, but what if you miss and pop the balloon inside me?"

"Nope. Won't happen. I do this every day. Trust me."

I really didn't have the energy to put Kelly on the spot for an in-depth statistical analysis on expander safety as she was preparing to make yet another hole in my chest and I did want to get to the museum, so I warily acquiesced, praying that I wasn't going to fall into that rare-occurrences category again.

Kelly moved the magic magnet around my sore little pitcher's mound and once she found her mark, grabbed a blue Sharpie, and drew a tiny little bull's-eye on my skin. I had no idea that Sharpies played such a large role in reconstructive plastic surgery. "Okay, we've got our target, Jude; I will tell you when to hold your breath." She picked up a very large, long needle attached to a fat syringe, which was attached to something else beyond my field of sight. "Okay, now would be a great time. Big breath in and hold it…" and she jammed what looked like a knitting needle into my chest with no anesthetic whatsoever and I could feel a slight pinch of the skin and the sensation of something probing deep into my chest, but surprisingly, it barely registered on my pain scale, which was a welcome relief. She then began pumping saline into me like I was a flat tire at a full-service gas station, idly chatting and complimenting my jewelry as my little mound started to grow right before my eyes. The stretched skin started to burn a bit and the new weight in my chest forced the expander to push further out in all directions, slowly, until it felt so full I thought I might burst and fly around the room backwards.

"Do you think we have enough in there, Kel?"

"Ohh, does it hurt? Maybe we went too big; let's back a little off for now."

Monica was completely checked out by this point and I can only imagine was praying to get the hell out of there ASAP to go look at something artful. After Kelly was done I looked down and saw my new minor league pitcher's mound protruding under skin so taut that it shone like a new silk suit. It still had my sad, doomed nipple on top but I knew that would change very soon. I never thought that 100 cc's of saline would make me feel better but I certainly didn't think it would make me feel even more freakish, which it did. I now had a ridiculously round Franken-boob.

Monica and I walked around the museum. I made small talk and laughed to take my mind off of it but I had real, honest-to-goodness pressure in my chest causing a great deal of discomfort. The Munch exhibit was interesting but grew more and more depressing until we reached his haunting "Madonna" with her long hair, perfect breasts and a face that appeared to be melting from regret forcing me to my cultural and physical breaking point. "Hey, how do you feel about taking a cab back to Grand Central?" I hinted with a sort of grimace-smile.

"Oh, Jude, does it hurt?"

"Only when I breathe."

APRIL 7

The day had come for me to part with my nipple and aureole. Jayne volunteered to come down from New Hampshire with her kids to drive in to New York with me. It was also the day I would interview one of the oncologists from Dr. Graham's list to see if I liked her enough to trust her with my life. The kids happily took two days off from school, but Jayne had valid trepidation about accompanying me to not one but two doctor visits in one day. But she was also very swept up in the fundraising success her team was enjoying, providing a fantastic diversion when conversation became too strained. Huge piles of cash were being donated on a daily basis and it affected her motivation and mood as if it were going into her own pocket.

Sitting in the waiting room of Dr. Graham's surgical office, I glanced at the kids over the top of my magazine. They seemed nervous, so I blathered on about something ridiculous until they reluctantly cracked smiles. Mac, her son, was just ten and her daughter Maggie would soon turn fourteen and they had been completely in the know since my diagnosis. When your mom works in a hospital you get used to hearing about bad stuff; Jayne did a good job of talking openly about the cancer and giving them just enough information so they understood the risk but are spared the more gory details. She was trying to get them to focus on what they might like to do in the big city, but I sensed they were waiting to see if their aunt came out of yet another surgical procedure alive before making that decision.

The surgery was disgusting. I was completely awake, without so much as a local anesthetic; while Dr. Graham used a process called electro-cauterization to literally burn the entire nipple off and carefully suture together the surrounding skin leaving me yet another ugly scar. It did not go fast and although he placed a sight-guard between me and the surgical site I felt incredible heat, saw blue-gray smoke rising from my chest, and smelled that god-awful odor of burning flesh—my flesh. When the heat became unbearable

I put up my hand and said, "Okay, *stop*. I know I'm not supposed to have feeling there, but I do. Can I have a local, please?"

"Sure, but I'm only about ten minutes away from being done here," which when translated means *I really don't care what you're feeling or not feeling, I'm on a tight schedule.*

"That's ten minutes too long," I said firmly. "Give me the shot." After the local took effect, he finished closing up the skin with a few sutures and it was done. I had lost another prized body part.

After he left the exam room so I could get dressed, the pent-up tension and revulsion released a tidal wave of remorseful tears. I became overwhelmed by the notion that this was somehow my fault and that it was just going to keep getting worse; that I must have done something to *deserve* this. It took a good five minutes for me to pull it together enough to walk out into the waiting room and rejoin my family.

Jayne and I walked around midtown Manhattan with the kids in the early spring chill. I was in some pain, although I believe it was more emotional than truly physical. Maggie, the consummate teenage girl in the heart of the fashion capital of the world, wanted to shop for clothes so we went into stores filled with young and beautiful girls—and their innocent and healthy breasts were everywhere I looked. I secretly felt like an unsightly monster. I tried not to ruin everyone's day, though, by behaving like one, so I bought stuff I didn't need instead, doing my part for the economy.

Our next stop after lunch was to visit a Sloan oncologist from the list that Dr. Graham had provided. The kids stayed behind in the waiting room with iPods and magazines while Jayne and I went in to meet Dr. Rivers, so named because we learned she lives in my neck of the woods close to the Saugatuck River. She is a tall, African-American woman who is the embodiment of confidence and steadfast control. Her voice is authoritative, commanding, and modulates perfectly as she scares the living daylights out of you.

My first meeting to discuss chemotherapy treatment was not in any way the nurturing environment I had anticipated somewhere in my needy brain; it was a business meeting. And Dr. Rivers's business case was clearly laid out on her desk in a spreadsheet she had prepared from Dr. Graham's pathology reports. The size of the tumors, risk factors, my age, lymph node involvement, and other key factors were all dumped into a giant cancer treatment database; then statistics-based algorithms formulated suggestions for the best treatment plan, which not surprisingly matched what Graham had suggested.

Her business plan also introduced me to something called my "survival rate." Until this point, I had not had a physician or any medical professional for that matter, look me in the eye and tell me my approximate chances of living through the next five to seven years. I am not sure why but I had not until that moment considered it could be so short a time. I felt a terrible heaviness in my heart every time she uttered this phrase. I silently pondered all the things I wanted to do and see before I became too sick to do so; but the painful reality of losing this fight was not a conversation I was ready to have. Despite her clinical and completely unemotional approach, I had enough confidence in her experience to sign her up to the Get-This-Cancer-Out-of-Me Team.

The chemotherapy plan being suggested was something called ACT which stands for three drugs: Adriamycin, Cytoxan, and Taxol. By this time I had been anonymously scoping out the discussion boards on breastcancer.org so this cocktail was familiar to me and downright ominous. Dr. Rivers explained that it was our "best shot" at killing off the cancer that is feared to have escaped into other parts of my body. She went on to say that while some women tolerate it rather well (all things being relative), other women become quite sick, as in *requiring hospitalization* sick, and have to abandon this particular protocol in favor of something less aggressive.

"Other than the cancer, my general health is quite good, so hopefully I'll do okay?"

"I wouldn't recommend this if I didn't think you could handle it, Jude. We won't know for sure until you begin treatment, of course..."

"I do Bikram yoga, Dr. Rivers. I can practice for ninety minutes in a room heated to 105 degrees. I might not look it, but I'm still pretty darn strong."

"Are you serious? Ninety minutes at 105 degrees?"

"Yes ma'am."

"Jude, no more Bikram," Dr. Rivers declared. "You simply cannot do it while on ACT; you'll be receiving maximum doses of this treatment which is toxic to your heart. Ninety minutes of exercise in a hot room could put you into cardiac arrest. Mild exercise like walking is okay, but nothing strenuous."

"It's toxic to *my heart?*"

"Yes. Some women whose hearts don't test out well beforehand are offered something else. We'll give you a MUGA scan to check the strength of your heart muscle before beginning treatment." Her comment forced a completely inappropriate giggle from me because I'm addicted to Harry Potter books and it sounded to me like she just said Muggle-Scan.

Dr. Rivers did not even acknowledge my lapse in seriousness and just plowed on as if ignoring a precocious child. "I will prescribe a number of drugs for you to take during your treatment to help with nausea and other possible side effects. Here is the list. You will also need to give yourself an injection of something called Neulasta on the day after every treatment to keep your white blood count at a reasonable level."

"Okay," I said, suddenly feeling the weight of all these additional drugs pressing down on my forehead as I let my fertile imagination wander off to the village of aliens hiding in my closet waiting to attack me in my sleep.

"You will lose your hair. There is no getting around it. It will grow back."

"Yes, I know."

"There is a special hat shop on this floor and I will give you a prescription for a wig."

"...a prescription?!"

"It is a head prosthetic, Jude. Your insurance company will not cover expenses without one and human hair wigs can be quite costly, I assure you. If you don't want to look like a Barbie Doll, you'll want the human hair and not a synthetic." *Please be making this up*, I thought. *A head prosthetic?*

"You will also stop menstruating. We call it chemo-pause; you won't actually be in menopause but the drugs will trick your body into thinking that it is. Estrogen-receptor positive cancer means your estrogen levels are in essence feeding the cancer cells and we need to stop them."

"So, I'm too much woman, is what you're telling me."

Dr. Rivers finally smiled a bit and said, "That's one way to look at it."

Jayne rolled her eyes but didn't admonish me. She knew what a crap morning I had and fully understood my unfortunate need for ill-placed tension-cutting humor.

"Well, can't say I'm bummed about not having my period."

"The flip side of that is you may indeed experience hot flashes, mood swings, a decreased libido, and weight gain; basically the same symptoms you would experience during menopause. You may or may not ever menstruate again and you can no longer get pregnant. Here is the list of other side effects you should familiarize yourself with. I'll also need you to keep a very specific log of your reactions to the drugs on a daily basis as well as take your temperature..." The hits just keep coming as Dr. Rivers matter-of-factly rattles off every horrible thing you can possibly imagine happening to your body during and after chemo, until my eyes glaze over and I look at Jayne as if I have heard quite enough for one day.

The side effects of these medications range from a decrease in white and red blood cells and platelets, anemia, severe mouth sores, nausea and vomiting, bladder irritation, diarrhea, constipation, nerve damage, jaw pain, hearing loss, nail discoloration (unless you consider black a color), nasal congestion, bronchial distress, total body hair loss including eyebrows and lashes, taste disruption, severe sunburn from sun exposure, severe heartburn, muscle aches, bone pain, numbness in fingers and toes, difficulty walking, and crippling fatigue or flu-like symptoms. Some women experience confusion or dementia-like symptoms and have trouble thinking clearly and difficulty with word retrieval, in some cases for years after treatment.

"You will have a severely compromised immune system so don't go to crowded places like movie theaters or public places such as malls. Avoid enclosed spaces where you could pick up germs; it could make you very sick. Always cover your head outdoors and don't go in the sun for more than twenty minutes unless you're covered from head to foot. If any of these symptoms become *unbearable*, you must let me know. The front desk will schedule you for your first round and you'll come back, every other week. Take these books to learn more about adjuvant therapy and we'll see you back here when you're ready to get started. But make it soon, Jude."

I was overwhelmed and trying frantically to locate a silver lining, partly for me and partly for Jayne, who was starting to look nauseated herself, "So you're confident my survival rate will improve after I get through all this?"

"The research says yes, our algorithms tell us yes, but I can in no way guarantee that you won't have a recurrence. No one can. That's why we'll get you started on another daily chemo dose called Tamoxifen when you're done with this series and you get your strength back. Unfortunately, estrogen-receptor positive breast cancer in pre-menopausal women with your background presents us with an *increase* in the risk of recurrence at about the seven year mark after treatment. So after your five years on Tamoxifen, we'll get you started on an aromatase inhibitor. (pause) There are no guarantees with cancer, Jude."

"So this could all be for nothing."

"It's been proven to help your cause, but there is no sure-fire method, no."

"And I'm on some kind of drug for the rest of my life."

For the first time in this sterile business meeting I noticed a slight shading of empathy in her voice. "That is what we advise, yes."

It must have been phantom pain—that sickening phenomenon that occurs after amputations when the amputee actually feels shooting pain in a body part that is no longer there—but on the ride home my nipple, the one that was just removed on top of my fake breast with no actual human tissue in it, throbbed in horrible pain. The harsh reality of what "treatment" really means is now lining up alongside all the other recent takeaways in my life to the point where I have trouble recognizing myself as a woman, much less a human being. I won't have my period; I can no longer get pregnant; I have one breast; I won't have hair; I'm going to get very sick over the next four months, and I could die anyway.

Jayne and I sat up in my room that night when we got home staring blankly into our glasses of wine while the kids played on the computer in the other room and we reflected on random snapshots from a very trying day.

"Jude," she said after a long silence, "are you okay?"

"No. No, I am not."

APRIL 8

This morning I am grateful that Jayne and the kids are still here. My new bed is being delivered today. My marriage is over and I need a bed I can feel good about having all to myself. My ex is finally moving out next week. I honestly don't even know where he's been living these past few months, but the daily ritual of scheduling when he can come by to visit the dog is draining. Sometimes when I can't be here, he lets himself in and leaves me notes—sometimes friendly, sometimes not so friendly. The last few times this happened I realized things were missing. Little things I can certainly live without but things that, to my mind, he had no right leaving with without discussing it with me first.

I changed all the locks. New bed; new life; new rules. He is furious.

APRIL 12

My left arm still has very limited range of motion. The exercises are slow going and they hurt. I am starting to get tingling in my fingers from the pinched nerves and every unnatural occurrence on that side makes me fear the onset of lymphedema. The mound on my chest looks ridiculous but I figured out that if I cut one of my more supportive bras in half, I can use the extra cup inside of a real bra to try and not look so lopsided and obvious. But the expander is hard and unnatural and feels like I have on a too-tight brassiere under my skin and there's really nothing I can do about that. My right breast is generally healed up from the lift although the scars are ugly and still very red and raised. Thankfully, my right arm is still quite strong.

I woke up in a panic because my ex was supposed to move out in two days and had yet to pack anything. His stuff was everywhere; clothes in the closet, a mountain of beer bottles in the garage; tools, books, toiletries, you name it. I looked around the house, *my house,* and saw only his things. It took me about five hours of non-stop activity but I put all of his belongings, every single thing I could find, out on the sun porch in large plastic bags. I played music, intermittently massaged my bad arm and didn't even stop to eat. I have no idea where this burst of strength and determination came from.

After dinner I picked up the *New York Times* and read an article titled "Studies Challenge Traditional Breast Cancer Treatment." The article was long and informative and in summary stated that while doctors traditionally use the *size* of the tumor to prescribe chemotherapy for breast cancer patients, a new MD Anderson Cancer Center study shows that there is a marked difference in the type of cancer that responds best to it; estrogen receptor *negative* cancer sees appreciable results; my cancer does not. So in essence, if I went through this horrible treatment, it could help my odds of living the next five years by a mere seven percent, which was not statistically significant enough to risk all the side effects and long-term toll this regimen will take on my body and brain. In fact, it might even make me sicker.

I was incensed. I was preparing my body, my life, my house, and my head for months of agony and MD Anderson experts were now saying it could be a complete waste of time. I called a Cancer Hotline. I was crying, sometimes to the level of screaming and intermittently provoking the poor counselor on the other side of the call until she insisted that I come in and meet with someone in their Norwalk, Connecticut, office as soon as possible. I made an appointment for April 19 at the Cancer Care Center although I didn't hold out high hopes for feeling any better after the meeting.

The article went on to cite that Memorial Sloan Kettering, my alma mater, weighed in to say it required more research and that these results are nothing more than "hypothesis generating" which sounded a bit like sour grapes to me, instead of a call to action. Sloan recommended just pushing ahead and leaving the decision up to the patient. How incredibly cowardly of them, I thought.

I have always suspected, but now I know for sure: it's a crap shoot. And I have a short window of time before throwing the dice.

APRIL 13

I had a dentist appointment today. My dentist is a dear old friend. Back in my younger and decidedly more artistic days, I worked as his assistant four days a week. When he came in to see me after the hygienist was finished polishing my smile, he had an uncharacteristically concerned look on his face and sort of helplessly searched my eyes before speaking. "Jude, I don't know what to say. Is there anything I can do?"

"Yes, actually, I could use a favor."

"Name it."

"Would you consider giving me a shot every other week? I know you're good with a needle and I'm just not sure I can do it. It's for my white blood count."

"Done. Give me a schedule; I'll come by your house."

"Thanks. I just didn't know who else to ask."

"As long as you let me decide where I give it to you," he said with a devilish grin that instantly erased the drama. I love him. And secretly wished I had ten more friends just like him. No, cancer isn't funny. But if you don't find a way to laugh from time to time, you might as well already be dead.

APRIL 14

After discovering that I changed the locks *on my own house*, the furious ex-husband, who had by now bought a brand new car with his first check from me, thought that coming to pick up Louis would be a perfect opportunity to give me a hard time about inconveniencing him as he now had to arrange for me to be here instead of letting himself in at his leisure. I am not making this up.

Last week, the absurd key dispute escalated to the point where he began yelling and storming around the house in typical fighting form, and I resisted yelling back until I finally cracked. I spewed pure hateful, pent-up venom at him that came from the depths of my soul, culminating with a very loud "get the fuck OUT," which I screamed not for effect but because I realized there was nothing he could do to hurt me if I did. We had already reached bottom. His parting shot to me as he was leaving was to poke me in the center of my chest and bark, "You have no fucking heart in there, Jude; no wonder you have breast cancer." I guess that was supposed to make us even.

Rage is a limited and insufficient word. He peeled out of the driveway as I watched, shaking with a fury I had not felt in years. I was so scared of my own next move that I called my brother Victor and told him what happened. I couldn't think of another person in my world that might have a rational response to this. He very calmly told me he would come down and be here when my ex moved out. And to please try not to get any more upset which, frankly, I didn't think was possible.

Victor arrived and we went out to a nice dinner. He was slightly uncomfortable at first and I could tell he only wanted to hear limited amounts of information regarding my health; the game highlights were more than enough for him, especially when the subjects ranged from cancer to boobs. I was indeed calmer now and so very glad that I had a composed and balanced older brother. Missing my dad's counsel, I realized over dinner that the apple didn't fall very far from the tree. I could hear my father's words coming out of his mouth and it was such a comfort. Victor and my ex at one time had been quite close and I hoped that his presence would help diffuse any drama. He was also tactfully trying to help me see things from another perspective.

The move went fairly smoothly. I spoke to my ex through my brother for fear of inciting another episode, so conversation was prickly but mostly civil; sadly, we couldn't even make eye contact with each other. One wonders how it comes to this. But I was a pathetic and nervous wreck watching Louis happily wander around the yard with Sophie, knowing that he was about to be taken from this house never to return, never to see either of us again; and he had no idea. Louis is a big dog, about seventy-five pounds of mutt that we guessed, after taking him home from the pound all those years ago, was the love-child of an Akita and a Labrador retriever. He is all white except for a reddish mask that makes him look like he is a Disney creation. His head is enormous and he would gently place it on the pillow next to me whenever I was sick and Sophie would sleep across the bottom of the bed. They have been my protectors and my constant source of undying affection. With everything else going on in my life I had forgotten to prepare myself for this. *Forgotten*. The brand new Subaru pulled out of the driveway for the last time, and the heart I was supposed to be missing shattered into a million tiny little pieces. Louis; my baby. Gone.

APRIL 15

It was just me and Sophie now. At three years old, she still had incredible puppy energy but thankfully, some older-dog wisdom; she knew I was immeasurably sad. She realized something was wrong when she walked over to her bowls and saw that two were missing. We spent most of the day moping and pining for our old friend the big, white dog. We were also now absent half of the furniture in the house, so the emptiness is not only visceral, it was also visual. We had been set adrift in our own home.

Julie, upon hearing the story about the final showdown, sent me something by email called a forgiveness exercise. It's her theory that, regardless of how badly you have allowed someone to treat you, it is only your capacity for forgiveness that will bring you any relief from the hurt. This exercise came complete with a script, which was very helpful because forgiveness was not currently in my lexicon. In addition, Kim suggested that I execute a white sage ceremony to banish the house of bad vibes and thoughts, and with any luck, a few aliens in the bargain. This was achieved by burning a bunch of sage and waving the smoke around as you move from room to room expressing out loud the kind of life you now expect to live in each location; not the one you had; the one you *want.* I liked that idea. Jodi and Jayne were much less magnanimous and just wanted his balls in a jar.

As I was cleaning up I found an old photograph of us from our theater days. We had just started dating and were very much in love, young and beautiful. I thought, *Here is my reminder. We did love each other. It wasn't a mirage. And the journey didn't end well but it certainly had its wonderful, magical stops along the way.*

I sat down on the floor with the picture mashed into my chest with both my hands and finally began to mourn my marriage. I didn't have to re-visit the decision to end it, but I did need to honor what it was. This was not about being sick or well, or living or dying; it was about remembering that it was, at one time, a wonderful romance that will always be part of me. And I had just as much to do with pulling it apart as he did when the relationship started to fray. There was no blame to be had; it was just the sadness of knowing that the two star-struck young lovers in the photograph hoped it would never, ever end, and it did.

After I reached the maximum amount of pitiable moping, I lit the end of the sage that Kim had left on my kitchen counter. I held it aloft in my left hand with the forgiveness exercise in my right and walked slowly from room to half-empty room, waving the smoldering herb like a magic wand, telling the universe exactly what I wanted. I then went outside and walked around the entire perimeter of the property; the riverbank, the pond, the meadow, and every area of the grounds and garden, whether the memories that hung in the air were good or bad, and told the earth and the water and the sky and anyone who would listen that Sophie and I recognized and acknowledged our past but wanted a new start. Another chance to get things right.

We may not be ready for what is coming down the river at us, and in truth I still have not decided on whether I am going ahead with the chemo, but we will always be there for each other no matter what. I did not once read from the forgiveness exercise I was holding because quite surprisingly, I had a script of my own.

I am not a religious person. I am a spiritual person when it suits me. But that day, I realized, for the first time I learned what it means to pray.

APRIL 18

I had a hair appointment this morning to cut my very long hair to shoulder length in anticipation of losing it. This was suggested by former chemo warriors because when the drugs start killing off your follicles, your scalp actually gets quite sore and irritated. The longer and heavier your hair is the more discomfort you will feel. So off it came. I didn't have enough for Locks of Love; I was just two inches shy. I watched it fall through the air and land soundlessly in huge piles all around my chair. I look very businesslike with shoulder-length hair and I really didn't like it. I haven't had hair this short in my entire adult life but I hoped that altering my look in stages would be less traumatic than going from Cher to Sinead in a day.

I drove down to Greenwich to the wig shop with my head prosthetic prescription and picked out a human hair number, very honey-blonde, that I named Stella. She wouldn't be ready for a few weeks which was good news because I was not quite ready for her yet either. When I called the insurance company to make sure they would cover my expensive new head prosthetic, they declined coverage. They said that my company neglected to add this feature to our group policy. I called Steve and told him that I just spent $600 I didn't have on a wig that our company thought I should have to pay for out-of-pocket because it was deemed elective and not necessary. Bless his heart—he called the insurance company and changed our corporate policy on the spot. It's good to be in HR sometimes.

I was going through all the motions as if I was still on track to begin the chemo. I was questioning all the preparation but couldn't seem to stop the momentum. I read more information about the recent Anderson study and feedback from all over the cancer world and every comment was coming back the same: *we just don't know*.

APRIL 19

Cancer Care of Connecticut is a non-profit organization that helps cancer patients with free professional services such as workshops, support groups, financial assistance, and Extreme Crisis Counseling for Crazed or Hysterical Breast Cancer Patients, which assured me I was in the right place. My visit today was with a woman named Patricia who has a masters degree in social work and, thankfully, three boxes of tissues in her office.

Our session started out on decent footing but quickly devolved into a horrible experience for both of us. Yes, I made her cry. I realized too late that I was ill-prepared to look someone in the eye and admit how incredibly tired I was of feeling helpless, how hard it was to suddenly be alone in the midst of this horror, and how angry I felt about facing down death at forty-six. I lost control of the little control I had left. Despite her best intentions, every therapist button she tried to push turned out to be the wrong one until I screamed at her at the top of my lungs, "IT ALL JUST HAS TO STOP!"

"What has to stop, Jude?"

I pause for a minute to catch my breath and think about what I really meant to say, feeling the full weight of the last few years squarely on my shoulders. "The bad news, the uncertainty, the pain. All of it. Has to stop. I have had enough."

"I know it's scary to think about Jude, but so many women have been through chemo before and…"

"I know where you're going with this, but a lot of them have died anyway and others have had lifelong chronic pain or illness as a result of the chemo. I am forty-six and have only been divorced a month and I don't even have the benefit of the medical community behind me because they just woke up and declared they don't fucking know what will work for my kind of cancer anymore. I mean, Christ, what would *you* do?"

"I really can't say."

"No, of course not; neither can I. I can only sit here and pathetically cry to a total goddamned stranger, trying to figure out my next move in this perverse game of chance." I can no longer breathe through my nose and have gone through an entire box of Kleenex. I rested my head in my hands on her desk.

"Are you taking anything…to help with the stress?" she asked gently.

"No," I barked. "I'm *fine*."

"I don't think you are. Call your doctor and get something, Jude. It's time. Most women do it after just a divorce. And *you've* been through…"

"Oh, so you think I'm behaving irrationally?! Okay, but I think I have a right to be a little unhinged all things considered—and you still haven't answered my question, Patricia, what in god's name would *you* do?!"

After a long pause, during which her eyes fill up as she internalized the terrible thought, she said, "I would keep my chemo appointment. I would not take the risk, Jude. I'm not advising you; I'm just sharing what I would do. I'm a mom, after all."

And I am not. And never will be. And I don't have a husband or kids or anyone else for that matter that would be affected in any long-term significant way if I picked the wrong door and checked out early. I know I have people who love and care about me but I am not a daily contributor to their lives and it would be sad for them for a while but life would move on.

So I drove home from my Cancer Care session leaving a visibly shaken Patricia (probably second-guessing her career path), contemplating my own death because it was easier than picturing four months of dose-dense chemo. I didn't feel any pain in this fantasy death; I just gracefully waft into the great unknown looking very peaceful and hopeful that I would be reunited with David and others who had followed the light before me. It is a dignified demise and I still have my long hair laid out around me on a fancy pillow instead of some cheesy wig, and throngs of people come to pay their respects and talk about me as if I were someone who mattered.

By the time I reached home I had convinced myself it might not be so bad, dying. I knew I didn't want to stop breathing but I also didn't want to continue feeling this paralyzing helplessness. I had reached a point where I could not imagine feeling worse so the concept of death sounded like a simple and lovely escape.

I will not make a final call on the chemo until the day before treatment. I did not tell anyone this. I called my doctor, my regular general practitioner, and told her quite calmly that I just got divorced and had a mastectomy and am staring at chemo in a week so I could really use some more Xanax. She called in the script immediately and I raced to pick it up. I didn't take any right away, but it helped to know it was there. I honestly thought about dropping some off for Patricia.

APRIL 20

In a better frame of mind today. Thank you, Xanax. I was in New York for my Muggle-Scan, as I was now calling it, to test the strength of my heart muscle. Another injection, more large noisy machines, and no pain, but when I got to the guy who was going to do the pre-chemo blood work, he's a newbie. God help me, what did I do to deserve him today?

"Seriously, you have done this before, right?" I asked after his third attempt at finding a vein that will squirt blood. My arms are thin. Most phlebotomists refer to my veins as "ropes" because they protrude and are so easy to find.

"I'm sorry, ma'am. Just one more try and I'll call in my boss if I don't get it."

"I've got a better idea. Call your boss, *now*."

Today's lessons: Yes, I am indeed a Muggle. No, am I still not very nice to hospital staff.

APRIL 22

The siblings and I all pitched in for the Big Event—Mom's seventy-fifth birthday—and bought her tickets to a Billy Joel concert at the Hartford Civic Center complete with a stretch limousine to take us to and from the venue. Jodi and I were her escorts. Big Syl loves this man. He's not Frank Sinatra or the Beatles, but he's close. And she will tell anyone who will listen, "He was our neighbor on Long Island!" when in reality he lived about two towns away and used to sing in crappy bars that she would never in her life be caught dead in. But it's a nice conversation starter.

I arrived at my sister's with my newly cropped hair and everyone made a big deal out of it, but I felt awkward. I also boldly put on a low-cut top even though I was grossly uneven; it helped to make me feel like a girl. If I can't have long hair, I need some semblance of cleavage.

Big Syl was dressed in a hip-hop outfit. We don't know why. She was wearing a burgundy velvet track suit, Skechers, gold chains, and a long leather jacket. She had never been to a rock concert before so I guess she believed Golden Girls Ghetto Chic was the way to go. We took pictures when the limo arrived and enjoyed a terrific ride to the Civic Center with Jodi's husband, Glenn, her son, Geoff, and my dad. Dad seemed engaged and happy to be out of the house but was barely communicative because he was never sure of what was going to come out of his mouth—intelligible words or some garbled version of what he really wanted to say.

The concert was magical. Mom sang along to every word of every song and was in a celebrity music-trance. She so needed a night out and couldn't stop talking about how she had "no idea they served wine at these things!" After we were dropped off, the "boys" went for dinner and then came back to pick us up in the white stretch after the show. When it arrived, pulling into the VIP section in front of the Civic Center, Jodi and I pretended we were Big Syl's bodyguards so on-lookers wondered if it might have been some relative of Mr. Joel's or perhaps Eminem's grandmother.

Thankfully, no one said a word about the fact that I was supposed to start chemo in two days other than Jodi, who volunteered to come with me and was talking logistics as we said good-night. It is a hard topic and I didn't want to talk about it tonight or mention my recent breakdown. I will however, confess to filling up during "Only the Good Die Young."

APRIL 24

Over the past few weeks, despite hourly vacillating about whether I wanted to keep my chemo appointment or not, the Virgo side of my brain was busy organizing, building my back-up team.

I needed to find a new cleaning service because the last one I hired broke an average of three priceless keepsakes every time they cleaned. I researched and secured a "green" pest management service because I was tired of listening to Mickey and Minnie in the attic when I was trying to sleep but don't believe in the more draconian methods for eradicating them. I negotiated with my refuse service to cart away the mountain of Sierra Nevada bottles still preventing me from using the garage for anything other than attracting more mice. And I miraculously found a lawn-mowing, all-around outside maintenance dude, who promised to come by on a weekly basis and "do whatever needs doing" which was music to my ears.

As much as I loved my John Deere tractor, on a good day it took me 2.5 hours to mow the weeds, masquerading as lawn. The garden that I used to tend on weekends or after dinner was completely overgrown, so I asked Lawn Dude for help with that, too. I called the company that opens and closes my pool to see if they would clean it for me after opening it this year, and finally, a friend's father agreed to help out with handy-man chores as needed in the house for a nominal hourly sum because he's retired and really just liked to get out of the house and feel like he's helping someone. I knew it was all going to be expensive, but I was determined to not only keep this house but chip away at making it my home. I also knew there might come a time when I would not be up for doing things myself.

Today Jodi and I had a double bill in New York: first, a second fill-up with McDreamy and then over to Sloan's other offices for my first blast of chemo. I decided that I would get through the first round or two and just stop treatment if I chose. It was my mental control game, and it was working so far.

Kelly came in to McDreamy's exam room and asked me, as if she already knows the answer, "So, Jude, do you know if you're having chemo?"

"Yeah. I start today, in fact."

"Oh, no. I'm sorry. Okay, well let's just give you a few more cc's today and then we'll resume when you're on your last round in a few months time." And as surreal as this ritual was the first time, I was now completely relaxed about the magnet, the Sharpie, and the needle puncture preceding the fill-up. Jodi is slightly squeamish, but she managed to hold it together because she knew this was just the pre-game show today.

The pressure in my chest was noticeable but not quite as bad as the first fill-up, and we headed over to Sloan's Chemo Chamber in fairly good spirits after a light bite of lunch. We were going to a new part of the Cancer Center that I had not seen before and, as we soon discovered, they definitely went out of their way to make it look more like the lobby of a three-star hotel: cushiony round seating areas and muted pastel tones on the walls and rugs and upholstery; piles of magazines and books; low, almost imperceptible

Muzak; handy places to put your coffee cups. It was all very welcoming and civilized. I don't know why I had expected a more dungeon-like feel with bald chemo-zombies wandering the halls chained to IVs. The patients all had on nice little caps or scarves covering their heads and didn't appear to be in any obvious gastrointestinal distress. Well, then; this might not be so bad.

When I was finally called, Jodi and I walked down a wide circular hallway that has a warren of very small rooms. Some of the sliding pocket-doors on the rooms were wide-open and others only partway. I tried not to look but noticed fractions of scenes from other people's lives as we walked by—a woman clearly much younger than me sitting with a friend; someone's grandmother attended to by her son and his wife; a teenage boy reading to his mom. It was all a little heartbreaking. The cloud of smells in this corridor is antiseptic to the point of being sour, adding to my trepidation; but realizing that I wasn't the only person being poisoned today helped me to keep putting one foot in front of the other.

By the time we got to our room a nurse had already prepped the space and was there to greet us. It was no larger than a walk-in closet with just enough room for a modified dentist chair for the patient, a slightly padded chair for a loved one, and a stool on rollers for the oncologist's assistant. The chair I was in didn't go all the way back like a dentist chair but it was just long enough so the back of your legs were supported and you could tilt back a bit, kind of like a mini-Barcalounger.

The assistant had no trouble finding an accommodating vein and easily inserted a needle connected to a thin flexible tube. She gave me several anti-nausea pills to take and then explained matter-of-factly that the Adriamycin is very toxic so it will be given as an injection through a salt-water drip and if I feel any pain in my arm to let her know immediately; it would be dangerous if the drug somehow ventured outside the vein. "Although that almost never happens," she added.

The Adriamycin looks like a bag full of iodine. It's bright red and makes its way into my body without incident. Jodi and I made small talk and ate stale crackers and generally made jokes whenever possible. The Cytoxan was administered in the same manner after about forty minutes and it took another twenty minutes. I was warned beforehand that "some women" have a reaction to it that feels like an allergic response.

"Can you be more specific?"

"Well, your nose might get itchy and you could feel the need to sneeze. Or you might even get a little lightheaded."

"I'm already lightheaded."

"I'll get some tissues."

As the Cytoxan made its way into my body I suddenly felt freezing from the inside out. I grew dizzier and put my head back to close my eyes before commencing to sneeze all over the room with a force that I feared would dislodge my IV; good thing it was taped to my arm. Not fun. I wanted to rip it out and walk out of the building and go to MOMA to look at depressing art instead. Jodi was a fountain of encouragement, but she knew I was not comfortable and was obviously trying to distract me. After an hour of "treatment" I was given a pile of prescriptions which we filled at their in-house pharmacy—anti-emetics, steroids, anti-anxiety pills, acid reflux reducers, and a truckload of other pharmaceuticals. Good lord. What was going to happen to my body on all these drugs if I couldn't take a sleeping pill without seeing aliens?

On the ride home I felt stoned; not a nice high, just a slow-motion fog. I stared out the window questioning my choice to go ahead with treatment, too tired to do much of anything other than recount the day with my sister, saying things out loud over and over again until I was convinced that it all actually happened: my fake boob was inflated again and I began intentionally poisoning myself so I can hopefully live past another five years.

After I got myself settled at Green Acres with some food and a change into yoga pants, Jodi went home. The second after she walked out the door I wondered what I should do next. I had so over-dramatized this in my head that I was shocked that I wasn't yet doubled over the toilet bowl making deals with god. I called my friend Dean from work. He had been checking in on me from California with stunning regularity and usually something funny to say. I don't know why I called *him* and not someone else in my family or Kim but I wanted to reach out casually to someone and let him know that, quite miraculously, I was still alive and not yet vomiting my guts up. I told him I felt very stoned and was just going to chill out for the remainder of the day with Sophie. He joked that, were it not for the cancer, he would like to switch places with me.

By the time the early evening rolled around, my belly felt very full and tight and I was nauseated. My temperature was up, my heart intermittently beat very fast, and I had several hot flashes for the first time in my life. I brought my laptop into bed and found a group called "Starting Chemo in April" on the breast cancer.org discussion boards.

Feeling like I'm at an AA meeting and admitting for the first time that I'm a drunk, I made my first public entry. *Yes, world. I have cancer, and I've started chemo. Stage 2B.* I realized at that moment there was no one else I could talk to about this experience except total, faceless strangers. Family and friends wanted to hear I was *coping*; they didn't want to hear fear. They didn't want to spend too much time with you talking about that scary place they couldn't rescue you from. I reached for an Ativan, the anti-anxiety drug that also miraculously helps with nausea, to help me go to sleep. Sophie sat at the end of my bed staring at me, wondering what was wrong because I'm never in bed before the sun goes down.

No, Dean, you do not want to switch places with me. It's Day One and I'm alone with nothing but my dog, my side-effects journal, strangers in cyberspace, and dread fear of the unknown.

APRIL 25

Kim checked in today to see how I was doing and I didn't want to tell her. I tried to make myself sound upbeat but calm, at the same time I was writing in my side effect journal for my oncologist: *Temperature up again to 99.9, very fatigued after noon, face is getting puffy and red from the steroids, headache, stomachache, and extreme dry mouth. I can't wear my contacts anymore because my eyes are too dry. Brain is very foggy. Force myself out into the garden for an hour and wind up just wandering around plucking a few weeds and sitting on rocks to breathe the fresh air because that is really all I can manage to do. This totally sucks.*

Jay the Dentist came over to give me my shot of Neulasta and I wished he could have stayed longer. I wish I had made more of an effort to be a friend to him and his wife when I was feeling better. I hope I get that chance because they're incredibly nice people. Jodi called to check in on me and asked me how I was feeling. "Like I'm eighty," I said.

APRIL 26

I make myself a decent breakfast and manage to keep it down. My stomach feels full all the time and food is starting to taste bad; everything has a metallic flavor to it now. It dawns on me that I have not gone to the bathroom in days so I take something else for that. By 2:00 pm my temperature has bounced up again and I am achy all over like I have the flu. I feel like total shit all day and barely get out of bed after 3:00 except to walk into the kitchen only to realize I have no interest whatsoever in eating because I now, on top of everything else, have menstrual cramps. What? No rain of frogs?

APRIL 27

Temperature is back to normal but I still have no appetite. I have my period, which I was not supposed to get, and a very swollen face with bright red cheeks and have so little energy I am worried about driving alone but I do it anyway. Today I am closing on the refinanced mortgage for my house, Green Acres. It is now officially, unequivocally, my very own house, with my very own swimming pool and my very own jumbo freaking mortgage. I had trouble dressing myself this morning. How on earth am I going to get through this?

MAY 2

My friend Priscilla offered to come along to pick up Stella, my $600 human hair accessory. I felt okay all things considered. Priscilla is another friend from theater but is also a neighbor and had swooped back into my life not just as someone who could be counted on emotionally but someone who found extra time to help out; which was shocking because she is a year or two older than me and had just given birth to *twins*, bringing her brood's tally to four, and holds down a full-time job while still finding time to do theater. I honestly didn't hold out hope that I would see her again until the twins were in third grade. But she and her husband, Kyle, had been checking in on me regularly and offering to provide company on trips to doctors or, as today, wig shops.

I squeezed Stella onto my head and although Priscilla was telling me I looked great, all I could see was Linda Evans in *Dynasty*, minus the shoulder pads. We joked about the other hilarious Elvira-like hairpieces hanging in the room and tried connecting celebrities with each one of the wigs. When I pulled Stella off after the Nice Wig Lady sized her for me and trimmed her up a bit, my scalp was very red, tingling and stinging. She said that it's not uncommon and advised that since my hair was so thick I should have it thinned out in their salon today for free so there would be less pressure on my scalp. She sold me some gentle wash for my soon-to-be-bald head and wig shampoo. Stella, it seemed, was very high maintenance. I watched as the hairdresser relieved my head of chunks of hair with her thinning shears until I could actually feel relief. It was still sore but not as painful anymore. I didn't even care about the fact that I could have done a better job with my rusty garden tools. My beautiful hair was starting to go away and I haven't even gotten to my second treatment yet.

MAY 8

I transferred to Greenwich Hospital for round two because I decided I did not want to schlep into New York anymore; that's a long drive when you're stoned. Dr. Rivers explained that the protocol could be fulfilled anywhere but she could still be my chief oncologist. I found through a friend a wonderful local oncologist I've named Dr. Bones (for his model-like cheekbones) who was perfect for me. He is affiliated with Greenwich Hospital, which is like the Four Seasons, bearing no resemblance whatsoever to a medical facility. Bones is younger than me, a veteran of NYU, and is also affiliated with Yale-New Haven. He is incredibly smart, funny, realistic, and so well-informed that I cannot trip him up. I tried, of course, but he was very much on his game during our first visit, so I fell immediately in love. He also did not shy away from the ambiguities of treatment success; his honesty coupled with a demonstrated effort to stay on top of the latest research and an *actual personality* was positively irresistible to me. He had photographs of antique rock and roll guitars on his walls and dropped the f-bomb immediately after I did. Bones also doesn't equate "big facility" with "best treatment" and explained what he saw as the difference. Finally—someone in the vast medical community that I could connect with. So I arrived at his offices today for my second round of treatment with Priscilla in tow. We were ushered to a small chemo room with two patient chairs and two stools—no private room today.

One of the nurses, a cheerful sort about twenty-five years old, tried very hard to get the needle positioned correctly in my arm but was failing miserably. At some point she said, "Okay, I think we've got it now."

"I don't think you do. It's not supposed to hurt," I said. "You can't have it in the vein correctly."

"Oh, okay. I'll try again." And she did with the same painful result. Finally an older nurse came in and said she would take over.

She peered over the top of her readers at my arm and said, "It looks okay to me. Start the drip."

"No, really, it doesn't feel like it's in there right. If the Adriamycin goes outside the vein—"

"Yes, we know," said the older nurse as she jiggled the IV to make her point, "But it looks fine to me. You're probably just sore."

So they started the drip and everyone in the room, including the other patient and her guest stared at me like I was a ticking bomb until suddenly a searing, white hot pain stung my arm as if I were being branded like a steer.

I screamed, "Stop it, stop this NOW, this is very dangerous!!"

The older nurse stopped the drip and took the needle out looking at my arm which was now swollen and pink as she *finally* realized her mistake. *She didn't listen to her patient.* And I now had a ruptured vein that is contracted and dead for all eternity in the one arm still available for injections. I demanded to speak to the doctor.

After a long ten minutes Bones came in and apologized profusely. He assured me that, although I'll probably not get the use of that vein back, I'd be fine. Since I'd never met a doctor who admitted mistakes before, I'm somehow calmed by this. Priscilla did her best to stay neutral but she was completely pissed off and frankly worried. I got through the rest of the treatment without further incident and felt the same allergic reaction from the Cytoxan to the point where it made me go to sleep from lightheadedness.

Priscilla got me home. Sophie greeted us at the door accompanied by a pungent and foul odor. She had, you guessed it, rolled in shit. Priscilla, who was dressed as she always dressed—like she's going to an evening of theater—helped me wrestle Sophie's stinky hide into the tub and hose her down. Every time the dog felt the need to shake, Priscilla and I just looked at each other helplessly as we got completely soaked with soapy watered-down poop spray. Sophie was looking at me with her ears down, shocked and appalled that I didn't approve of her special welcome home present. All I can say is that it's a rare friend who carts your butt to chemo and then kneels next to your tub in her Eileen Fisher tunic and cleans shit off your dog.

MAY 10

I'm losing my hair.

I wake up this morning, take a handful of pills according to the spreadsheet I have taped up in my bathroom and get into the shower. I do my stretching exercises for my arm then start to wash my hair. As I massage the shampoo gently into my sore scalp, handfuls of hair begin dislodging and dropping all around me in the shower making loud plopping noises. So I gently tug to see if this is more than just rapid thinning, and it didn't take much to realize that today is the day. I calmly step out of the shower, leaving a pile of hair in the tub, and throw on a towel.

I IM Kim who is working from home today: Hair falling out. Wanna drive me to Vinny the Barber's?

Okay, but why?

Cause I want him to shave my head. I don't want to look like a plucked chicken and he'll only charge me five bucks.

Right. Got it. Be there in five.

Vinny's barber shop is right next to Jay the Dentist and I could walk if I had the energy, but I don't. Energy is something that comes in spurts, usually only in the morning and never in the first few days after a chemo blast. Kim comes by to pick me up and my hair is still wet and I'm afraid to touch it. We get to Vinny's, which is a single-chair, old fashioned, red-and-white barber pole, Welcome-to-Mayberry kind of barber shop. Vincent is Italian, an immigrant who has been in this country for forty years and still has a just-off-the-boat accent—the kind that makes you hungry for pasta and garlic every time you hear it.

"Jude, so nice to see you! Been so long!!"

"Vincenzo! You look great. Hey listen, I would like you to cut my hair today."

"Okay," he says with a crooked smile because in the twenty-five years I've known him he has never cut my hair, but he always admired it and used to tell me so.

"Actually, I need you to shave my head. I'm on medication and it started falling out this morning. I just want it all off. It hurts." His face falls and he looks at me and knows I'm serious, and then at Kim, who introduces herself to break the tension.

"Sure, sure. Okay. Whatever you want. I do whatever you want. Come, sit."

"Oh, and can you give me a Mohawk first before you take it all off? I always wanted to know what I'd look like with one." I had warned Kim about this and she has brought her camera. Vinny realizes we're going to make the best of this situation and smiling, he immediately joins the team.

"You got it! We'll go nice and slow, I don't wanna hurt you. And you'll look beautiful when I'm done, I promise."

"Hmm. Doubt that very much," I laugh.

"You're always beautiful, my friend."

Vinny shaves my head carefully leaving just a strip down the center for my punk-rock star turn. He is going slowly but my scalp is so sore and irritated that he's nicked me twice and I'm bleeding.

Kim is taking pictures and making us both laugh and injecting as much humor into this scene as she can. After my Mohawk photo-op, Vinny shaves down the center of my head and it's done. I am bald. My head is cold so I tie on a baby blue bandanna and look at myself in the mirror before leaving the barber shop. Another step towards looking like the scary unisex cancer patient and away from the woman I used to be.

There was a car in the driveway that we didn't recognize. It turned out that another friend from theater named Sonnie had arrived on the spur of the moment after hearing about my situation and could not have picked a better time. We all went into the house and talked hair and cancer and theater. Sonnie told me she worked close by and would stop in with dinners once a week. She did not *ask* me, she told me this was her plan, which was exactly the right thing to do. I was beyond grateful not only for the promise of food I didn't have to prepare myself but because evenings were the worst; I could really use the company. She asked me what I could eat and took notes for menu planning. Kim quietly slipped into the bathroom and cleaned all my hair out of the shower for me before heading back home to work so I wouldn't have to face it later. She really does know how to take the sting out of just about any situation. With Sonnie's arrival today I started to feel the presence of a growing Inner Circle.

My head was tender and a little raw and the lack of hair was making me very, very cold. I wore a soft pink cotton cap to bed that the Wig Lady convinced me to buy. Sophie kept looking at me as if she did not recognize me. I figured out that I probably smelled very different to her because of all the drugs in my system. I gazed into the mirror in my bedroom trying to get accustomed to my latest persona: *Eraserhead.*

MAY 13

I am in New Hampshire at Jayne's for the weekend to celebrate Mother's Day. I have on a purple and gold Indian head scarf and my nephews are both avoiding me. I think I'm scaring them. My niece Maggie is trying valiantly to convince me that scarves can indeed look cool if paired with the right earrings and takes time to help me accessorize. I don't want to eat and have trouble keeping my head up for more than an hour at a time. The only thing that tastes good and doesn't bother my stomach is Edy's chocolate ice cream. Maggie and I devour an entire container. I am glad to be with family but feel as if I am disappearing before their eyes. I asked Jodi last week if she had anything in her closet that she could bring to Jayne's that I could wear to a wedding I was invited to in June. I am now a size four and everything in my closet is a 6 or an 8 and hangs off of me. I tried on the dress she brought and everyone told me how nice I looked but the fussing sounded forced and overdone. I look like a Number 2 pencil wrapped in black spandex. I have my laptop with me and Skype with Kim at 11:00 pm. I can't sleep. I tell her that it's all very surreal, this life of mine. She tells me to take an Ativan and call her in the morning.

MAY 17

Overall head clarity was much improved during the second week after a treatment. I could think things through without getting sidetracked. Word-retrieval was generally not as embarrassing as during Week One, when I had trouble finding and articulating words such as *box* or *door*, staring at these objects conjuring up all sorts of wrong guesses until minutes later the simple nouns return to my brain like old friends apologizing for being late for dinner. Under other circumstances I might have been able to find the humor in this, but considering my dad's current mental condition, this side effect was nothing less than terrifying. The same defect applied to writing as well. I am a list-maker extraordinaire; it is how I stay organized. But there were days when I got halfway through a simple grocery list and couldn't come up with the word for that long, orange thing with the green stalks that Bugs Bunny likes to eat.

The latest in my side effect world was the onset of some serious joint pain. In the mornings, my fingers were so stiff that I had to pry each one of them loose to get them moving but by midday I usually got all ten cooperating.

But today officially reached "good day status" because I received a call from my friend Tony, whose wedding I would be attending in June. I was so very excited for him; he has finally met the love of his life. A woman he re-met at his twenty-year high school reunion in Boston and they've been together ever since. I love this story. And I love Tony. He is the ringleader of my boy-posse from Priceline and we've been close friends for years. He rolls in and out of my life like a restless tide but is as solid, dependable, and trustworthy as a brother when I need him. When David died, Tony knew how impossibly hard my situation was and reached out to let me know he understood and took time to listen. He is a towering presence; tall and very broad-shouldered with a large, round, friendly face, an honest smile, and a charming working-class Boston brogue. One of the reasons we always hit it off as friends is that we could easily confide in each other about things that mattered and find silly humor in just about any situation, which to me is the recipe for a fantastic friendship. But when he called me today he was worried. He didn't like the sound of any of my answers when he asked how I was feeling because I was not sugar-coating. And I wasn't laughing. So he decided to pick up *the boys* and come up to Green Acres with dinner tonight for a visit.

The boys are Alex and Ravi, and another friend named Arjun who was born in Jakarta, also worked at Priceline with us, and is the youngest of the bunch. I have a soft spot for Arjun and have ever since we worked together. He always struck me as the most ambitious career-wise and yet the most unsure of himself when it came to relationships. He is lean and not as mocha-skinned as Ravi but exotic looking with enormous very dark brown eyes. I hired him and Alex and Ravi into Priceline; Tony was already there when I arrived. With the exception of Alex they were all still single. Since I was the eldest and, until very recently, married, I typically played the big sister or human resources life coach role. Long after I left the company I continued doling out relationship and career advice. We are an eclectic and, dare I say, interesting group. After enough wine and with the right lighting we could appear much like Dorothy and her friends the Tin Man, the Lion, the Scarecrow and Toto.

It was warm so I didn't bother to cover my head. When the boys arrived I panicked. I was suddenly terrified for them to see my naked head, so I grabbed an old knit winter cap from the closet on my way out the door to greet them. Tony grabbed me and gave me a big hug and realized immediately how thin I had become.

"Jesus, Jude, I'm afraid I'll crush you. Aren't you eating?"

"Yeah, but everything tastes like shit."

"I want that problem!" said Alex as he came around the car for his hug motioning to his barely noticeable love handles. Ravi and Arjun seemed happy to see me but were a bit less physically demonstrative so I ushered them all into the house to break the tension. I knew I was not the person they expected to see and it was palpable. I felt the same thing every morning when I caught my own reflection. After a brief tour of the house and grounds, they were officially in love with Green Acres.

"Omigod, this place is like heaven. It's so freakin' peaceful."

"Seriously, did you see the pool? It's like the pool that can be seen from space."

"She's got a river and a pond and a hot tub…Christ, Jude, do you have enough water features?"

I felt something new while listening to their comments. Pride in where I live; and pride in myself for hanging on to this very special place so far. When we got into the kitchen, Tony announced that they bought me a little Weber grill since mine was lost in the divorce, and that he was going to barbeque some steak tips tonight. They also brought cured meats and side dishes and appetizers, beer and, of course, wine, which unfortunately, tasted so bad to me now it was undrinkable, like sipping watered-down vinegar with food coloring in it. They buzzed around the kitchen asking where they could find plates and silverware and after the flurry of activity died down we all sat around the island in my kitchen and talked cancer. I was amazed at the questions they asked me, being a group of younger men who, I thought, would shy away from the topic entirely. Let's face it; they have boobs on their minds 24/7 but in an entirely different context. All four of them talked nonstop and barely let the other one finish a sentence as they fired off questions and comments about my situation.

"So, it looks like you've got something there, Jude. You're not flat or anything on that side…" Tony said as matter-of-factly as if he noticed a button missing on my shirt.

"Flat? What do you mean, flat? Tony, man, what did you expect? You had reconstruction, right, Jude?" asked Arjun as if he had read my medical chart.

"Yeah, well, I've got a ways to go yet..."

"Well, when Ravi and I saw you in the hospital," Alex remarked, as if to poke the other two who didn't come to visit me, "we thought you looked great and you still do. I mean, considering what you've been through, Jude, hats off to you."

"Nice, Alex!" said Ravi as he punched him in the arm for making the unfortunate comment that forced everyone to look at the stupid hat on my head.

"Jude. As your friend: that is the ugliest fucking hat I have ever seen," said Tony. Everyone in the room doubled over laughing and I put my hands on my head so they wouldn't yank it off.

"Seriously, Jude; I wanna see your head. You're completely bald, now right?" asked Ravi.

"Yes, Ravi, she's bald, just like *you*. Only much cuter," said Arjun. "C'mon, Jude. We all wanna see. It has to be better than that nasty hat."

"Okay, you wore me down. I didn't want to freak you guys out..." So I pulled off my silly knit cap and they all stared at my perfectly bald, perfectly round head with all the wonder of little kids watching their first parade.

"Cool, can I touch it?"

"Be gentle."

"That's fantastic! Some people have really ugly heads, like our friend Ravi here...but yours is, like, perfect," said Alex. "Seriously, Jude; I like it. You totally make it work." Alex was the arbiter of hipness and good taste for this group, so this was high praise and validation, indeed.

"Very Annie Lennox."

"No, no, Sinead...."

"Christ, no, not *her*!"

"Meryl Streep in *Sophie's Choice*!"

"Dude, I don't think Auschwitz is the way we want to go here..."

"How about: the New Jude; the Jude that will be better and stronger than ever when this is all over," said the ever-mature Alex as he raised his glass to redirect the conversation from any further mention of the Holocaust. Then they toasted me, my divorce, my house, my health, my good boob, my fake boob, my dog, my perfectly round head, and my new grill.

"So what's in there now? Like where your boob used to be?" This was Arjun. He is curious by nature and asks very pointed questions. He is the guy who always needs to know the *hows* and the *whys* in any given situation. So I explained the expander and the fill ups; the magnet, the Sharpies and the needles, and they cringed, making sound effects throughout my speech. They were seriously grossed out but hanging in there with me. It was hilarious.

"They just jammed it in there? Holy shit, Jude. You're like a fucking warrior. Seriously. This breast cancer is some bad shit."

"Oh, really? Brilliant Ravi, just brilliant; please enlighten us with more of your vast medical wisdom," said Tony who is forever punishing Ravi for his penchant for stating the obvious.

"C'mon, Tone," said Ravi in self-defense, "I didn't really know *anything* about this, I mean, did you? This is some fucked-up shit," which was the understatement of the century and one with which I completely concurred.

"Yes, indeed it is," I said, "but as long as I can keep talking to you guys about it and laughing, I will be fine. It's just so great to see you all."

"Whatever you need, babe; just let us know. But please do us all a favor and start eating some meat, will ya? You're too fucking skinny," said Tony.

"I'm a vegetarian."

"Yeah, I know," he said more seriously, "but that may not be the smartest thing for you to be right now. Have some steak tips. You need iron if you're gonna keep your strength up. You can go back to eating seaweed and trail mix when you're better." So I did. And I had forgotten how long it takes to chew meat and that saliva is a necessary component to breaking it down. My jaw was tired after two steak tips.

My new grill was sending wonderful summer BBQ smells wafting into the house ushering back happy memories of entertaining friends and family with casual dinners and festive pool parties. All of that seemed like another lifetime ago. But Sophie and I were both smiling and had one of the best nights we could remember in a very long time. The boys cooked, cleaned up, gave me pep talks about everything from eating to dating and stayed way past my bedtime. One by one they each kissed me and rubbed my head for good luck before they left like I was a human Blarney Stone. As I was turning out the lights I noticed the grill still smoldering on the patio and silently hoped there would be many more nights like this one in my future.

MAY 22

Kim came with me to Dr. Bones today for my third round of AC. She had not met him before but her reaction was similar to when she laid eyes on McDreamy. She was besotted, which made for lively conversation in the chemo-chamber, which we had all to ourselves. I felt weak and had a terrible headache. Bones came in and asked me how I was doing after the nurses carefully started the drip. He looked at the damaged vein which was still purple and now slightly indented from our last outing and again apologized. I rattled off a list of side effects, some new, some just hanging on, and waited for his counsel.

"Why didn't you tell me all this before?"

"Why, would you have stopped treatment?" I challenged him.

"No, but I could have given you something; I will give you something today for the breathing issues, Jude. We need to keep an eye on that." He was referring to the scariest new addition to my repertoire—an inability to take deep breaths without coughing when I'm lying down. I've been sleeping in sitting position propped up on a stack of pillows.

Bones explained that my bronchial tubes were very irritated from the Adriamycin and we needed to open them up with a steroid inhaler, another pharmaceutical for my collection. "But please, you must keep me in the loop on these things. I am *tracking with you*; I don't just load you up with drugs and send you home for two weeks with my fingers crossed. We're doing this together, right?"

"Sorry."

"I'm on this, Jude. But you have to work with me."

"I didn't want to bother you. I just figured it was normal."

"Well, you're anemic now, which is why you feel so lousy and I'll give you something else for that today. But it will have to be a separate injection; I can't put it in the drip. Are you still not eating red meat?"

"Yes. No meat or bird. I had two steak tips the other night to be polite but it took too long to chew."

"Fine, but when you leave here today your friend Kim is going to drive you to Whole Foods across the street and you will go to the meat counter and purchase a freezer full of hormone-free steaks and start eating them. I don't care how long you have to chew it. And get a few bags of spinach, too. We've got to get your iron under control."

"Do I have to?"

"Yes, Missy," said Kim. "Enough. Eat the steak."

We got several wildly expensive steaks and a bunch of other groceries that made me sick just looking at them. I felt awful. My eyes were becoming photo-sensitive and the sun was so bright that it hurt to keep them open, even behind my sunglasses. Between the aversion to daylight and the hunt for red meat I was beginning to feel like Dracula.

At home, I opened an invitation to yet another wedding—my brother's *other* son Kevin was getting married in Burlington, Vermont, in two months. The New York Kevin of Il Vagabondo fame is his son with his first wife; this Kevin, the one we dubbed Kevin-O is his stepson with Daryl. To make it even more interesting, they are exactly the same age and both went to college majoring in theater arts. The Kevins are quite close and love to mess with people's heads when they introduce themselves as brothers.

I love Kevin-O to pieces but the whole wedding thing sounded premature. My nephew was getting *married*. Didn't that make me really old? Wait, I haven't even met his fiancée yet! Somewhere in my befuddled brain I was happy for him but I was too conflicted and selfish to feel anything other than dread at the thought of parading around in front of family and a room full of strangers feeling and looking the way I did. I also was having trouble working up excitement about all these pending nuptials when I was still recovering from my divorce—which was *my* second marriage—so I didn't feel like it's such a great institution. I did not want to go and wondered if I could use the chemo as an excuse. What a total and complete shit I can be sometimes.

MAY 23

I wake up in a very thick fog with god awful pangs in my stomach and zero energy. It's four in the morning. I get up to see if walking around will help. It does not. Back to bed to stare at the ceiling thankful for my new steroid inhaler because I am actually breathing normally without coughing; however, I now have a burning in my chest like acid reflux from god knows what. I know I have a pill for that somewhere but I don't feel like taking it. I grab my laptop and one of the lemon hard candies from my bedside table and get on the discussion boards of breastcancer.org to see if any other chemo chicks are awake, miserable, and chatting. They are, and we commiserate on all sorts of intimate details of our plights while supporting each other with virtual hugs (( )). I fall asleep with my laptop on my belly and wake up again at seven.

Kim, who has radar, calls and checks in. "How goes it?"
"Bad."
"Are you eating?"
"Don't want to."
"How about I make you something and bring it over?"
"K."
"What do you want…I'm taking orders."
"Mashed potatoes."
"It's seven a.m."
"I need comfort food. It's the only thing that sounds edible other than chocolate ice cream."

One hour later Kim comes over with a huge bowl of freshly whipped potatoes with some peas thrown in for some extra nutrition. She lies on the bed next to me while I eat my gruel. It tastes like a warm butter festival which is exactly what I craved.

After I'm done she and I just lie in the bed talking; she is catching me up on work and other gossip when out of the blue she asks me if I'm afraid of dying.

"Sometimes; I mean I know it's a possibility that it could happen a lot sooner than expected."

"I'm scared, Jude."

"I know."

"You have to get better."

"Trying, kiddo."

"We have things to do…you and me."

"I don't have the energy."

"I know. You're sick all the time now. I miss my friend."

"I'm right here. I'm just not very much fun anymore."

"This sucks."

"You're telling me."

"Try and get some sleep, I'll call you later."

"Thanks for the spuds." I fall asleep for a good long while and keep down every last potato and pea.

MAY 24

After a month of treatment and just into my third chemo-blast, I got into a rhythm. I could predict with relative accuracy whether I'd be too sick to think or whether I would have enough energy to engage in things as taxing as speaking in full sentences or typing coherent emails. Right after treatment, the first three days were torture and then it began to ease up a bit every day so that I could function with the majority of my brain intact up to one or two in the afternoon, when extreme fatigue would take over. The morning was my very best time; even if I was too weak to move around much, I still had my laptop so I could *get things done*. By the second week, I could leave the house to fetch things I might need, like food or dog treats, or a meal at a restaurant. Sometimes I drove; sometimes I hoped someone else offered to take me out because I easily lost concentration behind the wheel. With all the warnings I was given about chemo, not one person mentioned any risk about operating heavy machinery, and they should have.

I was emailing my colleagues at work from time to time to let them know I was still alive and to be reminded of the part of my life that was waiting for me to join it again someday. I missed them. I missed our interaction and ability to help and coach each other in our respective disciplines. Steve had been diligent about calling once a week and when I spoke to him a few days before I said I was thinking about working part-time from home if that was all right with him. He mentioned a few projects that were mostly writing that he would be happy to hand over to me and I was elated to feel needed. He told me to think about it and let him know for sure in a few days. I would receive full pay for the hours worked and keep my disability for the hours I didn't. My bank account and my failing mental acuity desperately needed this. I ventured that I could work several hours a day and I would tell only my immediate team I was back on the grid so I didn't get bombarded. I really wanted to do something other than worry about keeping food down, paying my mortgage, and battling back each and every drug-induced malady that happened my way. Twenty-five hours a week. I can do this.

I sent Steve a simple email today: *Put me in coach; I'm ready to play.*

JUNE 3

Tony's wedding has, thankfully, fallen on the second weekend after treatment so I am, all things considered, feeling decent. Kim is accompanying me to Boston so I don't have to drive and hang out in the hotel alone but she is not attending the wedding. She is, as she likes to say, "Driving Miss Judy" this weekend. This is the first time I will be at a public social event since my divorce and I'm pale, skinny, and bald. I decided to go with the spandex number from Jodi's closet because shopping for an outfit would have been too depressing. My boobs are horribly uneven and every time I look at myself in a department store changing mirror, I get spooked. It's as if the Scary Jude Imposter keeps following me around and I can't get rid of her.

I made reservations at the Omni Parker House, one of my favorite hotels in Boston. It's certainly not ultra-chic or as luxurious

as it was in its heyday, but it has a magical grandeur all its own—
gilded and romantic and slightly faded in the shadow of sleeker
models just around the corner on Beacon Street, like an out-of-style
dress from your prom that you just can't part with. The location is
perfect and helps me orient myself in this wacky maze of a city.

We pulled up to the hotel on a busy side street and the red-
uniformed attendants circled the car to help us with bags. The one
who rushed to open the door for me noticed my uncovered bald
head and started talking to me like I might be mentally retarded.
Meanwhile, Kim popped the trunk. Unfortunately I forgot I had
bought a huge bag of dog food for Sophie the other day which was
carried to the car for me by the shop owner and was still there
because I didn't have the strength to carry it into the house with my
still-wimpy arm and its three-pound limit. We were trying to get our
entire stash of luggage out of the trunk with the help of our
bellhops, when we all noticed a blind man briskly walking down the
sidewalk towards us, a beautiful German Shepherd proudly leading
the way for him. Suddenly the guide-dog did something I have
never seen before; he pulled his master off the sidewalk and straight
for the back of my car, plunging his nose deep into the trunk while
the unsuspecting fellow he was attached to plowed right into my
back bumper in full stride. Kim raced over to keep Fido from
tearing into Sophie's food bag and to tend to the poor man, who
brushed himself off with great dignity as if this happened every day,
and proceeded on his way. No, it is never nice to make fun of blind
people under any circumstances. So we waited until we got into the
hotel and burst out laughing, and now the bellhops thought I was
retarded and mean.

Preparing for this trip was interesting. I had a separate bag just
for my drugs. I had programmed all of my new doctors' numbers
into my phone. I brought scarves and do-rags for my head and two
wigs—Stella and the new cheapie, named Ginger, that I'd ordered
from an organization called Hip Hats with Hair. She's real hair
attached to a bare skull-cap; perfect for wearing under a hat so your
head stays cooler but you still have some hair sticking out from
underneath. This one is reddish brown, long and straight like my
natural hair. She is much more approachable than Stella and
frankly, more comfortable. I also packed a lint roller for my head

because my hair, which has been trying to grow back, gets to about one-eighth of an inch long and then dies and wants to fall out again, so I have to roll my head with the sticky tape every day to pull them out so as not to shed embarrassing little hair dandruff onto my clothes.

Kim was incredulous as she watched me lint-roll my head and asked if she could please take a picture.

"Only if you want to sleep in the trunk with the dog food," I warned her.

All the rest of the body hair (with the exception of eye lashes which are still hanging in there) is gone, so I didn't need to pack razors. The legs are baby smooth as are the arms and the rest of the anatomy which, I must confess, is pretty freaking weird; I don't care what anyone says. I know some people think it's hot, but on this package it's just one more peculiar adjustment. I brought tons of makeup and my contact lenses, and a pair of very fancy silver high-heels that I was persuaded to buy one day when Kim and her sister Sarah convinced me that I have sexy feet and ought to show them off. It's the one body part I have left that still rocks. So the toes and the bright red pedicure would also be attending the wedding along with the black spandex dress, a wig, and an evening clutch, full of makeup and drugs, held aloft by a newly single woman teetering on four inch heels, attempting her first fancy evening event in over a year. I left the hotel feeling like a ten-year-old playing dress-up.

It was raining harder than a monsoon and the streets of Boston were flooding. I headed to the church in a taxi and was drenched by the time I reached the huge wooden doors. Between the heels and the tight dress I couldn't walk fast, and I prayed that my wig was still centered on my head. I had decided to wear Ginger with a smart black turban rather than Stella because the blond tresses were making me look too pale.

Tony was in the back of the church with Alex and a few other friends when I arrived. He was fumbling with his boutonniere and did not see me. I walked up to him with all the confidence I could muster.

He beamed when he saw me. "Jude, you look fantastic!" which was all I really needed to hear, because Tony would have told me otherwise were it not true, wedding day or no.

I helped him pin his stephanotis on his lapel, whispered good luck, and took a seat in the church with Ravi who had just arrived. I applied layers of makeup at the hotel including lipstick and some fancy cover up for my black under-eye circles and the ugly, broken, purple vein on my arm. I kept touching the front of my turban to make sure that Ginger was behaving and not giving me away. The service was gorgeous and I wept with happiness for my friend, grateful for waterproof mascara and Bye Bye Under Eye concealer, which is stronger than Bondo.

Arjun was there with his stunning girlfriend, Claudia, who is from Lima, Peru, and Alex was with his lovely and very funny wife, Alexandra. She and I had never met before and we hit it off amazingly well. We rode to the reception from church in a taxi together and she looked at me as if we were already old friends and said, "You look fucking fabulous. Alex told me about coming to see you in the hospital and at your house...and honestly, I don't know what I was expecting, but it wasn't this. I'm so glad to finally meet you. You've got it going on, girl. Damn."

Ravi also did not have a date, so he sat with me at the reception. I think he was being a gentleman and looking out for me because under any other circumstances he would have been glued to the youngest, hottest single woman in the room regaling her with stories of growing up in Mexico. He attentively fetched me very watered-down vodka and cranberry cocktails and we even danced toward the end of the evening, which was an interesting feat of balance and concentration for me. I had all I could do to not topple over. Several light cocktails had soaked into my chemical-ridden body and created an otherworldly buzz; the stilettos now felt like three-foot stilts. Our table was the liveliest one at the party and we laughed and took pictures and made plans for the next day's brunch. I glanced around the table and these people looked to me like a sliver of light peeking over the horizon at sunrise. There was something about their friendship that felt unobstructed and honest and natural, even though I had just met some of them. I loved that they made me feel like a pretty girl again, even if just for one night. I loved this whole evening and wished I could slip it into my purse and take it home with me. Aside from the rain, Tony's day was perfect.

Score one each for Ginger, the spandex dress, the silver stilettos, and the friend waiting up for me back at the hotel. I couldn't wait to yank this head prosthesis off and tell her everything.

JUNE 5

Fourth round with Bones, my last round of Adriamycin and Cytoxan. Jodi is riding shotgun. I am still flying high from my wonderful weekend in Boston and although I know it's going to end in about twelve hours when I feel like shit again, I take great pleasure in sharing the details of it with my sister. She cracks up when I explain the lint-roller segment of the toilette and latest wig acquisition. I am amazed when she tells me how her training for the 3-Day is progressing; she is walking over twelve miles in a day and actually sweating in public.

Bones comes in for a few minutes and asks how I'm doing. I give him the rundown. I ask him if I can go back to yoga in a few weeks since this is my last AC.

He furrows his brow and says, "I know it's important to you and we will get there. But it's still not a good time. Let's see how you manage the first round of Taxol in a few weeks. You must remember that the drugs are cumulative in your system."

"Meaning?"

"Meaning that they build up over time; that the longer treatment goes on the harder it is to manage the side-effects."

"Which is why I want to do yoga — to get my strength back!"

"Patience, Jude. You'll get there. But I do think you should have some genetic testing done. I was looking at your history and your mom has had BC, plus you have Jodi here and another sister, right?"

"Yes, Jayne."

"Any nieces?"

"Yes, Jayne has a daughter Maggie."

"Did Dr. Rivers talk to you about this?"

"No. But I know what it is."

"Well, I recommend it. Have the test done and find out whether you have the genetic markers because in your case, if you do, we might want to talk about a prophylactic hysterectomy."

"What?!"

"If you do have the gene, it means you are predisposed to ovarian cancer, Jude. Plus, you want your sisters and your niece to know if they are at higher risk, right? The tests are very strong indicators, but I can't say they are foolproof. Find out if your insurance covers it and we'll do the blood work right here in the office—I'll send it away to the lab and interpret the results for you."

I had heard about this before but pushed it out of my mind. The very idea of removing what little I have left of my womanhood is sickening to me and I already know I won't do it regardless of what the genetic markers tell me. But I should have the test so Jodi and Jayne and Maggie will have more information. As the drugs are flowing into my arm today I feel dirty, diseased, completely removed from the girl who went to Boston last weekend. Jodi drives me to Whole Foods for provisions and I fall immediately asleep in the car on the way home. Two days ago I was dancing on four-inch heels with a handsome Indian man to Stevie Wonder songs and today I can't carry my own groceries.

JUNE 17

Father's Day. Since he and Mom are cooped up in the condo 24/7 except for doctor's appointments or brief visits to Jodi's, I thought a nice brunch here at Green Acres might cheer them up. My brother volunteered to drive them.

I had guests for the day, which was very exciting, and in the same breath petrifying, because my Swiss cheese brain couldn't keep track of anything anymore so my kitchen had become a veritable tapestry of lists and sticky-notes. Dad was moving very slowly and cautiously but I could still catch a glimpse of his indomitable spirit behind the rheumy baby-blues every now and then, and I tried to capture each of those moments for safekeeping. Mom, on the other hand, was quite simply unraveling. Victor moved her outside to the patio and tried to coach her with tips on caregiving with limited success; this in response to my mother's frustration and complete inability to recognize that Dad was not going to learn anything new or remember what she told him from day to day. And that no, he was not going to make conversation with her anymore. He simply couldn't.

Daryl helped me in the kitchen and just kept telling me how great I'm doing. I didn't agree, although I didn't hurt her feelings by letting her know. I was glad to see everyone; but also very relieved when they left so I didn't have to witness my parents' anguish every time they looked at me. I had forgotten that with all they were dealing with, I am still their child, their daughter. And in some ways, I didn't really bear any resemblance to her anymore. My father looked at me with an unspoken sadness from an inability to help his sick kid. My illness was a burden they did not need. Seeing me didn't help them; it made them all feel worse. Damn.

JUNE 19

I had my first round of Taxol today. During the past few weeks, in preparation for my ACT cocktail, part deux, I spent time researching all the possible side effects online and in the pamphlets from Dr. Rivers. I then checked the only source I trust for empirical data on the topic: breastcancer.org. The discussion boards are so well organized that I can pinpoint other women on the exact same chemo-regimen that I am on — to the day — to see how they are faring. I can also go back into archive data to hear from other women and post random questions any time of the day or night and get answers ranging from the humorous to the academic to the heartbreaking. This is where I get my information now. I don't bother with other sites; I have virtual friends here whom I have never met; I have no desire to meet them but I know they are there for me. This is my "on call" support group and I don't have to sit in a room with bad coffee and uncomfortable chairs unable to escape from the abject suffering that this disease has caused some random stranger; I am not trapped in a makeshift breast cancer confessional where the nice person you just met last week during cookie break announces she is terminal, and have to come up with something to say when I really want to lunge for the door and throw up; I do not have to bear witness to my bitter and lonely soul if I don't want to; and I can maintain what is left of my dignity by not breaking down into a humiliating pool of public self-pity like I did in the Cancer Center session; I am as anonymous and revealing as I choose to be on any given day depending on my needs. This is my kind of community. Some women post pictures, preferring to be completely visible; others identify themselves only by their diagnosis dates and descriptions such as: BC Stage III, Jun. 04, positive nodes, etc. I can understand their need to do this but I do not. In fact, I don't reveal much of anything other than the latest in the side-effect ambush or to share helpful remedies that are providing a modicum of relief, such as my hard lemon candies for dry mouth, extra-virgin olive oil for sandpapery skin and scalp, and of course, Edy's chocolate ice cream; the most decadently delicious fat, sugar, and calorie supplement on the planet Earth for when missed meals begin to amplify all my various maladies. I have no idea what's in that stuff but it is the only food item from my personal test kitchen that is immune to tasting like a mouthful of dirty copper pennies. Please note that Dr. Rivers's Chemo Bible says to avoid all sugar and fats. What do they know?

On one particularly lonely night I did, in a weak moment, confess on the boards to being by myself, childless, and recently divorced, with family over an hour away. The response I received was overwhelming. One of my BC sisters told me of an organization called "Chemo-Angels" that helps people like me who are on their own or have some other major life struggle during treatment. I signed up with the Angels that night and felt terribly relieved that I was not the only loser out there crying alone into her green tea every morning after dry heaving. They immediately assigned me my own personal angel, like George Bailey's Clarence, whose job it immediately became to crochet me silly hats, send motivational greeting cards and inexpensive, uplifting gifts every week with the express intent of keeping me from wading into the river, rocks in pockets. I must admit that even though it bordered on services for someone confined to a nursing home or a mental institution, it did provide me a reason to walk to the mailbox for something other than a medical or utility bill. But the sad reality is that just like Blanche DuBois—a character I played years ago—I have been reduced to depending on the kindness of strangers.

What I found out about Taxol was interesting. Some women tolerate it like it's aspirin and others claim they would shoot their oncologists if given the chance. The bad stuff to be on the lookout for is the onset of joint and long-bone pain, neuropathy or numbness and tingling in the fingers and toes, nausea and our old standbys: vomiting, mouth sores, and shortness of breath. The esthetic issues are: loss of whatever hair you may still have, including eyebrows and lashes, and blackened finger and toenails which also occasionally just fall off for no apparent reason.

Several hours after my infusion, I do not feel as stoned as with the AC, but I am absolutely freezing; I have wave after wave of flu-like chills and cannot get warm; it's 80 degrees outside. Sometimes I wonder if cancer treatment is really just the evil brainchild of some sadistic asshole who flunked out of med school and devised this cocktail for kicks. I honestly don't understand how this can be helping me. Maybe those MD Anderson guys are right on the money. How frightening is that?

JUNE 22

I felt lousy today but was not going to miss seeing Dean, who had generously offered to take me to a favorite restaurant. He sent me an email last week after he discovered I was doing stealth projects for Steve and said he was going to be in town from California this week and would like to meet for lunch. Dean is the company's Chief Information Officer. He is married and has a son but I'd never had occasion to meet his family, though he talks about them all the time so I felt as if I had. I was looking forward to seeing him but I was not looking forward to him seeing me. It was a dilemma easily solved by remembering that no matter what I look like he is going to give me shit about it; he's like Tony, but with a bigger title.

I decided on a Tuscan wine bar with fantastic food and a tranquil dining room. I put on a skirt and flat sandals and spent half an hour standing in front of my mirror with a full complement of shadows, blushes, and cover-ups, trying every *Glamour* trick I know to not look pale, bloodshot, and achy. It was not working. My face had thinned to the point where my eyes looked sunken and hollow. In just three days the Taxol had already attacked my femurs and my hips and it was getting difficult to move from a sitting to a standing position. It was hard for me to believe that just a few short months ago I had Bengal tiger strength and was capable of doing sit-ups in a hospital bed ten hours after major surgery. Today it took me three full minutes to maneuver into the driver's seat of my car and clasp my seat belt.

Dean maintained a terrific poker face when he saw me; he graciously told me that I looked great as the maître'd escorted us to our seats by the window, past a lovely fountain splashing quietly in the center of the room. The floors are terra cotta and the click, click, click of my sandals echoes gently throughout the dining room. The sound reminded me of being a young girl pining after my first pair of heels so I too could make that uniquely feminine and grown-up sound. I was relieved we made reservations for after the lunch rush; the dining room was almost empty.

As we made eye contact, an involuntary expression of concern flashed across his face. "Honestly, you don't look as bad as you described on the phone..."

"Yes, I do. I look like shit."

"You do look thin, Jude."

"That's probably because I can't eat anything, Dean. I can't even drink wine; everything tastes like metal or medicine."

"That has to suck." He paused to decide whether to go down this road. "So, what's it like to be bald?"

"Plain old fucking weird."

He laughed uncomfortably. "I told the team that if they reach their goals this quarter I will shave my head."

"I'm sure you'll look fantastic; it's not such a great look for us girls," I said. Suddenly feeling wildly self-conscious, I tugged at the front of my bandanna and stared out the window, trying to think of something to say that wasn't gloomy or boring. I came up empty. I had absolutely nothing to offer except to natter on about my illness and rapidly disintegrating appearance. My eyes—I still could not keep contact lenses in for more than an hour—begin to fill up behind my thick, geeky bifocals. Were he not a good friend who traveled out of his way to see me, I would have excused myself, walked into the restaurant's kitchen and stuck my head in the oven.

"Was this a bad idea?"

"NO! This was a fantastic idea. Just talk to me and make me feel like I'm still part of the world. I don't even know how to do this anymore..."

"Do what, exactly?"

"This! Eating lunch and talking. Casual conversation that does not include the word cancer. You know—this! And I'm a nervous wreck because I forget simple words all the time; I completely lose my train of thought. Christ, I'm a walking buzz-kill. I'm sorry. Just talk."

So he did. I drank green tea and built up my confidence to engage in intelligent discourse and, haltingly, we managed to get back to the old Jude and Dean sparring on politics, books, and films, predictably disagreeing on everything except the idiots we hate at work. I miss him. I was beginning to recognize and need people who have a visible center of gravity and he was one of them.

He was not fazed by anything I said, even when I answered his questions about the surgeries and chemo.

I had trouble getting up from the table. I was embarrassed and felt ancient, holding onto the table to steady myself and stand up straight. Dean notices but, thankfully, let it pass. He walked me to my car, suggesting I come out to California when I am feeling up to it, because "everyone is asking for you. They miss you; not the same without you."

"You're lying. What employees in their right minds miss their HR person?"

"Think about it. It might do you good." It did sound like a wonderful idea, if I could get myself well enough to pull it off. We said our good-byes and I waited until he got into his car so he wouldn't have to see me struggle to get into mine.

When I got home, I took a nap because Sonnie and her partner, Frank, were coming over for dinner. I hadn't seen Frank in two years and I had some trepidation about it. But when he arrived, he gave me a gigantic hug and asked if there were any chores he could do for me. Instead, we decided that due to the intense heat and lingering humidity, a swim was in order, so we waded around in the pool and enjoyed the tranquil and perfect summer evening air. My pool is ringed on three sides by a huge stand of Norway spruces and is completely private and so picturesque; I sometimes forget what a luxury it is.

By the time we got in the house, my legs were in serious pain, but I didn't want to say anything and spoil the evening. I just moved to the couch and slowly stretched them out in front of me. Frank was preparing the vegetarian dinner they brought and Sonnie came over to the couch and asked what was wrong.

"My legs...it's hard to explain. It's like my bones ache on the inside...and my thigh muscles are very sore for some reason...."

And once again, Sonnie didn't ask what she should do. She just did it. She sat on the couch with me and massaged my legs while she talked casually about some random theater gossip, acting as if this was something that she and I did every day. Frank promised to come back and trim the hedges and help with some other odds and ends and I instantly took him up on his offer, because Lawn Guy was costing me a fortune.

THE LONG SLOW CLIMB OUT OF THE TREATMENT PIT

I am enjoying their visit and grateful for their friendship, but it all feels very unnatural to me; I still have not made peace with my existing and encroaching limitations. As I lie in bed tonight reflecting on the day I have a very clear image of myself shrinking until I am no longer visible. There is precious little left of the woman I was; I am not funny or interesting or attractive or healthy; my parents' situation is beyond tragic; I still can't afford furniture for my half-empty house and the work I'm doing for my boss could easily be done by a first-year intern. How long will these people hang in there with me before I wear them out?

JULY 1

Today I had to make my first mortgage payment. In order to do this and maintain some financial breathing room, I had to sell a good chunk of stock. My funds are low. I made my final payment to my ex last month and it was enormous, wiping out most of my liquid assets. Bills were on the rise because of all the help I'd had to hire for things I should be able to do myself but can't, and my medical bills are off the charts. Even though I had health insurance, I was still paying thousands in out-of-pocket expenses with all the drugs, lab fees and hospital extras that were so neatly folded into my policy that I never noticed them until the bills arrived. For example, the shots that Jay was giving me were about $1,500 apiece, not 100% covered, and they had to be delivered in a refrigerated container one dose at a time. But I have no choice but to get them or I will land back in the hospital anemic. Or worse. I have absolutely no idea how the drug and insurance companies get away with this—or how any of them sleep at night; it is criminal.

But the cash from the stock after taxes allowed me to make my mortgage with enough left over to get a few odds and ends I need for the house, although still not enough for furniture. My sister Jayne was coming down with her husband and kids for the 4th of July weekend and I was so looking forward to the company I could barely stand it. I missed Jayne; I hadn't seen her since Mother's Day. I tried my best to spruce up the house and the garden but was extraordinarily low on energy. To tend the yard I had to outfit myself like a beekeeper, so it took me longer to dress than the time I actually spent in the garden.

My mouth is dry and my throat is tight and sore from lack of moisture; it hurts to swallow. My eyes look feverish and feel like I have 20-grit sandpaper on them when I blink. The sun only makes them more irritated. I crave sugar and salt but everything except Edy's ice cream gives me crippling heartburn. The throbbing pain in my legs is getting worse and more frequent and the overall joint stiffness and fatigue is so debilitating I finally broke down and called Dr. Bones but he said there is "really nothing we can do until we're done with the rounds of Taxol." I guess this is the cumulative effect he was referring to but in his estimation I have yet to reach the "unbearable" threshold.

If I could only be sure this soul-crushing treatment is actually going to buy me time, I might not feel so hopeless; but I don't even have that to hang on to.

Friends and family, even Kim, are starting to get weary of my sadness, discomfort, and anger when they call. I hear their thinly veiled sighs of frustration and disappointment. Some have just stopped calling. I am entering a new phase of loneliness. Being sick is hard enough. Being very sick and alone makes every day feel like it could be logged in dog years. I never thought it would be so hard to reconcile not only having no one to talk to but no one to hold me; to just put their arms around me without saying a word and provide a few moments of shelter from an unyielding storm of pain and fear. It's a profound emptiness.

So, what the fuck do I say when someone calls and asks how I am doing? The honest answer is: the cancer is taking what was left of my life.

JULY 2

I was grateful to feel fairly human when Jayne, her husband, George, and the kids arrived with their new and outrageously adorable puppy, Rudy. Sophie and Rudy faced off for exactly thirty seconds until my beast established alpha-status and they became instant best friends and a constant source of smiles; the cuteness factor was off the charts.

I purchased a small television and had it delivered in time for their arrival because Mac and Maggie, like most kids, *require* access to television at all times. It would also be nice to have in the guest room (and it was on sale with a huge rebate, totally justifying the expense). I still don't have any living room furniture other than a couch, so my guests help me move some of my wooden Adirondack patio furniture from the pool into the living room which looks ridiculous but I don't really care. Jayne and George are being incredibly helpful around the house and the kids are treating me completely normally, praise the lord.

I put on my sun-proof beekeeper outfit this morning—which Jayne referred to as my Kate Hepburn look—so I could venture outside and pluck a few weeds. George, who is your quintessential handy-man, noticed I was venturing into the garden and offered to do yard work. I thanked him and asked if he would mow around the pool before it got too hot, and he was happy to oblige. I'd just had the tractor serviced so I had no reason to believe he would encounter any difficulties unless it needed gas. I opened the barn and left him to his chores. About thirty minutes later, Jayne and I were in the kitchen with the kids finishing the breakfast dishes when we heard a loud crack followed by an equally loud expletive.

George must have lost control of the John Deere on the downhill slope by the pool because in addition to lawn, he mowed down two sections of the split-rail fence along with a few perennials. He was still perched on the tractor that was pointing nose-down and lodged neatly into the gaping hole in the fence.

I said, "Well, that's one way to do it."

We both burst out laughing. When I walked closer to the crime scene I noticed he had mowed the lawn around the pool in maniacally perfect rows but had failed to notice in which direction the grass shoot was pointing, so he had also, helpfully, filled the pool with about twelve pounds of fresh grass clippings.

"I couldn't stop it...it just took off down the hill, and I—"

"George, it's a tractor, not a horse. Why didn't you just steer?"

"I *know*. I tried! I'm a moron...I'll fix up everything good as new; promise."

"You might want to get your kids out here to start skimming the pool before the filter jams."

"Oh shit, I didn't even see that!"

When I went inside and told Jayne what happened, she smiled and said, "Aren't you glad we came?"

So, we were managing to have some laughs and grill all our favorite summer foods; I made myself eat more than usual with very little gastric repercussion and although fatigued, I felt very *safe*. George brought along some fun ingredients for patriotic holiday cocktails—leave it to him to find red and blue mixers—and although I told him I couldn't drink a lot because of my medication, he said, "What's the worst that could happen? You already have cancer."

"Good point."

"Giorgio's Famous Vodka and Cranberries comin' up!"

"Antioxidants, Jude," added Jayne as she sliced up lime wedges for our drinks.

We enjoyed sparkly summer cocktails and I was thrilled to be pleasantly buzzed, in my very own home, feeling less pain than usual, laughing out loud and in great company. On the second day the New Hampshire Wrecking Crew was here, the mercury shot up to 88° and the Glastonbury contingent came down for a visit and a swim; Mom and Dad, and Jodi, Glenn, and Geoff arrived with swimsuits and snacks. I slathered my hairless, photo-sensitive skin with sunscreen #500 that we affectionately call "invisible shirt" because it is the consistency of marshmallow Fluff and requires a putty knife to apply. I put on a one-piece bathing suit, very dark shades, and a broad-brimmed straw hat so I could lounge at the pool with *la familia*. It was risky, I knew, but it was worth it; the warmth of the sun on my skin and my achy bones and the joy of watching everyone around me behaving normally and not treating me like a Fabergé egg was well worth the price of a sunburn.

Dad loved to swim and he tried to teach each one of us kids either in the ocean or our pool, but none of us ever took to the water the way he did. When we would go to the beach, the rest of us either body-surfed, bobbed in the waves, or tanned while it seemed he could swim forever with perfectly even strokes and never tire. Although he was now very unsteady on his feet because of his vanishing motor skills, we managed to gently muscle him into the pool. He was in heaven; his whole face lit up when the cool water rose up to his waist. He was shivering but his thin blue lips were smiling. Glenn snapped a picture of Dad and me in the pool together, standing side by side and squinting into the sun. We are pasty-white, thin as rails and ghostly compared to everyone else. I still couldn't swim a stroke because of my limited range of motion on the left side, but it was nice just to wade around and cool off.

The only pang of sadness I had all day was when I realized that Dad would most likely not be back in the pool with me next summer; hell, I didn't know if I was going to be in the pool next summer. There are some days when the loss was truly unbearable and then there were days like this one, when you just have to embrace what is right in front of you for as long as you can before it floats away and disappears forever. As the Glastonbury group was leaving, I hugged my dad and we took an extra-long time holding on to each other's bony frames when, clear as a bell, he whispered in my ear, "You're all right, kid." I rested my head on his shoulder and said, "I hope so, Daddy."

JULY 3

For my sixth round of chemotherapy I was escorted by Priscilla's husband. Kyle is a portly fellow a few years younger than me with an encyclopedic knowledge of theater, film, literature, and twentieth-century music. He is not the person you want to play Trivial Pursuit with unless he is on your team. Kyle is also an actor, writer, and teacher, simultaneously playing Mr. Mom for their four kids. He has written theater reviews for the *New York Times* and other newspapers and has interviewed some of the most interesting musicians of our time. Priscilla, aside from being an expert dog-washer, has a master's degree and studied at the Divinity School at the Sorbonne in Paris during her undergrad and speaks fluent French. She is a dazzling actress, singer, and mom. These two make everyone around them shake their heads and wonder, "How on earth do they *do* it?"

Kyle picked me up and took me to Greenwich to visit Bones and company. Today's session was hard because I was not feeling particularly great to begin with, so I knew the next few days were going to be some new version of hell on earth. We were joking and keeping spirits up in the semi-private chemo chamber but Kyle, like Arjun, is the inquisitive and curious child who asks five million questions per minute about everything—the cancer, the divorce, the surgeries, the family, and the job. Kyle has the soul of an interviewer and the brain of a hungry student of the arts. He can keep several threads of conversations going at the same time like an ADD talk-show host. It happens to be one of the many reasons I love his company, but today I would have much preferred listening to talking. The sound of my own voice was giving me a headache. But I did not hold back; I gave him all the hideous and gory details because, well, he asked. He committed every detail to memory for further probing while he quite unintentionally wore me out.

The nurse came in and struggled again with the IV. My tired veins were getting thin and ornery from chemical abuse and it was becoming harder for all my personal drug pushers and bloodsuckers to find cooperative veins; after several false starts she finally began the drip. I instantly became exceptionally woozy and experienced nauseating room-spins. As my stinging eyes rolled to the back of my head and I prayed that I would not further embarrass myself by tossing breakfast, I mumbled to Kyle, "Thanks for being here. This totally sucks, doesn't it?"

"Oh, my god, Jude; I had no idea."

I thought, *Well, that's a first.*

JULY 8

I do not want to go to this wedding. I look fifty times worse than I did a month ago. As much as I love and adore Kevin O, the thought of sitting in a car for five hours is not just psychologically daunting; my legs are likely to atrophy unless I can get out and stretch them every half hour. It's July so whoever drives will surely want the air conditioning on which means I will be stiff, achy, and freezing, plus I get motion sickness if I can't sit in the front seat. I feel like sleeping seventy-five percent of the time and am running out of chemo jokes that my family hasn't heard.

I didn't have anything that fit me except for a sale-rack designer dress I snapped up at the beginning of the summer. I bought it because it didn't accentuate my uneven bust line but I'd have to throw a cardigan over it because it completely exposed the scars under my left arm which I neglected to notice before making my "final sale" purchase. I couldn't wear heels because I slammed my toe into the refrigerator by accident last weekend after one too many patriotic cocktails, and it was very sore and bruised, so I now also walked with a distinct limp which added to the overall chemo-vampire-zombie image. The only flat-soled option in my closet that was even marginally wedding-worthy was a pair of Ann Taylor sparkly flats that were really just pimped-up flip-flops, but since the wedding was on a boat, I didn't think upscale beach shoes would be too out of place. However, the added adventure of traversing Lake Champlain on a ferry boat for several hours after the blessed event was making me wonder if I should also pack a small barf bag in my fancy sequined purse for the reception. I could jam it in next to my rescue inhaler, the Band-Aids to cover my bruised and blackened toe, anti-vomit drugs, a hankie for wedding tears, medicated lip balm, Evian facial spritz for hot flashes, hard candies for dry mouth, a mirror to check on Ginger or Stella, and a card for the happy couple. *I've got an idea*, I thought. *Let's not wait for the cancer; just kill me now.*

Glenn and Jodi rented a mini-van to drive the Glastonbury crew and me up to Burlington, Vermont for the festivities. I went with them, of course, because he's my nephew. Besides, my brother and Daryl were thrilled beyond measure that one of the Kevins had found his princess bride; how in good conscience could I sit this one out?

When we arrived at the hotel in Burlington after a less than comfortable journey, I checked into my room, which I had offered to share with Victor's eldest son, also named Victor, who lives in Buffalo, New York. I had heard that he was having some financial difficulties and recently had an emergency appendectomy so I offered him a bed in my double room to save him some cash. Why not? It's not like I was going to be hooking up and needing my privacy and chances are neither one of us would be shaking our groove-thangs at the after-parties.

Between the Victors and the Kevins things can get a tad confusing around the holidays or any family gathering involving adult beverages. My nephew, whom we have called by his full name *Victor Philip* from birth to avoid confusion, is still Victor Philip; even though he is nearly thirty. One might think that a four-syllable first name would get whittled down to initials or something more succinct after so much time, but we're creatures of habit.

I wandered down the hall of the hotel, which smelled like Lysol spray and stale vacuum bags, to see if Jayne and the kids had arrived. I found their room and they were just unpacking. Maggie and Mac presented to me with all the excitement of Christmas a wrapped gift— a pink Harley-Davidson scarf—for which, they told me, they had searched and searched. I was so touched that these kids thought enough about me to do this...I put it on my head immediately. We lounged a while before getting ready for the Main Event while George uncorked a pre-wedding Merlot and we speculated about Sarah, Kevin's betrothed, whom we have only seen in photographs but who was about to sign up to be part of our brood. She is gorgeous. Well, actually they're both gorgeous. Kevin O resembles Justin Timberlake and Sarah is a willowy tall blonde who, at first glance, could be mistaken for Cameron Diaz's younger and prettier sister. It was promising to be a beautiful summer evening and a perfect night to witness our very own Hollywood couple wed under the stars.

I had yet to decide if Ginger or Stella was going to accompany me so I wandered back to my room to get myself organized. I heard a knock on the door. It was Victor Philip and I soon discovered he was in worse shape than we thought. Just when you're convinced your world is the epitome of bad luck and crap timing, you hear someone else's story that makes you thankful that you're walking around in your skin and not theirs. This poor guy—it was like a black storm cloud was parked over his head and had not stopped raining on him in weeks.

"Dude! Welcome to Burlington, c'mon in!"

"Hey, Aunt Jude," he muttered, while still staring at the carpet. This was followed by a one-armed, half-hearted hug as he moved slowly into the room and collapsed on the bed holding his side and forcing an intentionally fake smile.

"Soooo...everything okay?" Victor Philip finally looked at me and my bald head and my skinny self for a second or two before snapping out of it and answering, "Yeah, yeah. I'm fine. How are *you* feeling? Christ, I..."

"You didn't know I was bald."

"No, I did, I just, I dunno." And I could see the lines on his forehead deepen as he registered my illness in a more profound way than emails from his father.

"It's okay, Vic, I know it's weird. I'll put a wig on for the wedding tonight. You want me to put one on now?"

"No, no...are you feeling all right?"

"How much time do you have?"

He laughed and said, "I know how you feel; my life is a fucking mess, too."

"What's going on?"

"You and I need to get drunk tonight. Very. Very drunk."

I let it go at that and went back into the bathroom to finish getting ready. I kept the door open so we could continue talking, thinking he might find it easier without having to look me in the eye. It turns out that my nephew was having "financial" issues because he lost his job at the restaurant he managed—a job he coveted and the place where he had met his adorable live-in girlfriend—the one who had just left him and taken most of his belongings, including his cat, whom he adored almost as much as the girlfriend. Then he got an eviction notice because he was behind on the rent, just before the emergency appendectomy from which he was still recovering while looking for a place to crash with absolutely no money because of a mountain of unpaid student loans.

"Please tell me you're making this up. Jesus, Victor Philip, you're like a walking country and western song."

"It's all true. How sick is that? I have no place to live, no money, no job, no girlfriend, no cat, and I'm out of painkillers. In one month. Believe me I did *not* want to be here but I knew I had to...."

"Neither did I. Welcome to Heartbreak Hotel."

"Seriously! We are in bad shape. I can't even afford to get Kev a wedding gift."

"You're here. That's all he cares about."

"Yeah, but what do I say when people ask me how I'm doing? *Well, at least I'm not dead!* This is so embarrassing."

"You're right. We *are* getting drunk tonight. Let's go find us some designated drivers."

I finished getting dressed for the wedding and adjusted Stella, who looked better with my pale green dress and cardigan than Ginger did. I was putting the finishing touches on my makeup and loading up my purse when the toe I injured a few weeks back quite spontaneously started bleeding all over the floor and my fancy flip-flops. I shrieked, scaring the daylights out of my nephew, who came running into the bathroom, recoiling at the sight of bright red blood smeared all over the white tiled floor. As I bandaged up my crazy toe stigmata I realized it was probably just the blood clot under the nail releasing. Victor Philip finally broke down laughing, holding his recently sutured belly, asking if I planned this scene just to make him feel better.

"No, Victor Philip, I did not drop a hair-dryer on my toe to make your world seem less tragic. Nor did it happen through any sort of telepathy."

"You never know. Women have all sorts of weird powers."

"Indeed we do, but if I really wanted to make you feel better I'd show you all the crap I have to carry around with me tonight to give the appearance that I'm still human."

"Touché."

What a pair. Separately, we were tragic figures, but together we were proof positive that comedy is cruelty. We went to the wedding in our highly compromised states laughing at the absurdity and determined to have a good time come hell or, well, since it was on a boat we wanted to avoid the high water if possible. It was strangely comforting to each of us that we were not the only lost souls at the party that night and we might just be able to help each other. He needed someone to listen—not judge—and give some grown-up advice; I even offered my spare room at Green Acres if he wanted to start fresh and get out of Buffalo. And I needed to feel needed.

The two of us stayed up very late, talking about all the misery that has befallen this family and how we're all still hanging in there for each other. We talked about life, death, and the best way to start over with a broken heart and a broken home. I said a prayer that my smart and sensitive nephew would someday find his princess bride, too. And was very glad I made the trek to Vermont despite realizing too late that Stella was crooked in all the pictures.

JULY 13

Kim and I went to an outdoor theater production tonight so I could see some old friends on stage as well as in the audience—theater chums from years ago who had since moved to Florida and other parts of the country are back in town for an impromptu reunion. I felt well enough to get out of the house and stay awake for a few hours, possibly even hold an intelligent conversation or two. We packed a picnic and entered the park for Musicals at Richter before sundown. It's a wonderful outdoor venue and I felt a nagging nostalgia as I looked up at the stage; I performed several times here but none was quite so magical as the show when I met my ex-husband. It was "Camelot" and he was in the role of King Arthur and I his Queen Guinevere. The pang of romanticism for a time long past didn't bring the sadness I expected; it felt more like pride, which was novel, and I thought rather healthy, all things considered.

I spied a huge group of old friends and was delighted to see them all together on blankets and lawn chairs with their partners and kids. I knew immediately that this must be awkward for them because they were being terribly polite when they saw me. Too polite. Typically, this group is loud, funny, very hug-oriented, and talking over each other while vying for center stage. But in their defense, none of them had seen me in almost a year so despite their innate improvisational skills they were temporarily at a loss. Kim fixed me a weak wine spritzer for courage and I started making small talk.

I suddenly spied my old friend Helen, whom I honestly could've kicked myself for losing touch with. She is a few years older than me but I always loved her intellect and warmth; we worked together doing theater and were, at one time, very, very tight. I plopped down next to her and started talking and she was smiling but extremely guarded. Something was up, and it was more than just my bald head and skinny ass.

After the show we all went back to a local watering hole, and not only was I awake but incredibly pumped from being in the company of so many friends. Eventually, most people got the hang of looking me in the eye and not freaking out; plus, Priscilla was there and always makes me feel at ease and part of the conversation. I sat down at a table with a few of the girls and called Helen over to sit with us. She smiled but demurred and sat at the next table. I was put off by that and wondered what I had done or said to make her want to avoid me as she was now obviously doing. Was my illness that difficult for her? I speculated with Kim on the way home and we came up with nothing other than *maybe it's hard for her to see me like this*.

JULY 17

Today I had my seventh infusion of chemo. I am beginning to sense a vague but hopeful light at the end of the tunnel; I only have one more round of poison after this. Thank god. I don't feel all that well physically but my brain is in fine fighting form. I posted a note in my kitchen today when I got home from Dr. Bones's with a wonderful saying I picked up from one of my You-Have-Cancer- But-Get-Over-Yourself-Already books, "The only side effect of fighting for recovery is becoming happier." It resonated with me that my goal should not be getting something back that I lost, but finding happiness in whatever I have. On some days this kind of folksy wisdom forces my gag reflex, but today I find it motivating, simple, and easy to follow.

I have lost my eyelashes and my eyebrows entirely, and sadly, my nose hair. Women don't usually think about their nose hair with any great regularity — at least not in the way I presume men do. But when it falls out you can no longer count on it to catch and hold whatever might be passing through. This comes under the heading of "you don't know what you've got till it's gone." I now have to carry my hankies with me wherever I go because I never know when random head congestion will decide to hastily exit my nostrils without warning.

The eyebrow thing is tolerable because I've been filling them in for years, but eyelashes? I try to apply some shadow to create contours forgetting that you actually need those little hairs for something more important than batting or applying mascara. The mauve eye shadow flecks fall right into my eyes and dust the hollows underneath them so now they're irritated and Uncle-Fester-ish— which was not the look I was going for. But at least I'm laughing about it and not letting it mess with my chi.

I called Priscilla when I realized I missed her birthday yesterday and casually asked her if she noticed anything weird about Helen the other night. She let go a heavy sigh and said, "Oh, my god, you *really don't* know."

"Know what?"

"Helen and your ex; they've been seeing each other for months, Jude. It's actually quite serious, from what I hear."

"*What!?*"

"I wasn't sure if you knew, but—"

"Are you joking?"

"No, Jude. I guess nobody really wanted to tell you."

"How long—Wait, no. Don't answer that. It doesn't matter."

"Sorry to be the one to have to tell you."

"Mmmmm (fighting back large tennis ball in throat)."

"I feel awful, Jude. You just didn't need this…"

"He's a free agent. I divorced *him*, remember? I honestly don't care so much about that…"

"That's ridiculously big of you."

"No, no it's not big of me at all. I just don't know why…you mean to tell me that *everyone* knows? Sonnie? Monica? You? Kyle? The whole goddamned theater community?"

"I'm honestly not sure."

"Jesus Christ, don't I feel like an idiot. I am the biggest fool in the world, aren't I? Everyone must have been…well, it doesn't matter. *None of this* fucking matters."

"Are you okay?"

"I don't really have words for how *not* okay I am."

"I am sorry."

"Not your fault. Thanks for finally letting me know."

I hung up the phone and stared out the window, wondering if I truly was shrinking; pound by pound, hair by hair, and would eventually become an undetectable and unwanted entity; a tick, a gnat, a flea, or one of those summertime nuisances that is so miniscule it gets in through the screens of your house. How could so many people believe that keeping me in the dark on this would be a good idea? In what world does that make sense?

In the scheme of things, I did understand the relationship; ever since college my ex and Helen had a soft spot for each other. It was *not* big of me; I got it. Everyone is entitled to find love again. But the lies of omission were like supernovas exploding in my head. I calmed down and called Kim, who was positively apoplectic. She couldn't believe that every individual we saw and chatted with, to a person, cared more about maintaining their risk-free "straddler status" than becoming involved in anything complex, messy, or truthful. I briefly reflected on the recent emails or calls, or the occasional visit from friends who were likely "in the know" and nearly collapsed under the weight of what felt like a betrayal.

Why is it every time I start to unearth the path of a possible future, a new life emerging, hope—something comes along and kicks me in the solar plexus to remind me just how insignificant, temporary, and disposable I am? I think I may have just tied with Victor Philip; possibly even taken the lead.

JULY 24

Jodi and I drove into New York to McDreamy's office to schedule my exchange surgery—the removal of the expander and insertion of the final implant. We spent the entire ride trying to change topics but repeatedly bounced back to the Helen and ex-husband storyline. Jodi, in her tactful way, helped me to understand that the people caught in the middle may have felt that they were doing the exact right thing by not adding to my burden and that I shouldn't fault them for it. Not sure why I didn't see it that way from the beginning, but my glass has been half empty for so long that the contents had curdled; and even after my head recognized the simple logic in her argument, my heart still felt surprisingly bruised and sophomoric.

THE LONG SLOW CLIMB OUT OF THE TREATMENT PIT

The good news was that I could schedule the surgery about a month after my last chemo round which was the next Monday so we were getting close! We waited patiently for McDreamy to come in to the exam room after my final injection of saline at Kelly's Filling Station. She injected enough solution into the expander to stretch my skin beyond where it needs to be for surgery because I am told it will more naturally contract after the implant settles in. My fake breast was so huge now it felt like it could burst through the skin and begin a life of its own, like the creature in *Alien*. McDreamy had finally settled into a nice rhythm with me; he knew what I expected: the latest research, complete honesty, his full undivided attention, and witty banter. This is not too much to ask, is it?

"Hi there! This is your sister, right? I think we met in the hospital," he said, extending his perfect hand to her.

"Yes, this is Jodi. She'll be your bodyguard today."

"Good to know." To Jodi, "She keeps me on my toes, your sister."

"There's a shocker."

"So, we're here to talk about you giving me the breasts of an eighteen-year-old, right?"

"Only god can do that and as good as I am, I'm not in that league. Yet. But we'll do something very nice for you, I promise." He looked at me with that practiced smile that could cause snow-blindness, so I knew another shoe would be dropping soon.

"How nice?"

"Well, I've been doing some calculations, Jude, and it seems we'll have to go just a tad bigger or smaller than your real breast — so I'll draw it for you and you can tell me which you're more comfortable with..."

"Why can't you match them?"

"Because of the whole I'm-not-god thing..."

"But how is that *nice*, if I'm still uneven after surgery? That sounds, well, unacceptable to me. Or the opposite of nice."

Under her breath, Jodi mumbled, "Oh, boy."

"Jude, I'll show you what I have and you can decide. But we're going to have to compromise somewhere. These implants come in very specific sizes. Here I'll show you..." He paused for a moment and then muttered, "*unless...*"

"Unless what?!"

He went into his email and pulled up a message. "Well, I've just been invited to participate in a brand new clinical trial for implants that are shaped more like a natural breast and have a bigger choice of sizes, but it's not been approved by the FDA yet, so we're still..."

"Show me."

He showed me the picture of an implant that wasn't shaped like a jelly donut, but like an actual, female breast with contours and sagging and all the bells and whistles with the exception of a nipple. Eureka!

"Oh, fantastic, look at this," he said, scanning the company's website, "They have one that is incredibly close to the size of your real breast; like almost exact! But I'd have to order it, Jude, and according to this it might not come until September."

"Do it."

"You sure you want to wait that long? I know how anxious you are..."

"And patient," deadpanned my sister.

"I have waited this long, I can tough it out for another two months if it means getting a breast that looks like a breast. I don't trust the FDA anyway. What do they know about breasts?"

"Done. I'll put it on order today and let you know when it comes in. You're right. This is the way to go."

"Pleasure doing business with you."

He shook my hand and winked at me and crooned in his smoothest caring-doctor voice, "We're almost there, sweetheart," and vanished, leaving Jodi and me in the exam room with silly surprised grins on our faces.

"Did I just visibly melt?" I asked her.

"No, but you might want to wipe the drool from the corner of your mouth."

We were very excited on the drive home, so we decided to treat ourselves to a nice lunch at the Westchester Mall, thank you Cancer Resource Services, and do a little furniture shopping at Crate and Barrel. I was finally in a financial position to purchase a couch and chairs for the living room, which was almost as exciting as getting this godforsaken expander out of my chest. We went to PF Chang's and had something yummy with salmon and bok choy. Afterwards we browsed around the furniture store, feeling very pumped to be back in "rebuild" mode rather than "tear-down." I was pricing an armchair when a dizzying wave of nausea came over me so abruptly that I had to dash to find a bathroom and beg to be let into the one marked "Employees Only"—which probably only works if you're old, pregnant, or bald.

"Fighting for recovery" means learning to balance victories, such as having access to cutting edge implants, with downers, such as projectile vomiting your lunch in nasty mall bathrooms. But the victories are starting to occur closer and closer together, like labor contractions. Or maybe I'm just noticing them more now.

JULY 31

Today is my final chemo blast. Hallelujah. Monica has offered to accompany me for this final dose of Taxol and, stomach permitting, to a celebratory lunch in downtown Greenwich afterwards. As we walk into the chemo chamber today, there is a woman who looks to be about my age in the next chair who is completely hairless like me, and improbably quite stunning. Her skin is perfect—not a blotch in sight and lightly tan as if someone dusted her with cinnamon—and she practically glows from her perfectly bald head down to her athletically square but feminine shoulders like a bride on her wedding day. I cannot stop staring so I introduce myself and Monica and we start a casual conversation while getting our IVs squared away. She has a different treatment regimen than I do and, sadly, is staged with a more advanced diagnosis than mine, but nevertheless appears to have what can only be described as an inner light that radiates outward during our chat. I conclude that she is content. She is not fighting herself; she is fighting only the cancer. I am wildly curious about how to arrive at this enlightened place. I want to get there! I want the magic formula for this state of mind; I want to be proud of having gotten this far in the battle, to appear comfortable in my smooth, hairless skin and disfigured body the way she appears to be. I am infatuated by her striking deportment, the strength she displays while attached to an IV that has less of a probability of saving her life than mine does. Where does this come from?

I start asking questions that might lead me to an answer, but they do not. After a few minutes, she looks at me as if she senses my mental unrest and says, "There's a little magic to be had in every day, Jude," and then she tilts her head back and leaves us for a nap. I am floored. I do not know what just happened but something is different. Monica is asking me about where we might want to eat and making small talk about theater friends and had no idea there was a seismic shift beginning in my head. I will be better—whether I live or die. I will not die whining. I have no idea whether this is the chemo playing with my brain or a truly substantive event but it feels good so I'm going with it.

After my chamber-mate's session is over she is unhooked from the needles and accepts one of the obligatory saltines from the nurse. When she stands, I notice how tall she is, regal. We are saying our good-byes and I ask her how she has managed to keep her skin so lovely and even, and how ever does she manage getting out in the sun without frying? She leaned over to me and whispered, "Bare Minerals with sunscreen. They sell it at Sephora. You'll look healthier in three minutes. Dust your head too and you'll look fantastic. More beautiful than you already are." And she was gone.

Oh, my god. At least on the outside it's make-up! I can do that! I tell Monica we're going to the bistro across from Sephora for lunch and she is delighted that we were going shopping too on this beautiful summer day and begins to rattle off her favorite products there.

My last session is finished. I have thus far survived dose-dense chemotherapy. I do not know what comes next but I feel strangely ready to take it on.

A perfect stranger called me beautiful, of all things. Beautiful.

AUGUST 4

The last Taxol blast was settling in to my joints and making itself known every time I tried to do anything other than lie flat on my bed without moving. I was trying to get myself packed up and out of the house so I can make it up to the first cheering station for the 3-

Day walk by two p.m. Everything I tried to do was reduced to slow-motion. This was my first big trip alone in almost a year. I reserved a room at the Omni Parker House (of course) and made arrangements for a dog-sitter for Sophie. Kim was coming up on Sunday for closing ceremonies, but I'd be on my own for the rest of the weekend which was thrilling and mildly terrifying.

My sisters have been literally gearing up for their big 3-Day walk with 3-Day hats, T-shirts, fanny-packs, water bottles—all the pink-ribboned Komen swag you can possibly imagine. Their mighty team of four raised over $14,000.00, and the donations were miraculously still pouring in. The spirit of The Sole Sisters has been positively intoxicating to our family, who long ago reached the tipping point of sadness and loss. Their team has also developed a band of loyal followers who promise to be at the finish line on Day Three to cheer them on through mile 60! I promised Jayne and Jodi that I would drive to Boston this Friday, spend the weekend, and visit them at the cheering stations along the long and tortuous route. I really could not be prouder.

I arrived in Framingham, Massachusetts, at about 11 AM, easily locating the cheering station. As I parked the car, I was considering whether to go "commando" or put a scarf on my head. I finally decided that if there's anywhere on the planet other than a hospital that this look should be acceptable it's a cancer walk. So I put on my flops and an extra dusting of Bare Minerals with sunscreen on my noggin, and I walked up to the town library to wait for The Sole Sisters, who would be completing mile 12 by the time they arrived. There was a stone wall where other supporters are gathered with signs and balloons and noisemakers. As I got closer I noticed that everyone was staring at me.

Oh no, I think, this is not what I want. I thought this would be okay and I would sort of blend in, but I don't. I become terribly self-conscious when suddenly I hear a few people start clapping and nodding at me. They are clapping for me. I am completely overwhelmed and tearing up behind my sunglasses. They don't even know me. I haven't done anything to deserve this; I'm not a soldier. I don't fight fires. I just did whatever I needed to do to try to save my own life and they would have done the exact same thing. I don't understand this "hero" title. Oh, my god. I am not prepared for this scene.

As the walkers began streaming by the library there were random bursts of cheering and hugs and all sorts of encouraging displays of support, very heartfelt and genuine. I was also drowning in an ocean of pink *everything*. Every now and then one of the walkers would leave the path and walk directly toward me for a high-five. One particularly strong-looking woman put both of her hands on my shoulders to tell me that she was a survivor and that I will be one, too. Completely unprepared for these open displays of solidarity from strangers and wondering where my sisters were, I retreated back farther into the crowd. I was receiving far too much attention. After about forty minutes I saw my team: the four Sole Sisters rounding the corner in all their proud pinkness—fanny packs, hats, T-shirts; even their matching black shorts had little pink ribbons on them. I jumped off the stone wall and raced right into the stream of walkers to grab my sisters and hug them as hard as I could. They were really doing this. Walking sixty miles. I was done with my chemo but weak and pale and as grateful as any human being has ever been. Mine are the coolest sisters anyone could ever have.

Jayne had a knee brace on and Jodi had a sunburned nose. Becky and Lisa, the other two Sole Sisters, whom I was meeting for the first time, were all smiles as they told me about back pain, blisters, and the rain shower they endured this morning. They had such a long way to go but by the looks on their faces they were incredibly determined to finish all sixty miles of their journey. We snapped a few pictures and I promised I would find them tomorrow somewhere along the route.

After the girls re-joined the walkers, I drove in to Boston to check into the Omni. It was still early and I wanted a walk myself to stretch out my achy bones, so I cruised the neighborhood and did some window-shopping. I was oddly elated to be alone. I did not have a schedule to meet or anyone else's itinerary to map to; I could do whatever the hell I wanted. *The sun is out,* I thought, *and I'm single in Beantown.*

As I walked back to the hotel at about four thirty I heard what sounds like after-work happy-noise coming from below street level. I noticed a drinking establishment that looked like it was in someone's basement. A few narrow steps down from the sidewalk there was an ancient-looking door painted barn red with a very small sign reading, "The Littlest Bar." Inside, through the tiny window at the top of the door, I saw the heads of happy-looking people. I heard swells of eighties music when the door flipped open and I suddenly felt as if this could be one of those *carpe diem* moments that, if I wimped out, I might regret for the rest of my life. *Can I do this? Walk into this bar, which appears to be a total townie hang-out, and have myself a beer? Alone? With no eyelashes?* I stood on the sidewalk having this conversation with myself while pretending to look for something in my purse. I am wearing a pink T-shirt and skirt, flops, and a bandanna on my head. I re-applied lip gloss, walked carefully down the steps hanging on to the wrought iron handrail for balance, and opened the door only to discover, way too late, that I was the only woman in the place. Dear god, are they all gay?

The Littlest Bar did not suffer from false advertising. It was the size of a very large walk-in closet made to look even tinier by the dark paneling on the walls and the bar itself that took up half the room. The sign said its capacity was fifty people but I suspect those people would have to be mashed up against each other or anorexic. The bar had a few wooden stools that looked like they'd been in that exact spot since the 1800s. With all eyes on me, I took a mini-yoga breath and assertively grabbed a barstool, like I did this every day, and ordered a Stella Artois. The acting experience comes in handy now and then.

"Nah, try something else. We gawt bettah beers than that. C'mon, try anotha. Look at all these local beauties I gawt on tap here...how 'bout some Sam or Ipswich..."

"Okay. How about you pour whatever you think I'll like." I had no idea if I would even be able to taste it because I couldn't remember the last time I drank a beer, but under the circumstances, I felt a Cosmo might not be the best choice.

"Now ya' talkin' pretty."

Hold on! Did that very adorable bartender with guns the size of Popeye and a gigantic tattoo of a snake rattling up his tire-sized neck just call me pretty?

One of his buddies came up to my barstool and asked me where I was from and I proudly said, "Connecticut. I'm doing that New England thing where we travel one state north for vacation."

Everyone thought this was funny and I caused a general stir with several patrons for the entire thirty minutes it took me to finish nursing the delicious blond ale Popeye poured for me *on the house*. I suspected that girls are a novelty here because I didn't think it was that funny. Several interesting guys wandered over to tell me where they vacation and one or two tried the arm-on-the-back-of-my-barstool trick—which did not in any way concern me. When I say *interesting*, I mean one was a drunken lawyer, one was a past-glory days ballplayer drinking a Diet Coke with a pot belly he kept trying to suck in, one was a Harley dude with fewer teeth than a hockey player and an English accent, and one was, allegedly, the owner of the place. I didn't care; I was flattered beyond measure. This was not a gay bar; it was an *everything* bar. All nutty drinkers welcome like the bar scene in Star Wars. Not one guy asked me about my bald head. Not ONE. It was fantastic.

As I was leaving, Popeye called to me, "Hey, Connecticut! Come back tomorrow night, I'll buy ya a propah drink; it's a pissah here on Saturday nights."

I'll just bet it is. I love this town. And The Littlest Bar.

AUGUST 5

I was ravenous because I'd been too tired to go out for dinner and ended up ordering room service which was completely unappetizing and inedible by the time it arrived. My taste buds have been re-awakening and some foods are returning to pre-chemo deliciousness, but mostly in the carb category. Veggies and fruits barely register on the taste-o-meter unless they are buried in salt, sugar, or vinegar. Wine still tastes like shit.

The mercury is heading up into the humid nineties. I strap on my Tevas, preparing for a good long walk. My legs are stiff but they are responding well to walking at a leisurely pace. My left arm is sore and its range of motion seriously tight, which I choose to blame on the hotel bed. I don't bring a map or my phone or any distractions. I take with me only a few dollars for breakfast, the ubiquitous hankie, and a desire to wander. I am experiencing that same wonderful sensation I felt yesterday afternoon which can only be described as freedom. I am done with chemo. I don't have anyone telling me how to arrange my day. I can just keep walking and eat at whatever restaurant I please. I am not tethered to anything other than my own physical limitations. Maybe these are delayed post-divorce endorphins kicking in, but it is so exhilarating that I find myself chatting up strangers and smiling like the first day I got my braces off, for no reason whatsoever. Creaky legs and gimpy arm be damned; this will be a good day.

I discovered an exquisite neighborhood hole-in-the-wall diner complete with original 1950s décor, where all the sweaty cooks behind the counter yell at you while you're ordering and the cashier is over a hundred years old. There was one waitress with leathery skin and dangly earrings who dotes only on her regulars and completely ignores out-of-towners wearing Tevas. The place smelled heavenly; one of those eateries where you walk in the door and a cloud of coffee and butter-bombs envelop your head and make you crave foods that tally up to your entire calorie count for the week. I ordered enough eggs and sides for a minor-league baseball team in training and sat at a tiny table with the *Boston Globe* in one hand and a fork in the other for over an hour. The air-conditioning was on life-support so there were fans strategically placed around the room rattling newspapers and blowing napkins to the floor at predictable intervals. Although she never made eye contact with me, the waitress was kind enough to keep filling my coffee cup as she performed her impressive breakfast ballet. I was glad she didn't linger because her perfume could've peeled the wallpaper.

Could this be one of those moments, I thought, *a simple pleasure full of glorious imperfections that I'm allowing myself to fully appreciate for once?*

I paid the centenarian and had just enough left over to tip my coffee-pouring friend.

When I arrived at the cheering station in Needham, it was swarming with screaming pink 3-Day groupies. It was a residential area and there was no place to sit unless you brought a chair or a blanket, which I had not. As I walked through the crowd I began to attract a bit of notice again but I was prepared for it this time. I felt awkward that I didn't have a sign or spray bottles of water to cool them down. I didn't have family with me, or noisemakers or candy or balloons. I wasn't even sporting any 3-Day swag.

As the pink army began streaming by mile marker 35, I cheered, "Go, walkers! Thank you for walking!"

One of the walkers left the path, came up to me and looked me right in the eyes. She said, "I am walking for you. You are the hero here—not me. Thank *you* for coming out today."

I was dumbfounded. As I watched her rejoin her team I started sobbing. I cannot pinpoint the emotional driver that was behind all these tears—all I know is they were completely necessary and I was not embarrassed.

A young woman with very short-cropped black hair and saucer-like blue eyes walked up to me. "Hey, there," she said, "are you okay?"

"Yeah, I don't know why I just became so weepy..."

"Um, maybe because you're just discovering that this is all for you? And me? Here, I have an extra beach chair and a box of tissues. Have a seat and we'll get through this day together. What do you say?"

So we sat and talked and I had my first face-to-face, down-and-dirty, private conversation with someone who could completely identify with the complex and surreal world of breast cancer.

My new friend's name is Hillary and she did not have a mastectomy but she went through a lumpectomy, radiation, and chemo and is just climbing back into life; she is thirty-nine years old.

To speak so openly to someone who is six months ahead of me on the recovery curve is fascinating and reassuring. And it's valuable to connect with another woman who is not supposed to be in menopause according to her body clock but is experiencing the side-effects and the anguish of being a formerly healthy young woman with an intact libido, and feeling woefully old before her time. As we get to the topic of "chemo-brain" I can see that this is still plaguing her as well and she confesses her worry that it will never go away. We try to joke about the topic but it's looming large with both of us that we might never return to normal brain function.

"So, is your onco telling you to try crossword puzzles?" I ask.

"Yes, which is the same advice they give dementia patients, right? I thought all I had to worry about was cancer, but noooo... On the bright side I can keep reading the same books over and over."

When she says the word dementia I shut down and go back to watching the walkers. The mental picture of my father trapped in his wordless world makes me feel like an ungrateful, self-absorbed whiner. Thankfully, she changes the topic to things currently within our control. Her hair is growing back and it's "wicked curly" but she's found a way to style it with barrettes. Her boyfriend and she just split up so she's looking for an apartment. She just rescued a puppy named Sumo who is the new light of her life. As I listen to her describe how she's sewing her shredded life back together, I begin sharing pieces, or rather, shards of mine. Hillary is staring at me with a look that is simultaneously sympathetic and shocked.

"Oh, my god, Jude. That's just not right."

"No, I guess it's not, is it. But it's the truth."

I told Hillary all about my amazing sisters and she promised she would wait with me so she could meet them. She told me how lucky I am to have them and although I knew that, I was proud to hear it come from her. The walkers had dwindled to just a few stragglers and there was no sign of The Sole Sisters anywhere. I felt terrible that I might have missed them but I couldn't imagine how because I'd been waiting for over two hours. The sisters had their mobile phones turned off to save the batteries. There was nowhere to recharge at the 3-Day camp and they needed to last through to Sunday. I had no way to reach them.

The crowd of supporters left little evidence that they were ever there, like the carnival that mysteriously shows up at the mall every summer and disappears in the night. I reluctantly told Hillary I was heading back to the hotel, fearing that I not only missed them but that something might have happened to one of them. As she walked with me back to the parking lot I glanced one last time at the walker's route and saw three pink figures moving, ever so slowly, in the distance. "Omigod, I bet you that's them!" I ran, as fast as one can run in flip-flops on fatigued legs, back through the parking lot and up the hill to the sidewalk just in time to see what looked like three wounded soldiers holding each other up after a rough day on the front lines.

Komen ensures that all participants are supported by, among other things, sweep vans that follow the route and help ailing participants by driving them in air-conditioned comfort to their next rest area or back to camp; these are affectionately known as the Boob Buses. Adorned with colorful brassieres and balloons, they are a wonderful safety net for walkers.

"Is that you, Sole Sisters?!!" I shout to them. They start laughing and waving their arms, punching their fists in the air like Rocky Balboa. I introduce Hillary as we all hug and take photographs.

Lisa had opted to board the Boob Bus a few miles back citing Entire Body Distress and is, by this time, probably safely ensconced at camp, showered and sleeping. Becky is smiling but nursing some lower back pain with handfuls of Advil. Jodi is sunburned and has three silver-dollar-size blisters erupting in her sneakers and a mystery rash crawling up her legs. Jayne is suffering from being A Complete Mess. She has a brace around one knee that is now swollen, an ace bandage around the other, and judging by her halting gait is in pain.

Excitedly, we speak over each other until the top story inevitably emerges: at approximately mile marker 25, after drinking gallons of water and Gatorade to ward off dehydration and hypothermia, Jayne was in desperate need of a port-o-potty. The next rest stop was miles away.

"Omigod, I was trying to walk while squeezing my legs together."

"Very ladylike, I'm sure."

"We didn't think she was going to make it! We started looking for woods or any place she could hunker down and go..."

"Jude, I honestly thought I was going to wet my pants."

"I must bring this out in you."

"And THEN a miracle," said Jodi. "We are walking through this neighborhood and a woman came out of her house just as we passed with a sign that said, "3-Day Walkers—Need a Bathroom?"

"Jayne was literally holding her crotch as she limped up to this woman's house asking, 'Is this a mirage?' It was hilarious."

"You make us all so proud, Jayne."

"I swear I must have thanked that Bathroom Lady fifty times. It was a miracle. I mean, what are the odds?"

I am worried about Jayne's knees but according to Jodi, she refuses to get on the Boob Bus. "One of her knees is in bad shape," Jodi said, moving the words sideways through the air like a ventriloquist, "but she will not quit. Trust me—she is going to finish all sixty miles." I need to learn how to speak without moving my lips someday.

"Is that safe?"

Jodi turns to me with an expression that indicates she has done all she can and needs older sister back-up. "You ask her."

"Jayne, are you going to make it? Can you maybe take the bus for a few miles to rest that knee?"

"Nope. Walking."

"But do you think that's a good idea, I mean...."

"Listen, I've walked over thirty-five miles which is more than halfway, Jude. I am doing this. If you can get through chemo, I can walk another twenty-five miles. Piece of cake."

And that was the end of that discussion. Jayne does not *assert* very often but when she does, she offers up an expression and tone of voice that lets you know the debate is over.

The depleted Sole Sisters were the very last walkers to pass through the Needham cheering station but I received a call when they made it back to camp, blisters, sunburn, injuries, and all. They sounded exhausted but giddy for having made it through Day Two. Then they went to sleep on the ground in sleeping bags, in little pink pup tents, so they could wake up and hopefully cross the finish line tomorrow. I am in awe of their powers of endurance.

Back at the hotel, I decided to take myself out for a nice — no, make that a fancy — Saturday night dinner to celebrate the end of treatment. I had not had to resort to consuming meat in a while, but I could feel an iron deficiency headache coming on so I decided on Ruth's Chris Steak House across the street from the Omni. It has an elegant dining room and a lively bar. I put on a pair of sandal heels with my little black dress and more eye make-up than usual. I walked into the restaurant without a reservation or anything covering my head and requested a table for one. The hostess looked taken aback but composed herself quickly and said, "Right this way, Madam."

I walked through the restaurant garnering a few stares and whispers but I told myself it's because they thought I was a huge celebrity. I took my seat as if it were my special reserved table. My waiter was very Italian and positively adorable, *and* he was flirting with me. I ate a petit filet mignon with a side of spinach. I was the only person in the dining room sans dinner companion, so I went to The Littlest Bar for a nightcap. Those guys seemed like much more fun than this white-tablecloth, martini crowd anyway.

The Littlest Bar was packed but Popeye, who was off-duty tonight, immediately noticed me and squeezed through the crowd forcibly moving people out of his way to reach me. "Hey, I knew you'd be back! You look gaw-juss, Connecticut. Gimme a sec, I'll find you a place to sit."

Every barstool was taken, but he reached for my hand and led me to a prime spot, the corner seat at the bar next to the window, and told the unfortunate occupant, "Hey asshole, get up and give the lady a seat." Which he did.

Popeye was my self-appointed Guardian Angel. As he was ordering my cocktail I noticed his yellow rubber LIVESTRONG bracelet, from Lance Armstrong's Cancer Foundation. He never mentioned it to me but it explained his brotherly attention. Somehow this disease had touched his life and in his own way he was doing whatever he could to help a survivor who stumbled onto his turf. There was no other motive. I was humbled and grateful. Before rejoining his buddies—who were likely wondering who the hell I was—he instructed the bartender to take care of me, and told me to find him if I needed anything.

I was happy to see I was not the only woman in the room this time but I was conspicuously, almost hilariously overdressed. About fifteen minutes into my vodka and cranberry and some banter with the bartender, a nice-looking man made his way over to me and initiated a casual conversation.

Okay Jude, I told myself, *here we go.*

He was a large burly man from Minnesota, clearly younger than me, in a faded T-shirt with a football logo who said he was here on business. He never formally introduced himself, but helpfully did all the talking, presenting like a sales guy into sports, domestic beer, and HDTV.

Back when my taste buds went on sabbatical, my olfactory senses became heightened, so when Minnesota leaned in closer, I got a noseful of a recognizable and expensive men's cologne. Delicious. But, my radar suggested, the scent did not match the man. My curiosity inched up a notch.

He swallowed a huge swig of his beer, stared curiously at my bald head, and finally ventured, "So, are you into men, or women, or both?"

"Men. Definitely men."

He smiled and said, "Yeah, me too."

I laughed, a little relieved that I didn't have to try to remember how to do the mating dance tonight and said, "So what do you think of the bartender?"

"Hands off, I saw him first."

AUGUST 6

Kim arrived at the hotel around noon and we had just enough time to grab a quick lunch and drive to the University of Massachusetts campus, site of the Closing Ceremonies where The

Sole Sisters would, fingers crossed, be conquering the sixty-mile mark. I am nervous for them. I'm seriously worried about Jayne's knee and all the other scenarios that could possibly befall "women of a certain" age walking their third marathon in as many days. I tell Kim all about my adventures though, with all the excitement of a young woman telling her mom about her first few weeks at college. I want her to be proud of me. She laughs when I tell her about the Littlest Bar and immediately wants to plan another trip so she can meet Popeye. When I share the events of the cheering stations we both get a little weepy and wonder how we'll ever make it through the day. We will be meeting with Glenn and George and their kids; Mom is taking care of Dad, of course, so we promised pictures. Victor and Daryl have other plans but sent all good wishes and generous donations beforehand, as did the Kevins, Victor Philip, and Kenny.

While waiting in traffic to get into the parking lot, we see walkers slowly streaming in to the campus. Some have abandoned their footwear altogether or are wearing flip-flops; others are walking with their arms around each other in pairs and teams; and some are walking slowly or, poignantly, alone. Kim and I are shocked by the number of walkers and the magnitude of willpower they possess as a group to keep putting one foot in front of the other on the third day of this marathon. I keep hoping I'll see the Sisters in their official team shirts that they saved for Day Three but so far, no sightings.

After we park, we begin scanning the crowd for familiar faces. We are estimating the crowd to be about four-thousand or more, and each and every one, including the local police, is wearing something pink. It's astounding. A large sign emblazoned with SOLE SISTERS is held up by Maggie and Mac and Geoff. Glenn has brought cocktails in gigantic thermoses and George is manning a cooler with wine, beer, snacks, and soft drinks. Becky and Lisa's families are present and accounted for as well and they have strategically selected a site near the finish line. The kids are wearing pink bandannas and scarves and excitedly tell me about the gifts they've prepared for their moms, and the calls they each received last night from camp. They are proud; you can see it.

Their moms are achieving the impossible today. George is on his mobile phone getting updates on the Sisters' ETA.

I stop to think if there has ever been an event, other than weddings or birthday parties, which we have attended or been wholly involved in as a family and can't think of one. This is a remarkable thing, when your family evolves from assorted relations into an authentic, T-shirt-wearing, banner-waving team. I look at Kim after taking it all in and, reading my mind, she says, "I know, Jude. Amazing."

Throngs of happy of supporters line the final route, clapping, shouting encouragement and thanks to every participant. Surprisingly we don't see many men walking but there are a few brave souls. There is also an all-male team of about twenty who call themselves "Men with Heart" and they walk with backpacks jammed with free items that might be needed along the way; band-aids, sunscreen, even tampons. They carry packs that weigh over twenty pounds and wear bright yellow shirts so they are easy to find in the sea of pinkness. The Men with Heart returned together as a team singing, "Doo-wa Diddy" at the top of their lungs and completely off-key. How could you not love them? After about an hour and a half, most of the walkers are back and have gone into the school to wait for their victory walk. We can hear the roar of the walkers from inside the building every time another team or individual enters the long-imagined air-conditioned holding area. At least two thousand walkers and staff members have crossed the finish line so far in conditions ranging from elated warriors to grateful wounded to les miserables.

A woman walks down the path towards us on her way to the finish line who is bald and in truly phenomenal shape. I gasp, suddenly overcome with guilt that maybe I should have been doing this with them! Have I been slacking off by not pushing myself harder? The feeling passes when I realize that I'm tired just from standing for over an hour. I walk up to her and throw my arms around her, this total stranger. We say nothing to each other; we don't have to.

Now I'm worried. The steady stream of walkers is down to a precious few and the closing ceremonies are set to begin in half an hour. All the staff is back. I keep hoping I'll see the Sisters in their

official team shirts that they saved for Day Three, but so far, no
sightings.

Where are the girls? Did Jayne's knee give out? Becky's back?
Jodi's dogs?

George gets a call that they're close so we ready our banners and
wait. Sixty miles. I think back to the New York hotel room the day
before Valentine's Day when Jayne declared that this was her mission
and she recruited Jodi as her co-captain; it was so foreign to me to
think of them doing anything athletic, much less something as strenuous
as this.

"There they are!" yelled Maggie. "Hey, MOM!!!"

We looked in the distance and saw pink logo-shirts attached to four bodies moving toward us as if through a river of molasses, but closer to their sweet victory with every step. The crowds along the sidelines were cheering with extra gusto for the final few walkers. The Sisters were smiling and waving to fans—strangers and comrades in this fight who were all here today because breast cancer had invaded their lives. It was a sporting event for thousands of people to battle one frightening and formidable opponent.

I ran up to them, not waiting for them to pass our viewing area and crushed my sister Jayne in a bear hug saying, "I can't believe you did this! I love you!!"

She was hurting but smiling and completely exhausted. "Oh my god, Jude. We made it!"

I grabbed Jodi, "You're amazing! How are you feeling?" I walked with them to our family encampment in the crowd. The kids were particularly astonished that their mothers did what they set out to do. There were hugs and tears and high-fives and pictures, but we had to let them get on their way so they could make it to the holding area in time for the closing ceremony parade.

Kim and I stood on a grassy hill waiting for the march of the battered sneakers to begin; I thought it somewhat cruel to ask them to keep walking after finishing the grueling route but by the time the throngs came out of the school and marched in formation before the crowd in matching 3-Day shirts they looked refreshed and triumphant; like one solid mass of undying love and support. Survivors who walked wore pink shirts and all other walkers wore white. As the parade passed by, walkers who saw me pointed and smiled, or blew kisses, or just respectfully nodded as if to say they walked for me and it was worth it. I collapsed into a non-stop flood of tears. At no time in my life have I ever allowed myself to publicly experience such unbridled gratitude. When The Sole Sisters passed by they held hands and raised them above their heads in joyful triumph. Kim put her arm around me and we screamed out to them at the top of our lungs. My pride was beyond measure and I wished more than anything that my mother and father, and the rest of my family, could have been there to understand exactly what Jayne and Jodi had achieved with their fundraising, and spirit, and this sixty-mile odyssey – a tangible measure of hope.

The closing ceremony was a blur but I remember the final moments. The walkers who are survivors were grouped together in the center near the stage; the master of ceremonies then instructed all the other walkers to remove one sneaker and hold it above their heads in recognition and in honor of their fight. There was a sea of shoes held aloft during a moment of silence, and that arresting tableau moved me toward understanding the healing power of ritual and community. After the ceremonies wound down, we all stood in the hot sun saying our good-byes and taking pictures of our very own pink warriors.

The thought crossed my mind that I didn't want this day to end; that I needed to hang on to the love and energy that knit us all together for this event and take it home with me. But they were exhausted; gingerly pulling off sneakers and lancing blisters, and sharing a last round of Advil in a crowded campus parking lot, baking on hot asphalt. It was 6pm on a Sunday night and The Sole Sisters were packing up their sleeping bags, hugging their kids and getting ready to go their separate ways back to Connecticut and New Hampshire for hot showers, cold wine, and the simple luxury of their own beds. I couldn't possibly ask them to do more, to spend just one more hour with me so we could continue celebrating and I could hear every story, every detail. So my solution as we posed for a last picture together was to whisper to Jayne and Jodi, "I will walk with you next year. I promise."

Much later, Jayne told me a story she had kept to herself for months. On the third day, she had come upon a young woman, a participant, who was vomiting into the woods along the route. When Jayne asked whether she should perhaps be on the bus, another walker explained that the woman was Stage 4 terminal, and wanted to finish on her own. Her children were waiting for her at the finish line and she wanted them to remember her in victory. Jayne seized upon that story as a transcendent example of courage in the tragic wake of this disease. To me, this was unfathomable strength of spirit.

AUGUST 8

I am finally going back to work in Stamford today. I somehow doubt that I'll be able to rely on my body and brain for the entire day but the drive and the much-needed change of scene will do me good. I am trying very hard not to overthink the whole re-entry process. My office is where I first heard the news of my cancer; it is across the hall from David's old office; it was command central for the divorce. Will everything be just where I left it in January, strewn all over the floor? I'm struggling with powerful memories on my drive in this morning and feeling excited but shaky; Kim no doubt has paved the way with everyone so they remember to treat me as normally as possible but I still have trepidation about trying to conduct a business meeting with no hair.

I work for a company that uses phrases like, "Our shareholders are anxious to see our margins improve through increased license revenue in the next two quarters so we must enable our strategic partner channels particularly in the Asia Pacific region." How am I going to do this without feeling like I'm play-acting? And will everyone be staring at my chest when they talk to me?

But I am so looking forward to seeing my work friends; they've been incredibly supportive and even made several treks up to Green Acres during the last few months. I still have an invisible line in my brain dividing my personal from my professional life. I guess it's part of my HR DNA. I am trying desperately to try to fuse these two disparate parts of my life back together but having

one foot still firmly planted in the sick camp makes it challenging.
My world has been about channeling enough energy to reach the
bathroom or clasp my seatbelt. I am wearing a sparkly pink-
ribbon pin on my lapel anxious for people to ask me about it so I
can tell them all about The Sole Sisters.

My assistant, Hideaki, stands in my office door just after I
arrive and with all sincerity says to me, "I missed your laugh. We
all did. It was incredibly boring here without you."

"Really?"

"No one laughs like you."

"You mean so obnoxiously loud so I can be heard down the
hall?"

"No. It's where you find humor. Seriously. I didn't understand
that until you... weren't here." He is looking into the doorjamb
now. I try to say something witty, or nice, or appreciative but
nothing comes. I just absorb his words and smile using my
rejuvenated gratitude muscles. I understand that the subtext of his
message is that he worried I might not come back.

The empty space someone leaves when they go on sabbatical is
radically different from the one left by someone who is fighting for
her life.

After David died, I realized there were parts of me that were
irretrievable because they required his humor, his laugh to make
them in any way relevant or meaningful. Three years later I can still
look across the hall to his office and fantasize about walking in with
my coffee and morning witticism; a mundane routine that is forever
catalogued in the Goddammit-I-Still-Miss-Him archives.

"Welcome back, boss."

Thank you, Zen Master.

SEPTEMBER I

I was having dinner at a favorite French bistro with a
professional acquaintance who recently had been making every
effort to be a friend. She also had known David and we spoke
briefly at his funeral mass, promising to keep in touch which, after
all this time, was finally coming to fruition. Little by little, we'd

been building the framework of a relationship that could move beyond the loss of a mutual friend. At first we could talk only about him because he was our sole connection; we then ventured into the "moving on" phase of our grief. But now we were getting to know one another so sometimes, sadly, there was little mention of him at all.

She was lamenting her current work drama as our appetizers arrived. Out of the blue, my head decided to relieve itself of several weeks' worth of congestion and lord knows what else. I grabbed for my napkin to stop the facial gushing but not in time before my dinner companion had to see, well, something not very appetizing.

When I explained the disappearing-nose-hair side effect, she registered a look on her face that was part concern and part morbid curiosity. It turned out that Lynn is insatiably fascinated by all things health-related and probably should have gone to med school, so we spent the rest of the evening in our lovely French finery, whispering about the bizarre world of chemotherapy and breast reconstruction. She asked such pointed questions it was hard not to answer in gross detail. It was the strangest dinner conversation I've had since Tony and the boys descended upon Green Acres, but we laughed and cried until about 11:00 p.m. when I finally ran out of energy and tissues.

What a nice feeling to know I have a new friend who won't dance around the safe edges of propriety when faced with the perverse realities of life—one who now has a renewed appreciation for her own nose hair.

SEPTEMBER 10

Spent today making plans for a trip to the home office in California and a visit with Julie; next week looks like it will work! I am determined to make the best of my time before heading into the operating room again and I miss my favorite cousin. We keep in touch by email and phone and she unfailingly sends cards on a regular basis because like it or not, she and I are products of the Hallmark generation. We understand the value of a well-timed

*piece of folded cardboard in the mailbox with clever writing on it.
And Julie is the master of finding just the right message. I save all
of her cards and re-read them like favorite books. But it's not the
same as hearing her laugh live and in-person. That's right up
there on the irreplaceable list.*

It was also my forty-seventh birthday and I wasn't sure how to
feel about that. Kim invited me to the community Steak and
Chicken Dinner, which is the annual fundraiser for the local
volunteer fire department and despite the fact that I didn't eat meat
and she was allergic to chicken, we went. I put on my favorite blue
bandanna and a jean jacket to ward off the chill. It was around the
corner from Green Acres and usually attended by just about
everyone in town and their kids. The firemen and a cadre of
volunteers cook hundreds of dinners over huge grills in a beautiful
picnic area under carefully limbed hundred-year-old pines. The
really hot "fire dudes" man the outdoor wine and beer bar, which is,
trust me, worth the price of admission. In this tiny hamlet, if you
are a guy who regularly pumps iron, I believe they make it
mandatory that you become a fireman and wear tight T-shirts. They
also string up white lights in the trees and by nightfall it's a magical
place to be supping off cheap paper plates and saying neighborly
hellos. It always feels like a sweet farewell to summer and a tacit
understanding that we may not see each other again until next
spring. This is New England, after all.

After we got settled at the picnic table with our gigantic dinner
portions of mostly mashed potatoes and some sweet champagne we
smuggled in, Priscilla and Sonnie and Frank and some other
friends mysteriously showed up bearing silly gifts and funny cards
and unexpected laughs. Kim had secretly called around and made
sure I wasn't going to celebrate this birthday alone. We drank
champagne out of paper cups and as if it were planned, I won two
prizes in the raffle. After an early autumn chill set in and I could no
longer keep myself awake or warm, Kim and I headed back to the
car and I thanked her for making it a very special night. I allowed
one picture to be taken of me and the gang tonight for the first time
in a long time and I liked the way my smile looked. Older, but
genuine.

SEPTEMBER 11

I drove in to Sloan alone for my pre-op appointment which by now, alas, had become as commonplace as dental hygiene visits. New Yorkers and tourists were wearing pins that say, *"9-11 Never Forget"* and American flags were ubiquitous. Street vendors were cleaning up, hawking photos of the old skyline with the Twin Towers and the newly iconic picture of two beams of light reaching into the night sky where the Towers once stood, a macabre *before and after* that still sends chills.

My exchange surgery was scheduled for the end of the month so I was signed up for a mammogram on the right side, blood work, EKG, and an interview with an anesthesiologist. I've gotten so used to these interviews I could actually tell *them* which drugs I wanted. As I sat in the waiting room for the mammogram, I took off my sweater as I settled in with a travel magazine. The woman sitting next to me glanced at my arm and asked, "Excuse me, but are you aware of those spots on your forearm?"

This might sound intrusive but cancer patients get into some serious in-your-face conversations in waiting rooms. "Staging" is a big topic because it immediately establishes the hierarchy: the person with the scariest diagnosis gets the full attention of everyone else within earshot, all of whom are presumably grateful for their lesser plight. It was understood that most of the time we were just looking out for each other because our stories, our *stage,* could change tomorrow. In some cases though, we simply needed to say out loud all the fucked-up words rolling around in our heads to someone else who was experiencing the same hell on earth. It's hard to pass up the opportunity once it presents itself.

"Oh, that. God it's so annoying. I finally get out in to the garden last week and managed to give myself poison ivy! I don't cover it though unless it spreads—which it doesn't seem to be doing. But I will tell you that it hurts. It's weird. Maybe it's poison sumac or something....."

"That's not poison ivy."

"No? What is it?"

"It looks like shingles."

"*What?*"

"Right after your mammogram, go tell your doctor. I assume you had chemo; it's not all that uncommon when your immune system is so compromised."

"Is this bad?"

"Depends. Just talk with your doctor. Good luck."

After my mammogram I skipped the pre-op appointment and went right into McDreamy's office to get his opinion. "Is this something I should be concerned about?"

"Oh shit. It's probably zoster. Let me get you in to see the dermatologist across the hall right away. When is our surgery?"

"Two weeks!"

I went across the hall and the nice dermatologist who, in comparison to me, looked like a pre-teen who stole her mom's lab coat, informed me that I had herpes zoster, a/k/a shingles, and must start immediately on an oral and topical drug regimen that she would prescribe. When I went back to McDreamy's office he was sullen.

"The dermatologist called me. I was right. We can't operate on you until it clears. Dammit. We're going to have to postpone your surgery. *Again*. I'm so sorry, Jude."

"How long is this going to…"

He cut me off, "At least six weeks to make sure we're clear."

I fought back the urge to scream, cry, and throw things only because he looked as disappointed as I felt. The pain in my arm that I thought was poison ivy was suddenly stinging, but the evil expander-alien in my chest breathed a sigh of relief knowing it still had several weeks before being surgically removed. The dominoes were beginning to teeter; my immune system was on the ropes. The longer-term risks and side effects of chemo were slowly rearing their ugly heads. I drove home in a daze with prescriptions for a new round of drugs in my purse and a six-to-eight-week postponement of my exchange surgery.

I wondered aloud if the universe was just trying to see how far I can be pushed, how many times I would keep getting up after being pummeled. "Really? The cancer wasn't enough so you had to throw in herpes!? Is this some kind of a sick joke? Hello, universe, are you listening?!"

I looked out the driver's side window at the New York skyline as I crossed the bridge for home, recalling a September 12th five years ago. I watched this same view from a park bench in the Bronx as the souls of thousands billowed soundlessly into the bright autumn sky. Death was no longer some abstract final destination or a morbid fact of life. It was the product of a violent war started in my backyard. Five years later I still felt the unrelenting horror I felt every morning reading the *New York Times* and seeing the pages upon pages of obituaries and photos of loved ones searching helplessly for their kin.

These memories formed a well-timed and finely tuned perspective reminding me that I am still *here* so I should just shut up and deal with it. Christ, it's only a few weeks, right? I'm not jumping out a window from the fiftieth floor to my death to keep from burning alive. I'm just taking more antibiotics and waiting for my new boob.

"Suck it up," answered the universe.

SEPTEMBER 18

I admit it. I love to fly. I hate the constant fear of box-cutter wielding maniacs changing flight plans and the endless series of indignities at security checkpoints, but once I'm airborne in a big bird with the Federal air marshal hiding in plain sight under the obligatory Yankees cap, I am in the zone. I'm not a big fan of turbulence but it invariably provides insights into the health of my psyche vis-à-vis the unrehearsed prayers it inspires: *Please god of planes and clouds, I'll be nicer to that asshole in accounting if you let me live after we plummet to the earth.* That sort of thing. But today I'm taking a different tack: *Please God of All That is Fair, please don't let me get lymphedema in my arm or a deep vein thrombosis in my leg from this flight. I've paid my dues on this one, don'tcha think?* I am at risk for both and although I was warned not to fly by the insensitive physical therapist at Sloan, I am taking the chance. All things considered, I simply cannot spend the rest of my life on Amtrak.

The flight to California was a direct to San Jose. Julie was driving down from Sacramento to meet me and stay with me overnight. We'd planned a drive down Route 17 to our favorite hot spots in Santa Cruz. I got off the plane feeling like I was meeting a long-lost sister even though it's only been a few months time. So much had happened since I last saw her. When she saw me at the gate, she screamed, "Jude!!" and we just hugged for about two minutes. I looked very different and she was doing her best not to let me see her cry.

It turned out neither of us had enough energy for Santa Cruz today, so we dropped off our bags at the hotel and headed back down to San Jose, only a ten minute drive, for lunch and some shopping. I was weak; the flight had completely zapped me. I kept checking my arm for swelling and holding it over my head to keep the blood flowing. I looked like I was hailing invisible taxis.

It is wonderful to see Julie and we effortlessly connect as we always do; like we saw each other yesterday. She listens to all the family news and asks ten million questions but is quiet and subdued when we get back to the hotel. We each take a bed and lie down. I take my scarf off my head and she looks at me with a sadness that I really have never seen before.

"I am afraid of all this, Jude."

"I know."

"I am very scared to lose you. It's too hard to think about."

"Please don't. I'm getting better. Really. There's just no guarantee that it won't come back, Jule. But I can't think that way or I'd never get out of bed."

"Are you tired? You look tired."

"What I look is old. And unhealthy. And yes, I'm tired. I only have energy for part of the day and I think I used up two days worth today. But it was worth it, Jule. I really miss you."

"Me too. I'm going to let you sleep."

"Please don't leave."

"No, no. I've got a book right here."

"Thanks. I'll get better, I promise."

"Please do. Because I seriously can't take much more of this."

And then changing topics to food, which is our fallback position whenever the conversation becomes heavy, "Hey, when you wake up we'll do some room service instead of going out, okay? That sounds like a better plan. Can you drink wine yet?"

"No. It's still awful."

"Chemo should be outlawed."

"I hear that, sister."

SEPTEMBER 21

Flying back to New York today. I am so relieved to have made the trip. To see Julie and my work colleagues—especially Steve and Dean—was integral to putting my life back together. The puzzle is still missing some sizable pieces but it is nonetheless beginning to take shape.

Our Santa Clara office is our global headquarters and home to about eight hundred employees of whom I only personally knew about fifty, but now they all knew me. The bald HR woman in the Ann Taylor dress created significant hallway buzz. When Godfrey, our CEO, saw me in the cafeteria, he put down his tray and he gave me a completely unprofessional and wonderful hug right in front of everyone, which no doubt added to the chatter. Godfrey also knew Steve's former colleague who was a survivor, and he is the father of all girls, and seemed genuinely relieved that I was back in circulation. I smiled and told him that it was good to be back, feeling as if every single pair of eyes in the room was now watching me in a very non-HR like embrace with our CEO. But the attention was *okay*. I have learned not to feel ashamed of what this illness has done to me. The hug felt nice. And let's face it; I have not had much activity in the Male Embrace Department of late.

I sat in on a few meetings with Dean and his team. One of his direct reports—Gary, someone I barely know—brought me roses from his garden one day. He had heard I was a gardener and thought I would appreciate them. It was such a lovely gesture that I didn't really know what to say. So I brought them to every meeting I had and placed them in the middle of the room, instructing anyone who felt the slightest bit of tension to put their nose in the bouquet and inhale deeply. Flowers work wonders. But this was so unlike the Old Jude that I'm sure they were all wondering if my treatment included a Complete Personality Transplant from someone who actually cared about something outside of work.

Steve took me to dinner one night and in true Steve fashion told me I looked very scary without eyelashes.

"Not a good look for you, kid."

"I know—it's ugly, isn't it?"

"It makes you look sicker than I know you are. You're coming out the other side of this beautifully, Jude. Just hang in there." In that moment, I felt it was true and loved the sound of those words strung together in just that order. I was thrilled that someone recognized that I was still healthy somewhere under all the exterior mess. We toasted to better days ahead but I overdid it a bit and was sick when I got back to my room.

I slept on the flight home when I wasn't spontaneously exercising my arm, driving the guy next to me slightly crazy every time. It was about eight p.m. when I landed. There was a driver to pick me up at JFK airport. It was a gorgeous night. I was so proud of myself for having made the trip, and now I was heading home *alone to my house.* Giddy would not be an exaggeration. I couldn't wait to tell Kim all about my adventures since she knew all the players.

I had promised Mom I would call her because she's a lousy flyer and says her own version of the rosary every time I leave the ground.

"Hey, Mom, it's me! I just got in from California, safe and sound. What a fantastic trip! How are you? How's Dad?"

"I...I can't talk about it." Silence.

"What? Mom what's going on?!" Now I am in a panic because in my mind I see my father in some sort of mortal danger. I am sweating as I wait for an answer. There is static on the line but no answer is forthcoming. She's audibly crying.

"Calm down, Sylvia. What is it? Tell me...I'm not getting into the car until you tell me." My driver is patiently waiting with my bags, smoking a cigarette, looking non-plussed.

"I went to the doctor. It's back. There is a lump.... I have to have a mastectomy." After she says the M-word she is inconsolable. Rightfully so. I am trying to convince her, through her sobs, that it will be okay when I know I have no basis for this argument. I digest the myriad implications of her recurrence in excruciating slow motion.

Oh my god.

SEPTEMBER 22

The Sole Sisters re-grouped. Calls and emails flew as we tried to think through all the scenarios of what this new diagnosis meant in real terms, and how in god's name we were going to get Sylvia through a mastectomy and reconstruction at seventy-six. She was the sole caregiver for Dad, who was failing at an alarming rate. Not to mention that I hoped to be heading back into surgery (with any luck, if you can call it that) in October, Jodi and Jayne had families to tend to, and Victor was sequestered in the mountains of Vermont as the sole proprietor of a home-based business. I called Mom and told her I'd drive to Glastonbury to pick her up to come to Green Acres for the weekend with Dad. She immediately battled back with fifty reasons why she couldn't leave the house and how hard it was to travel with my father. My response, roughly translated, was, *"Tough shit."*

"You're coming here and we're going to talk about what to expect from a mastectomy, Mom. Dad will be fine but we need to talk. Do you hear me? This is no time for heroics. Start packing. " I told Jodi that I needed to de-mystify this for her and she agreed. This was Big Syl Triage Weekend and I was emotional but pragmatic about the harsh reality of the situation. And it was the first time I felt like I could actually help someone else since Victor Philip's intervention.

After I get them settled in, Mom and I engage in probably one of the saddest conversations I have ever had with her. Helping your mom prepare for her mastectomy through the lens of personal experience is not a conversation I wish on anyone. She seems shrunken and fragile to me. Her eyes brim with tears and then she looks away trying to change topics, so it is slow going at first. My mother is fearful on so many fronts it is hard to know where to begin.

But finally, she talks. And as the layers peel away it becomes clear this is not about the surgery or losing a breast. It is not about the return of a deadly disease and her looming mortality. It's about the fact that her husband of fifty-four years cannot comfort her and tell her she will be okay despite the fact that he sits across the room from us, dutifully eating the apple she just sliced up for his afternoon snack. He looks up at us from time to time, grateful that we are with him, but mercifully just out of earshot of the sad words passing between us.

"He will never know." She whispers looking at him with an expression that borders on rage—as if he might somehow be at fault for abandoning her. Of course, she could tell him, and he would most likely comprehend it, but what is the point? My poor father will have absolutely no ability to articulate his own fear or support for her or to help in any way. His diminishing world has but one lifeline: Sylvia. And now she is sick again, possibly very sick. How crushing for both of them. This tragic epiphany instantly vacuums all of the oxygen out of the room because we are all three, at this precise moment, helpless to change any of it.

SEPTEMBER 28

About a month ago I was scanning the discussion boards on breastcancer.org catching up on research news when I spotted a post about an email lottery to win a free ticket to Martha Stewart's TV show, for an episode dedicated entirely to breast cancer survivors. It will air during Breast Cancer Awareness Month—or as I have come to call it, Boob-tober. For obvious reasons, I am as enthusiastic about "awareness" and support in this fight as anyone, but at some point when corporate co-profiteering strategically places the omnipresent pink swirl on everything from the trucks that deliver my home heating oil to a bag of romaine lettuce, I begin to feel a little queasy. Maybe because millions and millions of dollars and lives later, we're still without a cure or drugs that won't make us sicker. On the plus side though, Big Pharma is doing very nicely in the stock market. But I digress....

I am not entirely sure what possessed me to enter, but I did, and I won a ticket. Since Sylvia's recurrence, I was even more motivated to attend. I was also secretly hoping that I would be plucked from the studio audience to be interviewed about this mess of a disease, and enjoy an hour-long, uncensored rant about our health care system. It would be infinitely more interesting and instructive than listening to Ms. Stewart drone on about her latest craft requiring "simply a hot glue gun, some grosgrain ribbon, and a forty-acre farm." Seriously, she wears me out with her manic multi-tasking and hair that does not move. Who can compete? But now that I was going to be an imaginary guest on her show, I should be nicer.

I received an email from the producers of the show with information on when and where to arrive at her studio in New York City for the morning taping. I was quietly thrilled to be embarking on an adventure in New York that will not involve needles or blood pressure cuffs. It was a gorgeous September day and I have selected khaki capri pants and my Sole Sisters T-shirt, with a bohemian long brown cotton jacket emblazoned with "The Power of Now" on the back in big gold shimmery letters. I bought it during the divorce off a clearance rack as sort of a joke but for some reason it jumped out of the closet at me this morning and told me to wear it for La Martha. I waited outside the studio on the sidewalk in a long queue of survivors and their partners and realized I was probably the only person who was there alone. But I didn't really mind. I was enjoying picking up conversations with strangers who were admiring my jacket and asking the Cancer Questions, to which I responded: "Yeah, Stage 2B. Just got done with ACT; eight rounds of dose dense. One mastectomy, no rads. Feeling okay. Still tired. You?" I think I repeated that about ten times in a half-hour. But the bonus round questions always gave pause to the person asking. "No, no. Not married. Nope, no kids. Yeah, just me." Generally, people seemed to feel sorrier for me being alone than being diseased.

A producer's assistant shouted to us to go into the studio single file and show our IDs. So we all filed into a holding room where Martha's team served up cookies and tea which I hoped she had personally baked for us at three o'clock this morning while I was still cozy in my bed. As the groups were summoned and led into the sound stage, I was left standing awkwardly alone by the cookie table. There were just about five of us left now and the show was about to start. I was nervous that I had come all this way just to hear there was no more room in the audience. One by one the others were led away until finally a young stage manager type with a headset, a nose stud, and a clipboard said, "Follow-me, please." I walked dutifully behind her into the studio which was colorful and bright and buzzing with the excitement and spirit of hundreds of women, echoing like a gymnasium before a championship game. Huge cameras were scanning the room and throwing images of happy faces onto large screens, and row upon row of theatrical lights were magically simulating daylight throughout the studio. I followed the stage manager who walked me down the aisle of chairs next to the stage to *front row, center!*

"Have a seat, ma'am. Enjoy the show." I looked around and I was the very last person seated.

"I'm sitting here?" I suddenly flashed back to the fantasy rant I rehearsed in my head and allowed myself an audible giggle.

"Yes, you are," she smiled, "and thank you for coming today."

This is so incredibly cool. Martha Stewart walks out from backstage to much applause and is exactly five feet away from me in her perfectly appointed, gargantuan kitchen that although the set for a television show, is actually a working kitchen that most humans would die for. Tracy Ulmann was just announced as her special guest—omigod I love her!—and we are going to be treated to some of Ms. Stewart's favorite appetizers. The generous hostess then pulls an "Oprah" and announces a special gift for every member of the studio audience today: a pink Kitchen Aid mixer will be sent to our homes. Those things are not cheap. I am grinning from ear to ear at my momentary good fortune.

The show itself is not terribly interesting but it is breathtaking to witness up close the inner workings of a television show and be making eye contact with the brilliant Tracy Ulmann. In fact, she and I banter back and forth during a commercial break but I am so nervous I have no idea what I actually said. At the end of the show, the entire cast and crew comes out on stage and applauds us while Melissa Etheridge's cancer anthem "I Run for Life" blasts through the sound system, and I finally lose it; silly, sentimental tears for myself and frightened tears for my mother. I wish she could have been here today. It would have done her good to see so many survivors in one room, some of whom are her age or older. I say a little prayer for her before I leave the studio and smile at Martha Stewart and she smiles back. We are both crying.

On my walk back to Grand Central Station I congratulated myself for having taken a chance on the free ticket and attending alone. Even though I was not personally interviewed as I had hoped and the back of my spotty bald head would likely be on television when this airs in a few weeks, the bold words on my jacket—The Power of Now—would have to speak for me. Oh, and I discovered that some celebrities don't photograph very well, because in person, Martha is drop-dead gorgeous. And not just because she invited me to her show, baked cookies, and bought me a pink mixer.

OCTOBER 5

I am starting to feel like I'm in that Bill Murray movie, Groundhog Day. At Sloan for my pre-op appointment, I slog the same hallways and register with the same now-familiar receptionists on every floor. I slip into the open-front frock-du-jour and stick out my arm for blood work and pressure checks. I crack the same stupid drug jokes with the anesthesiologist, answer the same nine million personal questions that they already have the answers to, and sign the pile of paperwork giving McDreamy permission to do his thing. Again. I am receiving some enthusiastic high-fives from my regulars though, because my hair is making a return appearance by way of a fine, sparse white fuzz over most of my head with a delightful black swoosh directly down the center which I learn from the nurses is a phenomenon called "skunk head"—sounding more like a metal band than a side effect.

I am here because McDreamy says that the herpes zoster has been contained enough to safely operate next week. I call Julie to let her know that my official invitation to have surgery again had finally arrived and she insists on coming back east to get me through it and to see her Aunt Sylvia. I don't argue with her this time. I am very relieved because I really need her company and an extra pair of hands during our family's own version of Boob-tober. My exchange surgery is set for October 12 at Sloan which is six days before Mom's mastectomy at Hartford Hospital. You really can't make this stuff up.

OCTOBER 11

I looked in the mirror this morning and screamed because I saw my brother Victor staring back at me. With the addition of gray and black fur on my head, we now look frightening alike. He's a good-looking man but his head has no business being on my shoulders. I didn't dwell on it though because this was a big day. Kim was accompanying me to order my furniture from Lillian August, the pieces I had been lusting after for months, and Julie was arriving from California. Kim has a wonderful decorator's eye and has been teaching me how to think about color and design flow. I trust her instincts but we also have completely different taste; I am mid-century-post-modern-eclectic whites, reds, oranges, and yellows, and she is French country-antique-classic pale blues, beiges, and greens. But I give her enormous credit for saying nice things about what I selected, ironically, entirely from the Martha Stewart collection.

"Oh, it's really nice, Jude. Are you sure you want a white couch?"

"It's cream."

"Might I remind you that you have a dog?"

"I'll teach her not to go on it."

"Sophie? Your dog tells *you* what to do."

"What about the chairs?"

"We need another fabric here. I love the lines, but we've got to tie this together with the shape of the room. Let's look at samples." Kim and I painstakingly went through fabric sample books the size of the King James Bible until she finally selected the exact right piece. "Here you go. This is it. We're done."

"Really?"

"Do you want to have this stuff before the holidays? It's perfect for the room."

And she was absolutely right. It was perfect. So I went to the salesperson and signed my life away for a cream couch, two striped fabric chairs, two cane-back chairs, and a settee. It would take months to deliver but I didn't care. Sophie and I had grown accustomed to the old couch and patio furniture combo. When I thanked Kim for her help, she replied, "I'm going to be sitting on it, too, you know."

"Kim do you know what this means? I will have my *very own stuff*. Holy cow, this is big."

"It's another step, Jude."

Julie's flight and rental car got her to Green Acres in the early afternoon and I was thrilled to see her. She walked in with her latte and suitcases and declared, "Honey, I'm home!"

"Jule! C'mon in!"

"Hey, didn't I just see you a few weeks ago?" We laughed and got her settled in while talking hospital logistics for tomorrow's surgery, but it was just the preamble to the top story. Mom's diagnosis and the real possibility that she could be very sick rightfully trumped my plastic surgery. Julie looked just as worried as I felt.

"How did they find it?"

"She found it. In the shower. Self-exam. Same breast that she had the lumpectomy and rads. Left side."

"Jesus, she's got to be terrified."

"That's an accurate description. Although after a full court press, I think we got her dialed back from pure terror to understandable fear. She is going to have the DIEP flap surgery that I wanted to have, so it will be a much longer recuperation period. I keep telling her how lucky she is that she qualifies for it and that she will have a warm breast with her very own tissue instead of Hollywood Boob. But I have no idea how on earth she would get through chemo if she needs it. I can't even let myself go there yet."

"What about Uncle Vic?"

"He knows she's going in to the hospital but he doesn't know why. He's going to stay with Vic and Daryl again."

"Weren't they supposed to be going on some fancy cruise....."

"Cancelled. I think they got most of their money back."

"When is this all going to end for you guys, Jude? I mean, this is *crazy*."

"It does seem like overkill."

"Are you ready for tomorrow?"

"I've been ready for months. I just want this thing out of my chest so McDreamy can start to put me back together."

"I like your hair-fuzz."

"Shut up. I look like my brother."

"I wasn't going to say it."

OCTOBER 12

Back to Sloan with Julie and Kim, an empty stomach, a Xanax working its magic, and absolutely no fear at all about the procedure. The plastic surgery portion of my Total Recovery Plan was actually *exciting* both from an aesthetic and pain management standpoint, but all things considered, rather ho-hum on the risk factor scale. We were completely preoccupied with my parents' drama and talking about possible scenarios, all the while knowing, but not articulating, that I could also be facing a recurrence at some point. How these two incredible women were not completely exhausted by me, I have no idea.

I am pleased to see that Sloan's Surgical Smock Fall Collection has pink and blue stripes, so at least I am going into the OR with a fun, updated look and not the same old, same old. My furry head is covered with a bonnet and I shuffle into the operating room in my paper covered bare feet, chatting up the worker bees and doing my best to make them laugh; as if my fashion ensemble would not have been enough. I want this fucking thing out of my chest so badly I lie down on the table unassisted and ask why the anesthesiologist is late.

"C'mon, are we ready to do this, or what? Where's the Sleep Doctor? I don't have all day."

By the time McDreamy comes in with his entourage he is already grinning, because he's heard that I'm causing a commotion.

"Ahh, my favorite patient."

"Can I tell you how happy I am that you're going to put me to sleep today, Doc?"

"I share your joy, Jude. It's been a long time coming, but we're finally ready to roll. All right, let's do the countdown," he says

with a nod to the Sleep Doctor, "a quick little poke in the arm and you're going to wake up with a very nice addition to this body, I promise."

"Ten, ni..." and out.

I wake up in recovery several hours later with Julie and Kim by my side, waiting for me to be well enough to drink the Dixie cup of warm juice, eat the stale cracker without vomiting, and pee unassisted. That's the winning trifecta that will get me sprung from Sloan tonight. It's hard to move myself into a sitting position and shuffle to the bathroom, though, because once again, I have a goddamned JP drain hanging from my side.

"How do I look?" I squeak, trying to use my dry vocal chords.

"You've had better days, Jude."

"I mean my new boob."

"Movie star quality."

"Don't forget the painkillers, girls."

"Already packed. There's a pillow in the car so you can sleep on the way. You ready?"

"This drive is going to suck, but yes. Let's get out of here."

OCTOBER 18

So far so good. Hollywood Boob was definitely not as painful or large as the expander balloon and McDreamy managed to go in through the existing scar so I didn't look like the Bride of Frankenstein. There were several exterior sutures and interior ones that should dissolve on their own. The drain was a gigantic pain in the ass but Julie and I managed to make a sick game out of describing the exact color of the ick so we could write amusing descriptors in the log such as *Chinese duck sauce with a swirl of ketchup.*

Today was Mom's surgery which would be a minimum of seven hours so there were no plans to go see her in Hartford until the next day. This was also the day I could get the drain removed and immediately thereafter, *shower* for the first time in five days. Julie drove my car down to New York. I was on my mobile phone getting updates from Jodi on Mom. When we got to McDreamy's, he was happy to see me and after rather unceremoniously yanking the drain from my side, immediately began talking nips.

"This looks terrific, Jude. When are we going to finish you up with a brand new nipple?"

"You said I needed a few months for this to settle, so...."

"Let's get something on the calendar. There are several procedures you can choose from, so come back when you're ready for a consultation and we'll do something very nice for you."

"Again with the *very nice*."

"Okay, it will be gorgeous. Not the real thing, but you'll be happy. You'll have some symmetry back."

My head was not in this conversation. My nipple was really not the crazy, important thing it was a few months ago. In fact, it felt more than a little superfluous. Julie and I were looking at our watches because my mother was having a very complicated surgery and would be under anesthesia for most of the day; she is seventy-six years old and has breast cancer. Again. I kept thinking about the possibility of chemo for her. Between the M.D. Anderson report and firsthand knowledge of how tough it was, I would probably advise her not to do it. It would kill her before the cancer did.

OCTOBER 19

Julie and I arrive at Hartford Hospital around lunchtime. I didn't cover skunkhead and probably should have because I'm freezing. My new boob is settling in but the hole in my side where the JP drain was yanked from yesterday is very sore. I am eating Advil like candy. We are told at reception that Mom is in a step-down room which is one level below intensive care. She is right outside the nurse's station, already somewhat of a celebrity on the floor. Apparently, and I'm not sure why I didn't know this beforehand, this is the first time that Hartford Hospital has ever done this surgery. *The doctors and the interns and nurses who were involved in Sylvia's mastectomy and DIEP flap are in and out of her room constantly to check on her. DIEP or Deep Inferior Epigastric Perforator surgery requires very intense post-surgical monitoring to ensure that the blood flow is properly feeding the tissue. After hours of microsurgery to attach living tissue from her belly to the site where her breast was removed, the trauma lies not just with the patient but with the entire surgical team. This is a big deal. At one point several doctors wake my mother to ask if they can see and take pictures of their handiwork again and she deadpans, "Sure, boys, as long as these don't show up on the Internet next week."*

Julie and I walk tentatively in to her very complicated looking room. Sylvia looks small and childlike in the huge bed with noisy monitors ominously clicking and beeping all around her. She is wearing a pink-ribbon baseball cap and her eyes brighten the moment she sees us.

"Judy Ann, look at your hair! It's coming in all white."

"Yes mother. I am officially gray. With a black pinstripe."

"You look good, kid."

"So do you, Sylvia. Jesus. I expected you to be out cold today."

"I'm so-so. In and out. How was your surgery?"

"I have a new boob. McDreamy was great. Kim and Jules were with me. It's all good, Mom. I'm fine."

"She was a champ, Aunt Syl."

"I tell you girls, I don't feel a thing. No pain at all. It's just great. All this worry over nothing."

"You're on morphine, Ma."

"Well, whatever it is, it's nice." She puts her head back on the pillow; her eyes flutter and close.

"Yes. Yes it is. Very nice." And it dawns on me as I observe her drug-induced, stress-free contentedness that this is probably the most restful sleep she's had in over two years.

"Take a snooze, Mom; we'll go to the gift shop and come back later."

"Okey doke..." she whispers, already on her way to somewhere more peaceful than caregiver duty or a noisy step-down room. Take good care of her, Morpheus.

OCTOBER 23

The autumn sun leisurely reached out to each of the trees in my yard this morning with fingers of light, brightening the foliage until it appeared electrified. This is what New England is all about. Right outside my window was an explosion of color and beauty that cannot be found anywhere else on earth. I was thankful to be working from home today so I could use these images as a counterbalance to whatever human resource red-hot-nuttiness was menacing my inbox.

It was early so I decided to venture outside to get some exercise. I have been walking occasionally in the meadow with Sophie but I tend to tire quickly and she is easily distracted, so we usually don't stay out for very long. Fatigue still comes in crippling waves but something was telling me, some wildly positive voice in my head, to challenge myself. *How will you get back muscle tone and stamina if you don't push yourself harder? And how in the name of Nike will you get through sixty miles if you can't do ONE?*

For normal people it was a light fleece hoodie, no-hat-required kind of day. I was dressed for the Iditarod: a pair of yoga pants over my jeans, surgical boob-vest, turtleneck, two pairs of socks, wool sweater, barn jacket, hat, gloves, hiking shoes, pockets full of tissues and lip balm, and aviator shades. I was going around the corner. In Redding, that's about a thirty-minute walk, some of which is on a main road, but considering my achy legs, weak lung capacity (from general anesthesia) and sore chest, it would probably take me an hour. I planned on looping around to Jay's dental office and then home. My only thoughts were to stay warm, go slow, and not wimp out. *Finish the route, Jude,* said the annoyingly sunny voice. *Take in the gorgeous views and keep putting one foot in front of the other. You'll feel better.*

I have read about people with traumatic injuries who have to learn how to walk and talk again and the tremendous effort and fortitude they require facing every hour of every day. I was not five minutes in to my trek and wanted to turn around, go home, make tea and crawl pathetically back to my warm, soft bed. My thighs were burning. My ears were cold. My back was totally pissed off that I was walking on asphalt instead of the forgiving terrain of the meadow. But just as my brain began selling the rest of my body some lame justification for quitting, I remembered that this was the same path I walked in the snow the day David died. The exact same path. Oh, my god, how life had changed since then! I looked up into the bright autumn sky and summoned him out of thin air:

David, honey, I miss you terribly but you really, really suck. You should be here with me right now, laughing at my inability to hustle through this stupid exercise without feeling sorry for my pitiful self. You should be here helping me see the humor in…wait, is that you mocking me and my bag lady outfit? (beat) Well, frankly, you look pretty silly in that toga or whatever you're wearing. And I continued this conversation for the rest of the walk, actually making myself laugh out loud, which coupled with the outfit, was mildly disturbing to anyone who saw me. But it was so nice to catch up with him.

As I came down the home stretch toward the end of my driveway forty minutes later, I allowed myself a double fist pump and modified touchdown victory dance for the imaginary fans waiting for me at the mailbox. They were all wearing matching aviator shades, high-fiving and waving signs that read, "Whiners Finish Last." I was tired and a little breathless and dare I say it, sweating. I started my work day feeling like Wonder Woman in training (minus the cool costume and perfect boobs) and quite certain that David was somewhere in the great beyond taking credit for it all.

OCTOBER 24

Big Syl was doing spectacularly and would come home from the hospital in a few days. No news on the pathology report yet but fingers and toes were crossed that they "got it all." Jodi made plans to have a home health aide to help care for Mom and Dad when she couldn't be there. I know what I went through, and my surgery was not nearly as involved, plus I didn't have another patient to be caring for; Jodi was going to have her hands full.

Work was an interesting way to spend my time and I really needed the money, but I didn't have the same passion for it that I used to. I was enjoying the people much more than the tasks. I didn't really care so much about that asshole in accounting, or other minor nuisances that used to get me fired up. I recognized that once I let people in on my personal life, they were surprisingly easier to work with. I think they liked me better this way. Or who knows? Perhaps I'd been the closed-off asshole in HR all these years whom, during turbulence, everyone promised god they'd be nicer to.

Back in the summer, just after the 3-Day, Julie, The Sole Sisters, and I decided we would plan a getaway. No, make that a Vacation that Does Not Include Hospital Visits. Plus, it would be Jayne's fiftieth birthday in November and this seemed like the perfect way to celebrate: *by leaving the country, where no one could find us.* We tried to entice Kim and Daryl to join us but the timing didn't work for them. We decided on Mexico; an all-inclusive retreat with restaurants, a spa, yoga, a beach, and several humongous pools with, we hoped, hot cabana boys. We were so desperate to get something on the calendar we booked in August for a week in January 2007! But whenever our days were dark and stormy, we always had shimmery images of the Aventura Spa Palace in our heads as our beacon of hope for future peace, relaxation, and poolside umbrella drinks. Of course, we all bought ticket insurance, just in case.

The thought of being in a bathing suit in few months was a little daunting but I couldn't shop for one until the swelling went down on my left side. Even worse though, was the image of all this white and black fuzz on my head, which would likely be longer and more cartoonish come January. I had to do something about it. I called my hair salon.

"How long is it?"

"Well, it's very tight curls but if you stretch them out, oh, maybe a quarter or half an inch? It's short."

"Why don't we just wait until you have more to work with?"

"Because I look like Pepe le Pew."

"C'mon in. Let's see what we can do."

At Adam Broderick's, the wonderful salon that had not charged me a dime since my diagnosis and even trimmed Ginger for me for free, unknowingly assigned me to a young pregnant stylist whose mother had recently died of breast cancer. This was not an easy visit. She became very emotional and wistful when she saw me so we just talked for about fifteen minutes. I learned about her mother's indomitable spirit through three recurrences and her brave final days. She listened to the latest in my saga, which I confined to the end of chemo and The Sole Sisters because there were daggers of survivor guilt stabbing me in the heart. But she and I found common ground and sudden intimacy that went beyond standard cancer chatter. She was still very much in mourning and my mother's future still hung in the balance. It's a tired expression but at that very moment, I felt her pain. Even simple things like going to the hairdresser are just not the same anymore. The old Jude never would have engaged in this conversation so openly; I would have listened, but I never would have volleyed back. Once you unlock the truth door, like it or not, life charges in.

"I used to use this on my mom," she said, "she hated looking gray, too."

Then she gently applied an organic vegetable dye in a reddish-brown that she promised would not hurt my scalp or the skinny sprouts of hair pushing through, and would last several weeks. It looked so much better and my face appeared ten years younger under darker fleece.

I can't help but wonder why I have so far been spared in the breast cancer lottery. Why did the universe take someone's mother, who was about to be a grandmother, and not me? Does the world really need another HR person? On the drive home I convince myself that it's because there is something I am supposed to do. I must be missing the purpose, the grander scheme; the hidden clues to fully utilize this extended service plan on my life. I come up empty. But I feel like I'm on to something. If you make it to the lifeboat on the Titanic, it can't be random. There's got to be a reason.

OCTOBER 28

Big Syl was settling in at home compliments of Jodi's unrelenting patience and assistance. She also grumbled much less about her JP drain than I had done. She didn't seem bothered by it at all. Nor was she feeling any appreciable pain, which baffled everyone, including her doctors. When Mom got home after five days in the Big House, she refused to take her painkillers. "What do I need those stupid things for? They just make me woozy. Throw them away. I'm fine." Whereas I would have taken heroin if I'd had it.

Victor was ferrying Dad home from Vermont, stopping here at Green Acres, with a quick side-trip to New York to have lunch with some of Dad's cousins visiting from Chile. Vic met them through email via our cousins in Lima, Peru, and went to some trouble to coordinate this rendezvous. Which all sounded interesting enough, but we had never met these people before; however, it should be mentioned that the few times we have gotten together with the Peru crew, vast quantities of pisco and cerveza were consumed. I was debating whether this was really the best outing for Dad, but Victor was on a mission and would not be dissuaded.

I still don't understand the value of this trip, all things considered, but I agree to the plan because I want to spend the day with Dad. I can't wait to have time with him separate and apart from Big Syl. Taking into consideration her own health drama, she simply cannot appreciate him in his current state because she only sees what is missing from the picture while I have the luxury of appreciating and enjoying what is still there. I just want to walk with him and hold his hand and let him say whatever he wants in whatever manner it happens to escape his mouth. And I want to make him laugh. And I hope he says funny things to make us laugh. Despite his herculean struggles he is completely able to comprehend his environs—and thankfully my brother is uniquely adept at bringing out the best in him and puts the twinkle back in Dad's eyes just by being in the room. When you're the only men in a house full of strong women, the boys tend to stick together. They can still make each other giggle helplessly at things that require either the Y chromosome or a passion for golf, or both. Thick as thieves, those two.

It is beginning to turn cold so we put on our leathers and break out the scarves and hats before beginning our journey to Manhattan. Victor is driving and we're also accompanied by Il Vagabondo Kevin and his wonderfully skewed sense of humor that does not require the Y chromosome or a passion for golf. He's just funny as shit. When he was just five years old, the kid was doing SNL Dan Akroyd impersonations that today would have easily gone viral on YouTube. The group we are meeting includes two sisters from Santiago and two Chilean sisters who now reside in the United States, all of whom Vic has been communicating with these last few months. I suspect the family a world away is easier to latch on to than the one that is racking up medical bills rivaling the national debt.

We meet at a midtown restaurant eager to make introductions and try to close language gaps between Spanish, English and thick accents on both sides, all while speaking over each other very loudly and almost unintelligibly, at times resorting to simple hand gestures and exaggerated facial expressions for clarity. I'm sure Dad feels right at home. Victor and the cousin from Florida (amusingly named Charo) do most of the cross-continental translating once we settle down. Dad is smiling politely and does not speak a word of Spanish but his much younger female cousins are treating him with a reverence and kindness usually reserved for dying Mafia dons, so no translations are required. He is lapping it up. The man still knows a pretty face when he sees one. As lunch winds down there are toasts to my father and brother, "Salud con todos; Salud Victor y Victor" which sounds more like "BEEK-tor" to me and I decide is what I will call my brother from this day forward. I sit at the end of the long table with Kevin who surprisingly isn't cracking jokes but is earnestly and emotionally capturing the moment as something fleeting and worth remembering. I am glad to be out of the spotlight and watching it fall gracefully and rightfully on the most important men in my life. We did not need to speak the same language or speak much at all, really. There was food, sharing of food, wine, hand gestures, laughter, bountiful desserts, and the energetic and already forgiving smiles of newfound relations. Family is family. Beektor was right. Dad had a blast. I grin the whole way home.

NOVEMBER 7

I have been feeling the vague promise of muscle-building in my quads but it is very slow going. One of the reasons might be that I have not tried any hills yet. The "block" I have been traversing is flat and somewhat unsafe, a main road heavily trafficked by annoying trucks oblivious to the speed limit. So I decided to kick the exercise regimen up a notch and attempt (insert dramatic music) "The Loop." This was a just a bigger block that under normal circumstances was a nice walk but to me loomed as a death-defying hike with steep hills and curves for three long country miles. I did this walk many times in a healthy pre-cancer body in just under an hour without breaking a sweat, but I had no idea how long this would take me today. I figured that, at my current pace, I should bring water, trail mix, mobile phone, toilet paper, and my health insurance card.

I started out at seven thirty in an ensemble that included scarf and fanny pack, looking positively ridiculous. The bracing wind was forcing my face into an unflattering grimace like the one Sophie wears when she hangs her head out of the car doing seventy m.p.h. on the highway. My thigh muscles were on fire when I rounded the corner, heading up a street called Umpawaug, where Kim lives. I was very short of breath but kept telling myself that this would help me; that a strong body would not fall victim to more disease. I kept putting one foot in front of the other wondering how the simple act of walking became an Olympic event. Everything hurt, but I pushed it.

I passed by a farm at the halfway mark, the second one on the Loop, and stopped to watch the horses; old skinny nags grazing in the field. The reddish one walked slowly over to me hung her head over the fence to say a neighborly hello. I was so taken aback I began talking to her like we were old friends. As I got closer, she put her head on my shoulder and the weight of it felt so warm and comforting I didn't want to leave. I took off my glove and began petting her long nose and telling her about my plan to walk sixty miles someday and her tail began whooshing back and forth, slow and steady.

I took a mental snapshot of the moment because it was such a lovely reminder of how many times I walked past that farm and never gave these creatures a second thought. I told my large equestrian buddy I would be back and she actually watched me walk away, head still hanging over the fence, as I disappeared beyond the hill. I now had a wonderful reason to make it to the second farm on the Loop every time I walk.

I got home and looked at the clock on the stove as I shed my layers: eight forty. Nailed it! My legs felt like rubber, my dogs were blistering and my cheeks were windburned but damn, it felt good!

Today is Dad's birthday. He is seventy-eight. I call him and do all the talking. He sounds like he's smiling whenever he ventures a few words back. I hit all the hot topics: golf, the Yankees, Derek Jeter, Mom, and the weather. I'll go visit them this weekend. And see if I can get Big Syl out for a walk.

NOVEMBER 8

I had several appointments coming up to discuss Tamoxifen with my Keep-the-Cancer-from-Coming-Back Team: Drs. Rivers and Bones. Tamoxifen is apparently the drug of choice, an "anti-estrogen" drug for pre-menopausal women that I was supposed to take starting sometime in December for the next five years of my life before switching to something else, to be determined, if I'm still here. I read everything I could put my hands on about Tamoxifen and had been on the BC.org discussion boards about it—and I was seriously considering not taking it. I read about women who go off of it within months, even weeks. I heard horror stories, laced with very few success stories which I was convinced were written by moles from the drug company. All told, the side effects are numerous and present risks that can do permanent damage:

"Most women tolerate it quite well, but common side effects include bone pain, back pain, headaches, cough and breathing difficulties, high cholesterol, indigestion, anemia, mood swings, hot flashes, hair loss, hypertension, osteoporosis, rashes and hives, blood clots, ovarian cysts and decreased libido. Severe side effects only occur in about 19% of the women who take it. Those include abnormal vaginal bleeding or discharge, coughing up blood, loss of balance, blistering skin, severe depression, vision and speech problems, new or increased breast tumors or pain. This is not a complete list."

Nineteen percent of women experience one or more of these symptoms and millions of women are on this drug? It's heralded as statistically offering me the "best shot" at preventing a recurrence and marginally increases my survival rate, so I guessed that alone was supposed to make me feel good about jamming this pill into the back of my throat every day because, as the marketing slogan *should* read, "At least you won't be dead."

I'm incensed that this drug even got past the FDA, but on balance, I was learning that the quality of life meter is on a completely different scale for cancer patients. *And* there are women who actually *do just fine* with a few minor annoyances and the occasional trip to the doctor for some onset of one of the above. Is this really the best we can do? We figured out how to build a robot to perform surgery but we can't concoct an antiestrogen drug that won't cause abject misery "in a small percentage of women"— which, by the way, considering the millions who are taking it, comprises a rather sizable group.

Here was the dilemma: I wanted to feel better. *Someday.* I wanted to be healthy again. I did not want to be tethered to yet another drug that could take me down a path of being sicker elsewhere in my body. This was like a scary game of whack-a-mole—beat one thing back and something else pops up. It felt wrong on so many levels I almost convinced myself, and a few people in my Inner Circle, that I should not do it.

"Not taking it."

"Okay, let's talk about this. Why not?" queries the ever-patient Kim. I read her the side effects list with appropriate dramatic inflection until she begins officially wigging out. Which was the desired effect.

"Oh, my god, Jude. That's hideous! Isn't there anything else we can do?" I am flattered that she says the word "we" as if this is her disease too, but it catches me off guard. "Have you looked into holistic approaches?"

"Eye of newt, perhaps?"

"Be serious for a minute, what other options do we have? There must be clinical trials or alternative medicines..."

"I've looked into the only two options available to me in this country or covered by my insurance: taking this drug or doing nothing. The holistic approaches out there have no scientific data to support them so it's the equivalent of doing nothing while choking down crushed white sage pellets, or some other

naturalistic sounding crap invented by some stoner in Utah with a marketing degree."

"So you've made up your mind, then. Why are we having this conversation?"

"Because I wanted your reaction."

"Well, now you have it. Let's keep looking."

"I'm just tired of doing this, Kim! I'm tired of hearing I have to sacrifice whatever quality of life I have left for—"

"You are not out of the woods yet, missy," said the Kim who sometimes sounds like my mother when she's annoyed.

"I'll never be, so it really doesn't matter does it?! I should just spin the roulette wheel and see where I land, because this is all just one huge fucking crapshoot anyway. If I don't want to take a chance on this drug, I'll deal with the consequences. You don't have to!"

There is silence on the other end of the phone because we humans have a terrible habit of masking our worst fear with our ugliest anger. And hurting the ones we love most.

NOVEMBER 23

Thanksgiving. Jodi and Glenn are hosting. I feel horrible; as if someone has thrown mosquito netting over my head making it hard to see things clearly and move with any grace. My head is pounding and my bones are aching and weak which is all adding up to me feeling like the Tin Man in need of a lube job. I think about cancelling and staying home with Sophie in my bed watching old movies but I keep picturing my parents waiting for me to arrive so they can see I'm okay.

I slam back several green teas for a caffeine jolt and drive the hour to Glastonbury. I am still not eating meat so I power through dinner eating mushy sides and over-compensating for how shitty I feel by trying to be funny—which isn't working. I sit myself next to Dad before dessert and put my head on his bony shoulder when Jodi says to me, "Why don't you go lie down, Jude. You look exhausted."

I take her cue and wander into the other room to sleep under a warm blanket on the couch, listening to the faint whisper-talk

*going on in the dining room as I nod off. I worried them. I should
have stayed home and not ruin a nice dinner. Dammit.*

NOVEMBER 30

I met with Drs. Rivers and Bones separately today. With each of
them, I had long, protracted, some might say, heated debates about
whether I should take this frightening drug for the next five years or
roll the dice. After listening to the ever-clinical Rivers rattle off her
Scary Stats List without a hint of doubt or sensitivity, and watching
Bones stare straight into my eyes without blinking to assure me, "If
it were my *wife...*"

I caved. I realized I was beaten. For this round anyway.

Rivers whipped out her "survival rate" scenarios all of which left
me either dead or in serious danger seven years from now, and
Bones, more careful in his approach, shared his deep, personal
concern if I were to do nothing. He sweetened the pot by adding
that I could start on a small dose every other day and build my way
up to the recommended dose to see how my body reacts. He also
said that it was highly unlikely, considering my youth and otherwise
excellent health, that it would be a game changer in my quality of
life. And he meant it. I asked him ten different ways whether there
was a better option and he told me, "Not until we rule out
Tamoxifen as something you can tolerate *well*. It's the best we've
got." Bones has learned not to mince words with me so after I
succumbed and agreed to take the poison pills there appeared a
new look of concern on his face.

"Enough time has passed since you completed the chemo, Jude,
so we're going to start today by taking blood samples so we can
begin checking your markers on a regular basis."

"How regular?"

"Every three months."

"What are you looking for... exactly?" In my heart I already
knew the answer.

"Any sign in your blood work that tells us the cancer might have
returned. It's not foolproof, but it's a baseline we can measure against."

"You're worried."

"Cautious. Think of it as a maintenance plan."

"Every three months sounds pretty serious. For how long?"

"Jude, we'll do regular blood work for at least the next five years while you're on the Tamoxifen; and then likely for some time beyond that. But let's take this one step at a time," which is his ever-so-diplomatic way of trying to keep me from burying him in bullshit questions for the next thirty minutes, "and get through a few months on Tamoxifen first."

"Jesus, I'll never be rid of you."

"C'mon, I'm not that bad. You'll grow to like me. Take some cookies on the way out after your blood work. They're homemade."

The older nurse came in to extract three vials of blood from my right arm since I cannot give blood or have any injections in my left for all eternity, and she couldn't get a line. She tried three times. I swear I'm cursed.

"Your veins are so thin and weak," she said, as if I didn't eat enough vegetables as a child or this never would have happened.

"Yes, well, you might remember that little incident with the Adriamycin and four months of poison coursing through them. It wears a girl out, you know," I said pointing to the long divot in my forearm that is forever purple and ugly and every inch her fault.

"You should have gotten a port."

Now you tell me. She's the kind of person who is always pointing out something that is crystal clear only in hindsight—as if she knew better all along but opted smugly to keep it to herself.

"We'll call you in a few days to let you know the results," she said as she wrapped tape around my arm. "Don't forget to schedule your follow-up appointment." And just as I was about to say something I'd regret, she added, "Good luck, Jude."

Right. Luck is about all I can hope for. I can't believe I have to wait again; wait for another proclamation on whether the cancer is really gone or just hiding in a vital organ somewhere waiting to kill me. And that I have to go through this torture every three months! I know I should be grateful that these tests even exist but I still want to punch something very hard until my knuckles bleed.

I leave Bones's office with a prescription for the Tamoxifen Russian Roulette Regimen. I have chosen Christmas to begin because Jayne and her family will be with me so if I choke or die from immediate drug-induced consequences, I won't be alone. I am legitimately nervous. I am trying to squeeze as much positive energy as I can into these new developments telling myself that it will keep me alive long enough to have a second shot at a life. It might mess with my chi, but at least there will be chi to mess with.

A new sticky goes up in kitchen: "The only side effect of fighting for recovery is becoming happier." Please, please let that be true.

DECEMBER 1

On the bright side, just before Thanksgiving weekend, I received a call from one of my work colleagues in the UK who was lamenting the sorry state of sales recruiting in the EU and politely inquiring, *would I consider coming to visit the London and Paris offices* to help her make the case for adding more recruiting resources and investment to the global budget. I am not making this up. Apparently the same quandary I was supposed to look into back in January on my rather dramatically cancelled trip was still lingering eleven months later and causing executive consternation that was rolling downhill, gathering steam and headed straight for her.

"Well, I don't know," I said with a tone that was supposed to sound put-upon rather than jumping out of my fucking skin with excitement, " I'd have to check with Steve..."

"Right, I spoke with him already, Jude, and he thought it was a splendid idea. You can come out to the Manchester office and then we'll scoot you off to Paris to meet with the sales leadership there. I really think this will help." And she went on a bit about the failed strategies to date before saying just a little too cheerfully, "Plus, everyone would love to see you, you know! You gave us quite a scare there, Lovey. Feeling okay now?" As if I had the flu.

"Uh, sorry." I've only met this woman once and I didn't even think she liked me very much. "Feeling pretty good, yes." No point in dredging up the laundry list of after effects from the chemo.

"Well, we're just delighted to have you back. Now, get on the phone with travel..."

"Wait, when would you want me to be there?"

"First week of December? We have all the sales guys in that week into the next. Can you pull it together by then?"

I was sitting in my office looking at the same white board I had thrown random unsecured objects against almost a year ago, when involuntarily the most shallow (yet stylish) part of my brain, the one that still purchases and reads Fall *Vogue* every year, envisioned the shoes I bought at Shoe La-La last December sitting boxed in my closet like some sorrowful shrine to Things That Might Have Been; never worn, but dare I say, tailor-made for Paris. I flushed with girlish anticipation. I can finally take the trip I planned lo, those many months ago, and be in Europe *by myself*, on the company's dime, with kick-ass pumps. How incredible is that?

"You know," I continued, forcing my bored-work-monotone, "I'm looking at my calendar (that had absolutely nothing on it) and it looks like that *should* work...."

"Grand! Oh, I knew we could count on you, Jude. Just let us know when your travel is booked and we'll set up your meetings for you. Excellent."

Professionally close call. Hung up. Jumped up and down in office. Shouted with glee.

"Boss, everything okay in there?" queried Hideaki, who had learned to question me rather than allow me to emote unsupervised.

"Oh yesssss!" I yelled back. Then I stuck my head out of my office and whispered to him a tad more discreetly, "Just a little trip to London and Paris in two weeks for the EU sales team, *merci beaucoup.* "

"Ah. Madam, may I stow away in your suitcase, *s'il vous plaît?*"
"*Parlez-vous français?*"
"Nope. Japanese."
"Next trip."

Packing for a business trip has never been so exciting. Europe is much more formal than our offices in the US so Jodi and I went sale-only shopping last week and I loaded up on gorgeous skirts and feminine looking dresses, therefore everything going into my suitcase this morning is NEW. And I am starting to feel just a little bit of my female-ness returning ever so slowly. My hair is thickening a bit and curling like mad. It is looking less like a furry helmet and more like it could actually be a style of some sort. A car is picking me up at 4 am tomorrow for a flight from JFK to Heathrow. I have a very ambitious trip planned with just a wee bit of down time in the City of Light, but it will be more than enough for me. The only nagging reservations I have in the back of my head, other than being eight hours away from my parents are: will I have enough energy reserves for the jet lag, and that pesky, terrifying specter of lymphedema. Two very long plane rides with shorter hops in between and a ton of meetings is beginning to sound stupid and risky but I immediately push it down and lock it into the place where I compartmentalize things such as how hot dogs are made. Yes, it's gross and scary but if I choose not to eat hot dogs I can sidestep the revulsion. This is how I decide I'm going to battle back these fears today: by selecting not to digest them.

The phone rings as I'm painstakingly pouring toiletries into three-ounce containers. It is Lillian August: my furniture is in! They've got it on the truck from the warehouse in Norwalk and they can deliver today. I look around the house I have strewn with clothes, shoes and scarves and remember I'm also supposed to be attending A Gala Art Exhibit tonight with Jay and his wife Michelle to benefit the Mark Twain Library. Holy crap. How am I going to manage this? There's too much to do. Martha Stewart would have it under control of course but she has a fucking staff and probably doesn't even have to wait five minutes for furniture with her name on it. The good people from Lillian August are patiently waiting for an answer while I work this through. Everything is good, right? None of these events involve injections or pain. These are more building blocks to my Life Reassembly Plan: travel, old friends, supporting the arts, a place to entertain, a place to sit in my living room that doesn't smell like dog. Okay, this all makes perfect sense now and almost seems serendipitous. My beautiful new furniture is coming just in time so it will be here waiting for me when I return from Europe. I like this now. I calmly tell the delivery team that they can come by anytime before five today. I'm leaving at 6 pm to go to the art show at the library and at 4 am tomorrow for the airport. I'm crazy-excited but I'm already kind of tired so I decide that I need to sit on my yoga mat and just breathe to collect some energy from the universe. But that doesn't work, so I call Kim.

"Omigod, my furniture is coming today!"

"Really? Fantastic...I thought you were leaving..."

"That's tomorrow morning. O-dark-hundred. Tonight I'm going to the Gala with Jay and Michelle."

"Well, look at you."

"I KNOW."

"Who's got Sophie?"

"Her vet's assistant is staying here...I will tell her not to let her on the furniture. Promise."

"How do you feel? Are you okay?"

"Like I'm fifteen and going to the prom with a hot senior." I do not tell her I am waiting to hear back from Bones's office about my blood tests.

"But are you feeling up to all this?"

"I don't care if I'm not. I will make myself be up for it."

"Don't over-do it. Bring your Xanax on the plane."

"Yes, Mother."

"...and your fancy shoes."

"Already packed, still have the little shoe-trees in them."

"Oh, my god, those fucking shoes. Remember when you were crying over not being able to wear them because you had breast cancer? Do you recall that insanity?"

"I wish you were coming with me."

"Me, too. We'll do another trip; one where we don't have to squeeze in any work. Just you and me and the open road."

"Sounds like a plan, Thelma."

"Tell Paris I said bonjour."

"Kim, if anything happens to me..."

"SHUT. UP."

"K. Ciao."

The annual Mark Twain Library Art Show is *the* event for Reddingites. I had never been because of the hefty admission price just before the holidays, but had always wanted to attend since I moved into this town. It's a wonderful opportunity to see local and national artists' work displayed and for sale throughout the library which Mark Twain funded and built in memory of his beloved daughter, Jean. Some of his books are here. It's the closest thing to a church for writers and Twainiacs in the area, rivaled only by his Hartford homestead an hour away. Attendees dress in their holiday finery for this affair so I re-worked Jodi's spandex number from Tony's wedding with rhinestone everything and, when Jay and Michelle arrived to pick me up, teetered out the door on the only heels that weren't packed for my trip.

The leaves were all down and we had yet to see snow this season but it was coming. I could feel it. I looked up into the clear night sky before getting in their car and it was so bright with stars it looked counterfeit, computer generated, like the pre-show at the Hayden Planetarium. We are far enough from a big city so we don't have any ambient light to encroach on our ability to see stars and tonight they are dazzling, as if heaven decorated itself for Christmas.

I walked into the event with my neighborly escorts; we were all dressed to the nines. They were very attentively looking after me like some friend-parent hybrid unit but I didn't mind. It made me feel protected. They were both full of advice and mischievous fun, as always. The library had been absolutely transformed. Wait-staff walked around with appetizers and champagne and there was so much artwork it looked as if a museum, a bookstore, and a white-tablecloth restaurant all happily collided for our benefit. It was twelve degrees Fahrenheit outside, a freezing cold night by anyone's standards but some of the younger Redding women were showing some skin while others were strictly L.L.Bean, right down to their duck boots. I might've been a tad overdressed but I didn't really give a shit. It was all very magic. I separated from my escorts to give them space and be on my own to wander dreamily from one piece to another, hoping I would find one that I loved and could afford to support the cause.

One of the participating artists was the wife of my ex's best friend. She saw me but made subtle efforts to avoid making eye contact. At one time she and I were quite close—like spend Christmas Eve with her family and sing around the piano close—but she'd moved quickly and decisively to the groom's side of the courtroom shortly after the divorce. I miss her. And I have always liked her. But I didn't ever have hopes of trusting her again. When we happened to make eye contact later in the evening and further into the champagne, she realized she had no choice but to acknowledge me amongst the thinning crowd.

"Oh, hi, I didn't know you were here, Jude!" First lie accompanied by fake smile.

"Hello there."

"Sooo…" awkward pause, eyes darting around room looking for a way out, "how've you been? You look great!"

"I'm really fine. Nice to see you as well. What a wonderful event." And I was going to keep it very short and impersonal but then she stepped in it.

"Yes, yes! Always a nice evening." Concerned face accompanied by second lie. "You know, I've been *meaning* to call you…"

"Oh? You know, that's okay. I've been pretty busy." But that's as far as I was going to save her now.

"Yes, well, you know how it is, the holidays and everything…" Now she's given up completely on looking me in the eyes.

"Hmm. Yes, I do. Please tell everyone I said hello, Mike, the kids."

"Oh, sure, sure. Will do."

"Merry Christmas, friend." I reached out and gave her a kiss on the cheek and she looked frightened and pained. Eleven months ago, my divorce and disease disrupted the lovely order of things for her. I suspect she and her husband had intended to erase me entirely, now that my ex was safely ensconced in his relationship, and that kiss just broke the force field that had been protecting her conscience all this time.

I walked away without saying another word, mentally closing the chapter on our friendship. I told myself I simply did not have room in my life for her anymore, quite certain that she reached the same conclusion about me long ago. I wandered the shelves of books and randomly hung paintings and came upon something perched on a music stand that was so lovely and petite and thank god, affordable, I purchased it without hesitation.

At dinner after the art show, Jay and Michelle and I laughed about the evening, our neighbors, some harmless gossip, the upcoming holidays and, of course, my trip that was to begin in just a few hours. We got tipsy and made plans to be in each other's lives more. I had the same feeling wash over me as I did with Tony and my Priceline posse; these are the people I must invest in. They have been true friends. They did not avert their eyes.

I showed them the painting I bought and Jay said, "Love it, Jude. It totally belongs in your house." He then ordered a very special French chardonnay that under other circumstances would have been quite exciting but I knew its gifts would be wasted on me. I didn't want to be impolite as Jay was waxing poetic about the vintage, so I took a sip expecting to taste chilled liquid metal when something miraculous happened. I tasted *grapes*. It was not a superb taste though because it had been so long since I had a glass of wine that it came across as slightly sour, almost bitter. But it sat there on my tongue for a moment making itself at home and gently invited me to sip again. Oh, it became more luxurious with every mouthful, every swirl of the glass! If that were not enough I looked out the window of Clemens, our restaurant that is also named for Mr. Twain, and it was gently snowing. Where did these snow clouds come from? It was clear just hours ago. I had to catch myself to make sure I wasn't time-channeled into a Frank Capra movie. Christmas miracles were everywhere.

When I got home that night I walked in the door, kicked off my heels and padded into the living room, having forgotten that a room full of furniture had arrived earlier in the day. I propped up my gorgeous little painting on the mantle of the fireplace and admired it amidst the brand new atmosphere for a few precious minutes before going to bed. My house was becoming my home.

I am building a life. I can taste wine! And I am just as excited to leave for Europe as I am about coming back.

I turn off the lights and go to sleep full of pride for my latest acquisition. It is a watercolor of a tree; a single, strong, bountiful tree in a meadow, held by a thick, black, sturdy wooden frame.

DECEMBER 10

Arrived back home at seven p.m. Checked my voicemail as soon as I got to JFK and there was a message from Bones himself, telling me that everything looked good in my blood test and to have a great holiday. I breathed an audible sigh of relief and chatted up my driver on the long drive home with an enthusiasm that can only come with hearing that you're free and clear to live without worry—at least for the next three months.

I very fortunately traveled with a colleague named Beth who is a dear friend and a fantastic companion, plus she had never been to Europe. So after our tour of duty in London—where I finally got to wear my utterly fantastic black pumps to much applause—I got to play beret-wearing, scarf-tying tour guide in Paris and show off my favorite haunts: the Left Bank, the Musée d'Orsay, the Champs-Élysées and all the other touristy and dreamy sights in Paris that make you wonder why we all weren't born French. Life would be so much prettier.

Beth and I stopped for a hot chocolate at a tiny café and sat outside under the heat lamps to people-watch, Parisian style, when out of the blue she asked me if I was happy. I didn't hesitate for a second before answering yes. She smiled and said that for some reason I seemed happier now than I have ever been and considering my recent life events, wondered why. She has worked with me for seven years and to her eternal credit, came to visit me after the mastectomy all the way from Texas. I remember her sitting in my living room at Green Acres with my mother pushing tea and cookies on her, and the honest look of fright on her face whenever the word cancer was uttered.

"Beth, I'm sitting at a café in Paris weeks before Christmas after shopping and sightseeing with my friend on a trip I did not have to pay for. I believe that qualifies for pure, unbridled joy."

"I was so worried about you..."

"I worry every day. But this, right here and now, is a perfect example of why I need to worry less and focus on staying healthy—body and mind."

"So you can travel?"

"So I can drink liquid chocolate on the Left Bank and know it's still not as important as the simple and luxurious gifts we take for granted every day."

"Like the new boots you just bought?"

"Exactly."

Beth and I comfortably meandered through topics large and small on our whirlwind Parisian tour, and she even allowed me the indulgence of a heartfelt reminiscence about David, although politely steered me back to our plans for the holidays so I didn't veer too far off into the Depressing Lane. I was beginning to get excited about entertaining on Christmas Day because I've never done it by myself before in my entire adult life, so she was providing wonderful coaching tips, having raised a houseful of hungry boys. Beth also recognized that I had not talked about my divorce very much and deftly forced a good, balanced conversation out of me that was long overdue. Good friends, friends who push on you with just the right amount of pressure to penetrate the bullshit layer, are pure gold to me. I thanked her again and again for being one of mine.

Being in such a magical place so far from home truly transported my soul and held it aloft, high above the fears that were always looming, waiting for an opening so they could smother out the joy. It was well worth risking the myriad things that could have gone wrong. But the phone call from Bones was the icing on the croissant. *Magnifique*.

DECEMBER 13

David has been gone for three years today. It doesn't seem possible. He is not fading, he is not ghostly. He is still smiling and telling jokes, tucked away in the hollow of my heart alongside a warm and sorrowful ache to someday hear his voice again. I miss him every day. I stop to wonder if I had died—if the surgery went south or the cancer gained momentum—might there have been someone, some friend dragging my memory around three years later, crying and thrashing a perfectly good pillow? And would they still be hoping it was all a big mistake and I was really hiding on an island somewhere, waiting to sneak back in to the country with tales of intrigue? Because I'm sitting alone in my kitchen tonight carrying a torch a big as Lady Liberty's for a friend I still cannot believe is dead. He must be here somewhere. When does this go away?

DECEMBER 25

I have been preparing the house and working on the menu with a surprising merriment that I never feel at the holidays. It escapes me. I am not a Christmas Bunny who hoards things red and green all year waiting for the big day; I don't believe in the notion of a virgin birth and honestly despise the shopping, not because I don't like buying things for friends and family, but I dislike that this forced expectation gets confused with actual giving. Plus, I detest Christmas music in all forms with the possible exception of "The Nutcracker." I have been known to run out of stores yelling harsh things with my hands clasped over my ears when songs like Dolly Parton's "Jingle Bell Rock" or its mutant cousin, "The Chipmunk Song" comes tearing at my eardrums. Or when one of the many female octave-jumpers tragically and ironically *screams out* "Silent Night" with vocal riffs apparently only dogs and I can hear. It's enough to make you want to run away and curl up to sleep in a manger until January.

But this year I have a chance to spend time with my family on my own terms, in my own house, play whatever music I want and what's more: *I like them.* We make each other laugh. And now I know that, no matter what, we have each other's backs. What could be better?

I don't have a tree but there are plenty of options outside. I string up white lights in the Russian olive tree just outside the big window facing the circular garden so you can see it from the house. Gifts are wrapped; house is clean, food is prepped, wine is chilled, and I'm exhausted. I hope I can fight off the evening fatigue until after dinner. I call Kim and let her know I wish she could be here.

"Merry Christmas, Howard." I've taken to calling her by her last name and she has selected a nickname for me in response.

"Hey, Booty."

"All set for your family extravaganza today?"

"Oh my, yes. It's always a Very Howard Christmas at my mom's house. She's been planning since July."

"Give everyone my love. We'll get together after the families disperse."

"Quite a year, kid."

"And it's almost over, thank god! Please let us get through it without any more drama, shall we?"

"My thoughts exactly. Tell Jayne and the crew I said hello. And have yourself a blast. You deserve it."

"I would not be here without you. You know that."

"Nope, we were partners—or it never would have worked."

"Love you."

"You, too."

As I'm getting myself ready before everyone arrives, I look at the bottle of Tamoxifen that's been sitting on the bathroom counter for days. What am I doing? Do I really need more drugs in my system? I'm still dealing with the after-effects of the chemo. There is a ten-minute-long fiery debate in my head while I stand motionless staring at this ominous-looking bottle until I hear tires in the gravel driveway outside. I take one out of the bottle and wash it down with cranberry juice, cringing, as if there might be some immediate and horrible reaction right after I swallow. Nothing happens. I look in the mirror and say out loud, "Just work. That's all I ask. Don't mess me up and do your job. Keep it from coming back."

There is a knock on the door and they let themselves in en masse. Merry Christmas to us. Everyone.

DECEMBER 26

Morning. Head very large. George poured some special concoction after Christmas dinner last night that may have had rocket fuel in it because I believe I traveled to the moon and back. Dinner would have been a big hit except for the fact that Maggie and Mac won't eat anything that's not chicken fingers or hot dogs and I served neither so they rolled their eyes and picked at their food for an hour waiting for dessert; the heaters out on the porch dining area weren't strong enough to keep us warm so we ate in our fleece jackets and scarves; the sauce for the ham I burned for them congealed into a single mass the consistency of toothpaste; and the wood in the fireplace wasn't fully seasoned so the house filled with a thick smoke that forced us to open windows on a twenty degree December night. The Georgio cocktail du jour really hit the spot.

But it was morning now and we all had to get ourselves pressed and dressed and drive to Jodi's over an hour away for the Official Family Gift Exchange and Fattening Food & Sugar Marathon. My tiny house was overrun with suitcases, dogs, wrapping paper, boxes, gifts, and the chaotic noise of five people fighting over two bathrooms. Breakfast was a blur and we made it out the door leaving the canines, Rudy and Sophie, to enjoy some peace and quiet, and the mess we left behind.

Everyone is here at Jodi's with the exception of Vic's boys and, despite all the loud overlapping conversations and routine background chatter, there is an undeniably heightened awareness that in this room are several people whose illnesses make them appear more ethereal. After our first round of holiday cocktails, there is decidedly more hugging and hands resting on shoulders and around waists. We are laughing louder and surprisingly not taking any pictures. Mom is looking strong—albeit thinner—but she is anxious and overly doting on my father. Dad is very thin now and stays seated most of the day. His speech is still a mixture of actual words peppered with fragments and sounds that are meaningless to an outside observer; but we can read his intentions and inflections well enough to understand most of it and keep him involved in the conversations with some gentle coaxing support.

Jodi is doing her time-honored hostess thing and making sure a sweet compliment or funny remark is extended to each one of her guests. The rest of us are in various stages of nursing hangovers, recovering from long drives, mixing drinks, or trying to find a place to sit near the food.

"Crab dip!" I swoon, excited to see something warm and not covered in salt or sugar on the hors d'oeuvres table.

"Don't act surprised—she makes it every year," intones Jayne.

"Yes, but it's good every year."

"Thank you!" yells Jodi from across the noisy room. "Tell Jayne I can hear her."

To an outsider it's a normal, casually dressed, loud, suburban Christmas tableau with bad holiday music in the background and kids running around showing off their loot from yesterday; to me it is an everyday miracle. I am smiling and drinking in all the tradition that I used to scoff at because for the first time in my life it feels comforting and necessary and kind of fun. The gift exchange portion of the day is progressing as it has since I was five, including furtively darting my eyes over to Dad wondering what he is thinking and listening to my mother scold people for opening their gifts before the last person has finished with theirs. Jodi is my Secret Santa this year and she hands me a box with pink wrapping paper which I think is odd for Christmas but it looked very pretty. Inside was a box full of breast cancer swag for the walk including Komen 3-Day shirt, baseball cap, and pin that all say "Survivor." It's a thoughtful gift from a thoughtful person and I was in the process of saying thank you to her when suddenly the significance of that word made delayed contact with my brain, exploding on impact, so I could not complete the sentence before I started bawling; large embarrassing Christmas tears. Lo and behold, I am a Survivor.

JANUARY 6, 2007

It was dawning on me that being single, I did not have to endure the comments, criticism, or scheduling conflicts of another human. It was also dawning on me that I had always wanted to belly dance. Julie told me she used to belly dance and was quite good at it, so it had been on my Highly Competitive Personal Checklist ever since. I searched online and found a class that is the next town over and only $13.00 for an hour. How bad could it be?

The act of walking out of my house into the unknown world of belly-dancing, knowing I did not have to tell anyone how it went, *even if I totally fucked up*, was exhilarating. The class was in a yoga studio so they're very Zen about it, burning incense and low-talking. There were ten other women of all ages attaching colorful and noisy jingly-jangly belts to their midsections, which ranged in size from teeny to gigantic. I was the only new student.

I suddenly felt as if I had a grotesque goiter on my neck that was repelling these women from me. The music was some mashed-up version of salsa, Euro-pop, and Middle Eastern funk—if there is such a thing—and our teacher was, I'm guessing, a Cirque de Soleil alum because she appeared to have no spine or connective tissue whatsoever. She was Gumby. And I am an old, middle-aged woman with bad memories of hula-hoop humiliations engulfing my brain. The messages to my hips and ass—to gyrate and shake to the music as if attached to a colossal vibrator—are flatly ignored. The noise from the belt was giving me a tension headache. *Why am I here? What was I thinking?* At the end of class we assumed a meditation pose to reflect on our hour of dance and contemplate our complete waste of $13 when Gumby solemnly distributed—I am not making this up—weird tarot cards to each woman lying prone, sweating, and completely out of breath on the floor. We were told that she passed them out randomly but that some larger, Jiggling Belly Dance Spirit would direct her to give the right card to the right person and she hoped that it told us something; sent a message.

Other people were *ooh*ing and *ahh*ing over their messages from Gumby and sharing their results as if it represented some divine guidance. Mine had a picture of a Prince holding an apple and told me that it was time to "Take a Lover." I believe my laughter was heard in the next county.

JANUARY 9

Today was the beginning of the anniversaries. In the past I never understood how people could get so worked up and sentimental over recognizing a particular date on the calendar every year, imparting to it such solemn reverence or inflated importance. It always felt forced and Hallmark-induced to me.

For years I observed my parents go into hyper-drive on their wedding anniversary: the formal dress, the sought after reservations at white-tablecloth establishments, the exchange of cards and flowers and gifts, the quest for sane babysitters; it often made me wonder why they just didn't behave that way all year long. Why were they suddenly more important to each other on June 7?

Or historical anniversaries, like when JFK was killed for instance, which I believe must have been the genesis of the phrase "game changer"—still stirred a wariness in me each November that I'd be asked to re-live, yet again, the horror I felt when at four years old Big Syl insisted I watch the black and white footage of the casket lying in state in the Rotunda for hours on end explaining this morbid assignment with the directive, "This is history you're watching, Judy Ann. No cartoons today," immediately followed by "no feet on the couch" as if Jackie herself would have judged me disrespectful and uncouth.

But I was learning that when the date you're commemorating represents the day your life changes forever—and not in a thrilling *married-the-love-of-your-life* kind of way, or a shocking *assassination-of-the-leader-of-the-free-world* way, but in a bracingly personal and intimate way—you must take notice. You have to honor the passage of time. I guess I can more readily associate September 11 in this way; everything before it was experienced through different eyes and in different skin. Fundamentally something changed. There is a bold line of demarcation, drawn with a thick black Sharpie across your chest and underneath in small print it reads: There is no going back.

One year ago today was the mammogram that started me on this journey, creating a terrifying parallel path to my divorce. One year. I find myself staring motionless at the calendar resting on the kitchen counter unwilling to throw it out in favor of this newer, fancier 2007 model that is already filling up and vying for center stage. Every day of 2006 beginning with January 9, is burned in to my brain and carved on my soul, forever. I don't ever want to part with it; even the hardest dates, the times of excruciating loss, or the revelatory days uncovering my own embarrassing stupidity or emerging strength—I cannot simply discard these days like the used wrapping and boxes from Christmas. These months and weeks and black numbered squares kept me going; the plans I made or the ones made for me, were pure salvation because I needed to wake up every day to meet obligations, good or bad. I would sometimes jot in the most mundane chores just to create a tangible purpose for being awake and alive on that day.

I pour a glass of wine, sit on my new couch with Sophie at my feet, in my very quiet house, around the corner from my best friend, on a freezing cold New England night, and read through every anniversary, every last date from 2006; each person, every appointment, every inglorious or triumphant moment I had the privilege of living. My hand reaches up to the center of my chest and I spread my fingers out wide, across both my breasts, as if to hold on to my heart; hold it in place, while I allow myself to remember.

JANUARY 21

I don't believe that under normal, pre-cancer circumstances, this foursome would have assembled for a vacation *anywhere*, much less in sunny Cancun, Mexico, at the all-inclusive Aventura Spa Palace. If Jayne and Jodi had not had a crisis-filled year that had taken them away on other occasions so that their families actually understood the concept of functioning without mom, and Julie had not become an honorary Sole Sister by virtue of her unfailing selflessness when my life imploded, I feel pretty certain that suggesting this trip to my sisters would have been met with a polite, "Mexico? Without the kids? Are you freakin' kidding me?" Julie, on the other hand, is always up for an adventure.

But the year progressed as it did and what started as a promise between Jayne and Jodi and me to take a trip to New York that didn't involve general anesthesia has grown into a gigantic all-inclusive vacation in a place where we need passports and a bed for Jules. We very much wanted Daryl and Kim to come but after they declined we decided that we were going to forge ahead and find a cheap place in the sun that would spoil us for a week so we could tan, drink, eat, and watch the boys go by. Nothing more. Plus,

Jayne's fiftieth birthday passed in November without too much fanfare or recognition because of the unparalleled family events in Boob-tober, so we really owed her a party. I ordered a car service to get us to JFK International Airport to begin our all-chick adventure.

After we arrived in Cancun and took the 45-minute taxi ride to Aventura, we were beyond tired. Jodi gets all kinds of cranky when she misses a meal and Jayne was physically fading and crazy worried that her luggage might not actually be "on the next plane" as promised by the pimply baggage dude, but rather, sitting on an abandoned baggage carousel in Bora Bora unceremoniously emptied of anything of value. When we pulled up to the place in a sweaty cab that stank of cigarettes, the travel drama immediately took a back-seat to the panoramic views of this gorgeous property; the sound and smells of the ocean and the enormous Vegas-worthy entryway welcomed us to our long-awaited holiday. Oversized gemstone-colored flowers, manicured pathways, and a bright orange sun that was just about to droop lazily in the dusky purple sky provided stunning views wherever we looked. We each breathed a sigh of relief and propped each other up for one last burst of energy so we could end the day on a high note.

This was quickly replaced by razor sharp disappointment, however, when the two rooms they tried to move us in to, were in a word, *appalling*, and nothing at all like the photographs we'd been dreaming about lo these many months. I should have guessed because as we were winding our way toward the building on our chauffeur-driven golf cart, I noticed that we were moving farther and farther away from the ocean and closer and closer to a behemoth crane ruining the landscape and standing guard over a new Aventura construction site. The rooms were on the lowest floor looking out over the volleyball pit filled with sweaty, margarita-fueled *turistas* reliving their high-school glory. Not only that, the rooms were just below ground level so we had to look *up* for this blubbery cellulite vista, which also completely blocked out anything resembling light or sky.

After one look at our subterranean rooms that were one small step above a college dormitory, miles from the water, I turned to the nice gentleman who escorted us there and politely, through slightly gritted teeth, told him to put our bags back, *por favor*, because we were not staying. "We explicitly ordered and paid for ocean-view rooms and did not travel all this way to sleep in the basement of a gymnasium."

Jayne and Jodi were doing the eye-roll and trying to calm me down. "It's okay Jude, we can *make do...*" which was really just their way of saying if they didn't get something to eat and drink soon, they were going to run me over with the golf cart. "Look, on the map here, it's just a short walk to the pool...really, it's fine!" Jodi said, dangerously past the point of low blood sugar.

"No. Not fine at all. Nowhere even close to fine."

So yes, just over three hours in the country and I made a scene. I hustled everyone back into the golf cart with all our bags and our weary, hungry bones and I walked up to the check-in desk that issued these hideous rooms to explain the obvious mistake, but the busy person behind the counter was firm: sorry, but there are no other rooms. I argued with him for ten minutes, in hushed tones but clearly letting him see my seething American anger until I finally wore him down. There were also now about twenty people on line behind me getting increasingly annoyed that they were not in their rooms yet drinking something tropical.

Out comes his manager in a fancy suit. In a smoother, more eloquent Ricardo Montelban-ish manner, the manager told me the same exact thing, adding that "there is no guarantee that these rooms will be available when you book so far in advance, *señora*."

So I asked to speak to his manager. Mr. Fancy Suit took haughty offense to the fact that I didn't buy his schtick, furrowed his brow to register his annoyance with me, then had the audacity to raise his voice as if scolding a child.

I gently took him aside and said in my best Shirley MacLaine, "Listen to me, I know for a fact you've got these rooms because I'm the one who booked them and we paid a premium for them. I don't know who's enjoying them now, but they'll have to leave or I will go knock on every ocean-view room and tell them what you're trying to do. Understand? I'm not backing down."

Dramatic pause.

"My sisters and I will have ocean-view rooms." This was enhanced by my ability to stare someone down without blinking.

Jayne and Jodi were at a side table positively crimson, pretending not to know me. They have seen me in action before—in hotels and doctor's offices—and understand that I am as stubborn as an ox and it's best just to give me room and let me make a jerk out of myself. They were also pissed, tired, hungry, and craving wine. Not a good combo.

After several tense *minutos* when I wondered if we were going to spend the evening in a Mexican prison for Smart-Mouthed Americans, out comes *his* manager from an area where I supposed they just lined up managers in order of importance waiting for cranky customer issues, but he was in an even *shinier* fancy suit wearing the pained and practiced smile of a mediator.

Manager *numero dos* was accompanied by a shapely young woman holding a tray of champagne and, much to my relief and delight, a book containing a floor plan of the available rooms at the Aventura Spa Palace, inquiring which ones me and my dear sisters would like to occupy for the next week.

I beckoned to Jayne and Jodi, hand them each a glass of bubbly, and announced, "Nicer rooms, comin' up!"

Julie arrived around nine p.m. after some travel nightmare with her connecting flight, Jayne's luggage finally arrived, unscathed, and we all convened in the room Jules and I were sharing. Miraculously, we now have rooms with lovely views, balconies, humongous Jacuzzis complete with hand-towel origami, and undulating, warm ocean breezes. Just like the pictures. We all lie about the room in various stages of joyful unwinding. Jayne's iPod is playing the Beatles and U2 in the background, wine is being poured, room service has been ordered, and the ritual recognition of the fancy pedicures and toe-rings is underway. We are all feeling very Samantha, Carrie, Charlotte, and Miranda at the moment and that's about as good as it gets after the year we've had. There is an excitement in the air coupled with relief that after five months of planning, anticipation, and fear of derailment, we actually pulled this off. We made it to *Mexico. Buenas noches, amigas.*

JANUARY 22

Up early and had a way-too-big breakfast. Something happens to perfectly normal-size brains and appetites when the signs say "all you can eat" or "all-inclusive" or "it's free so gorge yourself till you burst like a balloon." We are not big eaters by any stretch of the imagination but we made several trips to the egg bar, the bread table, and the fruit stations. Just because. However, if you asked Jayne she would justify it by saying, "I'm in training."

Wandering around the massive complex to get our bearings, we stopped in the tour office to make reservations for a bus trip to the ruins of Tulum. The tour operator looked at the four of us and said, "No esposos (husbands)?" Julie took the lead because her Spanish actually includes verbs and replied, to make things simpler, that we're sisters. To which he replied, as if the insult that we're traveling husbandless wasn't enough, "Sisters of Charity?"

After leaving the tour office on the way back to our rooms to get ready for the pool, Julie stopped at the walk-up bar and ordered a Margarita; rocks, no salt. It's ten a.m.

"Sisters of Charity, my ass."

JANUARY 23

Bus trip to Tulum. Interesting ruins but it rained the entire time we were at the site. And somehow, Jodi still managed to get sunburn.

JANUARY 24

This morning was sunrise yoga and our instructor, for whatever reason, kept calling for us to spiritually connect with the Earth Mother, which was a pleasant enough sentiment except she did not have verbal command of the "th" sound so we were chanting to the Earsh Maahsher for over an hour. I looked at Jayne after the third time she said it and we both had to bury our heads in our towels to keep from disturbing the chi of the rest of the class.

Our next adventure was a simple walk to the coffee bar near the yoga studio. Only it's closed. It's nine a.m. and the only way we got Julie to come with us to yoga, instead of staying cozy in her bed, was the promise of fresh-brewed caffeine afterwards. She had what can only be described as a meltdown.

"Ten o'clock? What kind of coffee place opens at ten? I mean, how hard is this? You have beans and you grind them and heat them with water...this takes until ten to prepare? Ten o'clock isn't even morning anymore. It's early friggin' afternoon, in my book. Is there a goddamned Starbucks around here for Pete's sake?!" It was not pretty. The Earth Mother was probably wincing but Jodi, Jayne, and I were screaming laughing. Who knew she was such a junkie?

The afternoon took us to the spa for something called hydrotherapy, where we huddled in a sauna, then jumped into a hot tub and then into the "freezing cold plunge pool" which to me sounded like torture and I was right. Except for the fact that afterwards my skin was tight and perfect and I was completely relaxed. Better than yoga.

We called Mom for her birthday, and all the kids, and had an amazing dinner at an Italian place killing several bottles of red grape juice. Omigod, can we just stay here?

JANUARY 25

Okay, I'm pretty sure this was not brought on by the plunge pool, but I started getting serious and regular hot flashes. I immediately blamed the Tamoxifen but Jayne assured me that it was probably normal and not to freak out. I didn't understand that when the searing heat comes from the inside and you feel as if your vital organs have erupted in flames, there is no escape. What an unsettling feeling. I tried to push it to the place where hot dogs are made.

While we were sitting around the pool today with our cocktails du jour, we started playing the game where you combine the name of your first pet and the first street you lived on to create your porn name. Mine was Tawny Catherwood, which sounded more like an accountant than a bodacious movie queen. This amused us for about an hour until we decided that because we have four names all beginning with J, we should select and vote on new party names for our vacation. Julie snapped up Samantha, and while she was perfectly content with her *Sex in the City* alter ego, that left Jayne, Jodi and me fighting over Carrie because none of us wanted to be Miranda or Charlotte, even though Jodi *is* Charlotte right down to the little pink plastic bows on her flip flops, and Jayne would give Miranda's dry barbs a run for their money; they just didn't scream PARTY. So, Jodi decided that she would be Amber (very porn-ish), Jayne picked Sophia, which was a sexy Italian and bold alternate ego for our resident brainiac, and I selected Ginger—after my wig, and of course, my childhood idol from Gilligan's Island with the perfect everything. It made for a more interesting afternoon. I think our combined egos were still in recovery from the Sisters of Charity comment and this helped us get back in the groove.

We each brought books for pool-side lounging but interestingly, Samantha, Amber, and I were all reading the same series, Janet Evanovich's Stephanie Plum novels. They are mindless, hilarious romps and perfect for the beach. We are each on a different number in the series so we're careful not to share spoilers but are giggling about our favorite characters, particularly the hot men. Sophia was reading a book about a war-torn village in Afghanistan. Enough said.

When we got back to our rooms to prepare for dinner, Julie was in a panic. She couldn't find her book. She and I turned the room upside down but it was nowhere to be found. I loved that this was the most upsetting event of the day and I watched her go just a little nutty over it.

"I mean, Jude, it was just at the point in the book where Stephanie and Morelli are going to...."

"I know. But they do that in every book. It's okay, we'll find it. All else fails, I can send you mine when I get home."

"Well, what if we don't find it? What will I read? I need that book!"

"Why don't you call Amber and Sophia and see if maybe they packed it in their beach bags by accident?"

"Oh, my god, you're right. That could be it!"

She was mildly frantic, so I dialed the number for her and handed her the phone. Then for some inexplicable reason when Jodi picked up, Julie blurted out, "Ladies, we have a situation!" and slammed the phone back down.

Now, it could be that my cousin spent a bit too much time watching "24" or other life or death CSI forensic cop-dramas, because a lost book doesn't really rise to the level of a Code Red. But by the look on her face, you would think that something, somewhere very near to us, was going to detonate if said book was not located, pronto.

The sisters came running into the room seconds later with rightfully concerned faces only to find me on the bed laughing to the point of snorting, "We have a situation?! What are you, the fucking FBI?"

"Oh, my god, what's going on?" demanded Jodi, the Clear-Headed.

"My book..." Julie had now dissolved into mild hysterics laughing at her own made-for-TV reaction and could no longer complete sentences.

"What book?!"

"...is missing. I think something's... happened to it."

"Jesus, like what? What could have possibly happened to your book other than you lost it?"

"Hey, Samantha, maybe it was kidnapped. Is she serious?" asked Jayne with half her hair curled, still holding Mr. Tool.

"Serious as church."

"So, this is just a Lost Book Situation?" queried Jodi.

Muffled gales of laughter from faces buried in pillows.

"Jesus," declared Jayne, "you made it sound like an Evacuation Situation—I thought the fucking building was on fire!"

"Maybe the maid took it..." squeaked Jodi who had now collapsed on the bed, still trying valiantly to make some logical sense of this.

"Now, why on earth—?"

"Wait for it...then it would be a Domestication Situation."

"Or at least an Investigation Situation."

"Sounds like somebody needs a Medication Situation. Can I please finish curling my hair now?"

And so on. At this point we were laughing so hard we were holding our bellies, weeping. It's not at all funny unless you were there to see the look on Julie's face when she realized her momentary insanity, but for the rest of the vacation, when we reminisced about every last detail of the trip, they all, of course, became Situations.

When we finally got to dinner, our makeup ran all over again as we embarked on our nightly Intoxication Situation.

JANUARY 26

> *"How are you feeling?"*
> *"Awesome, Jule. It's really so great to be here and —"*
> *"Okay, but in case you hadn't noticed, you're bleeding."*
> *"What? Where?"*
> *"Don't panic. On your chest."*
> *"Jesus, what the hell?" I take a look down my shirt and sure enough, one of those fancy sutures that was supposed to dissolve, decided to dislodge instead and is poking out of my fake boob accompanied by what looks to be real blood.*
> *"Shit, shit, shit."*
> *"Let me get a tweezer…"*
> *"To do what?!"*
> *"It's comin' out anyway, let's just help it along."*
> *"Okay. Give it to me. Bathroom surgery, Mexican style. Can you pour me a wine first?"*
> *"Comin' up."*
> *"Now we've got ourselves a Post-Operation Situation."*
> *"You did not just say that."*
> *"Oh, yes, I did."*

JANUARY 28

Hard to leave. We gathered up our belongings and said woeful good-byes to things like room service and balmy breezes, Jacuzzi tubs, and swim-up bars — and the totally relaxed and freckled faces that would be our temporary souvenirs from a glorious week in the sun. We asked a golf cart attendant to please take a picture of us before we boarded the limo to the airport and in it our smiles are broader and brighter than they have been in over a year. We had much to celebrate but didn't ever feel compelled to enumerate or toast or even talk about those things; we just showed up for a special once-in-a-lifetime trip and rolled with it. Adios Aventura. Ciao, Sisters of Charity. Always in my heart.

FEBRUARY 14

I don't even want to talk about it.

FEBRUARY 25

The freezing cold temperatures of the last few weeks persisted and the sun seldom visited for more than an hour or two. February in New England is all about staying warm and finding ways to amuse oneself indoors, wearing woolen socks and other unstylish L.L.Bean attire. If you are not a skier or someone who particularly enjoys the excitement of de-icing your car, there is really just not much to do. Nor is there anything pre-ordained to February, as there can be in other chilly months that fits the description of "fun." I mean, President's Day loses its luster after you stop eating paste in second grade. And there is no mercy to be had in that god-forsaken holiday known to some as Valentine's Day and to me as The Day the Surgery Didn't Work. I was still slightly tan from Mexico but there are only so many times I could look at the pictures before I started kicking myself for ever leaving the Aventura Spa Palace. I needed a diversion.

But the great news is I was finally feeling as if I might be able to rejoin a yoga class. My new Holly-boob was settling in and no longer hugely swollen although my left arm was still incredibly tight and sore; I couldn't straighten it over my head yet without it feeling as if I was pulling taut a rubber band at risk of snapping and breaking my shoulder. It has been like this for months. I didn't know what I'd been doing wrong but I decided to go back to yoga today. If I couldn't do all the poses, they would just have to deal with it. I also rather boldly decided that I was going to walk first.

Outdoors. In the COLD. I was desperate to start building some muscle mass (I'd become pure mush) and get out of the fucking house for something other than work. This was going to take some work. I couldn't do it just ambling around my tiny home wishing for it to be so.

It is easily in the fifteen degree range today which is an improvement over the last few weeks so I put on all the clothes in my closet for warmth and my Sorel snow boots that I believe were invented for NASA lunar missions. I can move my limbs in a swaying motion but not actually bend them in any way, so I'm maneuvering as if in a body cast. I have also packed a bag for Bikram yoga so that after I completely torture myself on the Loop, I will drive forty minutes to practice doing the weird bendy thing in a room heated to 105 degrees. I have cleverly convinced myself that it will be my reward: non-stop warmth once I get through this obstacle course of freezing pain. I have put a generous dollop of Vaseline on my lips and the apples of my cheeks so they don't chap and pull my knit cap down right to my aviator shades so I have the distinct look of an over-stuffed ventriloquist's dummy. Please don't let me see anyone I know, or slip on the ice, or die in this outfit.

Sweet Jesus in heaven it's cold. Everything in the landscape is covered with snow and ice and there is a nasty wind swirling and darting around the tops of the trees and swooping down on me every few minutes. There is not a soul on the road. No one is driving or loopy enough to be out for a stroll, like the Current Resident of Green Acres. My eyes naturally go to the lights on in the houses and I imagine warm, central casting family scenes; something cooking on the stove, mundane February conversation around a warm fireplace, a gentle laugh track, a nuclear family where everyone is growing and no one is dying. I start singing to myself and it sounds very loud because my wool hat is holding the sound next to my ears; like a breathy soundtrack to this slow-moving film about my neighbors. Not even the horse is in the field today. I hope she is under a warm blanket eating hay and watching Mr. Ed re-runs.

I made it back to the house, uncomfortably numb in a few toes and fingertips. My bag was already packed for yoga but I wondered if I was overdoing it. Should I have told anyone I was doing my own Iron Man today? The car was slow to start and I went easy on the roads. By the time I got to the yoga class my digits were back but stinging a bit and I was longing for the wet heat of the yoga studio. I stripped off all nineteen layers of clothes down to gym shorts and a tank top and walked barefoot into the completely mirrored studio. The last time I saw my body in a full length mirror in this outfit I had a left breast. And a rocking body. Now I had a too-round lump of obvious silicone. I stood at attention with all the other students. The teacher came in and began our series.

I can't look at myself without filling up and crying. This is harder than I thought. I want to put all those ugly clothes back on and melt into the mat. I will never look like I did, ever again. I have no muscle tone; the skin on my arms and legs is sagging and I can't even do basic poses without cringing. I keep pushing and sweating and trying to move my thoughts to something else. Something not so finite. Nothing comes. During Srivasana, or Dead Body Pose, I suddenly realize that my real boob flattens out when I'm on my back and the fake one stands at attention. I curl up into fetal position and give up all hope of a peaceful meditation.

I treated myself to a long hot bath. My muscles were in upheaval and my heart was in a civil war between completely opposite emotions: pride for walking through the frozen tundra and shame at my ego-filled childishness in yoga. I lit a candle and did my best to work it through. The home phone rang at nine p.m. It was Steve.

"Jude? Sorry to call you so late."

"No problem. Everything okay?"

"Well, it depends on how you look at it."

"Please no bad news. I forbid it."

"It's still very confidential, but I need you to be in the know. We're selling the company. To Oracle. We'll probably close the deal by June."

"Holy shit."

"Yes, well. My thoughts exactly. Which is why I'm calling you at this late hour."

"Will I have a job?"

"Don't know yet, kiddo. There is a lot to do before we get there. And I'll need you on the integration team. But I doubt they will keep many HR people. My guess would be—make a plan for no."

"Because I haven't had enough disruption in my life, I now need a new job?"

"Look on the bright side."

"Looking, but not seeing..."

"Larry is buying us at bust-out retail. And your stock will automatically vest."

"Which means very little to me, since I sold most of it to pay off the ex and keep my house, but I appreciate your optimism." I do a quick calculation of how very rich my colleagues will be from this deal which I will walk away from almost empty-handed. I try to be happy for them but it's not working.

"Relax, you'll be fine. Look at what you've been through already; this is a blip. Trust me." The tectonic plates are shifting again. I know this is very hot information so I can't share it with anyone unless they are "in the know." It really is a curse to be in HR sometimes. I want to talk more about it to Steve, but the tone of his voice tells me he's wrapping up the call.

"Just let me know what you need me to do, boss."

"I need you to not worry too much about this. But do what you need to do to protect yourself. That's all the advice I can give you."

"Is Kim in the know?"

"Not yet. The news will cascade over the next few weeks. Just hang in there."

"I am really beginning to hate that expression."

MARCH 3

I've been working long hours on the acquisition, training when I can, visiting my parents, making doctors' appointments, working on the house, revving up my network to find a job, and trying to get my body to do things it used to do. The Tamoxifen is causing some annoying issues like joint stiffness and pain and hot flashes, but the biggest side effects are still from the chemo: fatigue, short-term memory loss, and word retrieval. I still can't sleep on my left side and I can't find bras that make sense so I just stopped wearing them and bought a bunch of spandex camisoles with elastic shelves in them. I am not accustomed to any of it and hopefully never will be, but I make efforts not to bitch about it or whine openly in public; and I try to share only new developments with Kim.

I waited for the results of my latest blood work from Bones and started to wonder if I was deserving of more good luck or if I was going to join the ranks of the women on breastcancer.org who did everything right and followed the rules and it still came back. I can't help myself but after a doctor visit, when I'm reminded that I am now and will always be in the sick camp, I allow myself to read the posts of Stage IV terminal women. I read and cry and pray. And force myself to stop after a time.

> *I know I shouldn't linger there, but I'd be horribly remiss if I didn't pay my respects. I send pithy worthless comments into cyberspace for dying women and hope it does something other than help me absolve myself of survivor guilt.*
>
> *Today I am writing a fundraising letter to raise money for the 3-Day and it's suddenly daunting. How can I possibly ask the people who have been so kind and generous with their time to now give me cash to support a finding a cure for breast cancer? I draft the letter about ten times asking myself if it's too self-serving, or too serious; not personal enough or over-the-top "too much information." Then I read my sisters' messages on their personal fundraising web pages, and the pages of new Sole Sisters they have recruited to join our team, and reflect on my cyber sisters who are discussing re-drafting their wills and remember that this is not about me, for god's sake. It's about taking steps, enough to get us sixty miles, to find a cure so that we can end this thing once and for all. But despite all the logic behind it, I am still weirdly private about this and vacillate for hours. It's like admitting to this very large distribution list that I have cancer and am missing a breast even though they probably already know. Plus, there's Big Syl in the mix and I can't write a letter without explaining that my own*

mother is also affected. Nor can I ignore my inspirations for this incredible undertaking: The Sole Sisters in all their unselfish pinkness. This has got to be personal. And it's got to be real.

I hit the send button and feel as if I just dove off a cliff. My Inner Circle and large outer circle just got a note in their inbox asking them to help me reach my goal of raising $2,200.00, the minimum amount I need to raise to walk sixty miles in August.

My letter is long-winded and sentimental and jarringly personal. Jesus, who wrote this thing?

MARCH 15

One year since the divorce. One year. Sophie and I take some time today to remember good things about the time we had here with my ex and Louis. We sit next to the great room window of Green Acres staring out at the bare trees and cut ourselves some slack for feeling very sad. Not for letting go, but for still having a hole in our hearts where the love escaped.

MARCH 16

One year since my mastectomy. It's a crushing memory that seems to just be catching up to me. My real breast was replaced by this cold, hard imposter. The breast I still have is badly scarred and strangely tentative and out of place; it has no partner. I am out of balance, out of sync with this prosthetic that was supposed to make me feel less freakish. It does not. I am still in mourning over my once-beautiful body. But my harshest fear was now behind me. It is something to remember; to reflect upon. Nothing has replaced it other than fear of recurrence and whatever drama that would bring. On darker days I still cry about it. Mostly in the morning when I wake up and remember I'm deformed. This is one of those mornings.

But I checked today and the epic fundraising letter had done its job and then some. Donations starting pouring immediately, and not in $5 and $10 increments, but $100 and $200 and up, so I brazenly raised my goal to $5,000. I felt as if I was in a non-profit casino placing bets on people's generosity. At the same time, I was starting to get antsy about my job. There was now a rumored possibility that Oracle wanted to hire me but I got the underlying sense that it was a ploy so I would stay on board long enough to help close the deal. There was some financial reward for me staying but it wouldn't even scratch the surface of what I lost in the divorce. Plus, I just don't trust these people. I needed to actively look for a job now if I was going to sleep at night. I couldn't survive without good health insurance. I couldn't afford COBRA for very long, and I was alone with a monster-size mortgage.

The responses from headhunters and companies in my network were positive but from very far away: North Carolina, Boston, California and Texas. But then I remembered that anything is possible. I honestly didn't want to be that far from friends and family; my folks in particular—but that's what airplanes are for. And Skype. I didn't need to be in Redding, Connecticut. As much as I completely loved my house and the land, it's five acres and I'm one person. I began getting more serious about a possible move and set up interviews in Marin County, California, Boston and Raleigh, North Carolina. This cliff-diving was getting easier.

Oh, but could I ever really bring myself to leave?

APRIL 10

"Open your robe, please?"

"Yessir...how do I look?"

"Pretty great, actually. You heal fast. Do you mind if I manhandle you a little bit?"

"Do your thing, doc." McDreamy cups both my breasts to feel for lumps in the healthy one and how the implant is settling in.

"Well, it looks like this one is a little bit bigger than the good one...did you lose weight?"

"Four months of chemo ring any bells?"

"Oh, yeah, right." He then paused and stared at my breasts for what felt like an eternity, held them again with a troubled expression, looked up at me and said, "We'll make it work. Just decide which nipple procedure you want today and we'll get it done. You'll be good as new, Jude. Not perfect, but something pretty that you'll be happy with. I promise. I'll send my nurse in to review your options with you."

"Is everything okay? You look worried."

"Sure, sure. I just thought we had gone smaller with you. You'll gain some of that weight back though; it should be fine."

One of his nurses came in with the Big Laminated Nipple Book and pitched me like a diamond salesman. She started with the simplest, most affordable gems and then began teasing me with multi-faceted, bright, shiny nips, one of which could be all mine if I just wanted to be put under general anesthesia again and go through scarring and recovery time. At one point during her spiel when I was looking perplexed and overwhelmed by the pages and pages of headless pairs of boobs she regrettably said, "You know, this is the procedure I would choose if it were me. I would want to look and feel the most natural."

"Well, thank you, but you're not making this decision and I pray you never have to." I mean, really. We're not buying shoes here; I don't really care what you'd do.

Option one, and the easiest choice by far, was the tattooed-mama approach where during a routine office visit and without any anesthesia, McDreamy would tattoo me a new nipple; simple, easy, almost fun in a *well-this-is-different* kind of way. The pictures of the tats looked reasonable at first glance but upon further scrutiny looked flat, cartoonish, one-dimensional—poor excuses for nipples. It was as if someone took a pale rose Magic Marker and drew on a target. I guess it would be acceptable if I had two of them, but my fake nip will have a sister and I wanted it to look like it was part of the family. (It's ironic that for my entire life I have repeatedly said there were two things I would never do: 1. Plastic surgery, 2. Get a tattoo. Enough said. Things change.)

Option two was the Tweak and Tat, another in-office procedure whereby McDreamy would take some of the existing skin, stretch it and literally pull it up into a small clump to make a tip, sew it in place, again without any anesthesia, and then tattoo his handiwork after it heals, several weeks later. This made more sense to me and I almost jumped at that one, until Nipple Nurse dramatically turned the page to the Top-of-the-Line, Ultra-Deluxe Nipple Reconstruction Package.

Ta-daaaaa!! There it was. Looking like a nipple ought to look. Option Three was a skin graft that preceded the Tweak and Tat so that there was actual new skin forming the nipple and it was...*very*, very nice. This is what I needed, I told myself: something that came from another part of my body to restore the area that was now missing. It sounded très organic and naturale and circle of life-y to me. She called it "skin origami." On the flip side, it required another stay in the Big House as an outpatient because the skin would be grafted from the upper part of the inside of my thigh and it would require anesthesia and stitches. I quickly calculated that I could take a two-week break from training for the 3-Day and still be fine. Not crazy about more scars in new locations, but I was starting to become like those women who get hooked on plastic surgery and say, "What's one more?" And it looked absolutely perfect in the nipple book.

So I left his office that day excited about seeing the end of the tunnel. I called Kim to let her know we had a surgery date in May for my fancy nipple replacement. Only a best friend could muster a "Yippee" upon hearing this news.

APRIL 16

Sophie and I are jolted awake by the sound of a jet engine roaring in the back yard. It's four a.m. It has been raining hard for days. Last night was particularly balmy, filled with crackling thunder and heavy downpours that had my ferocious beast alternately diving under my pillow and climbing on my head throughout the evening. We race out the back door in the dark. The light sensors trip so that we can now easily see the source of all the noise. It's the river. Overnight while we were cozy in our bed, it surged, broke the banks and is rushing with a force that only whitewater rafters or weather forecasters can get excited about. The fire pit is submerged, as is most of my outdoor furniture, by a torrent that is rushing a mere twenty yards from the back door. It is loud and scary, a strangely magnificent show of strength but also capable of washing my house away if it continues on this path.

Green Acres is surrounded on three sides by the Saugatuck River but the danger is not in the back yard where it flows away from the house; it's in the front yard which is smack dab in the middle of a FEMA-recognized flood-way. I run into the house to grab a raincoat, rubber boots, and a flashlight. Sophie and I walk up the long driveway mucking through deep puddles and can hear the pounding of the water over the bridge that lies just to the right of the mailbox up at the roadside. As we get closer, I see—holy crap—the street is under water! The river swelled over the bridge and there is a steady flow coming straight down the incline of my gravel and dirt driveway cutting a big chasm into it and continuing on into the sodden meadow.

I am shining my flashlight around in the humid, rainy darkness and in each shaft of light I see water moving everywhere around me; rushing, raining, shimmering, pooling, rising, dripping. I am going to lose my house.

I splashed through growing puddles back down the driveway, with Sophie leading the way. We ran into the house dragging half the mud from the driveway with us. My heart palpitated as I thought through my options and grabbed some breakfast. *I may as well eat something while I still have power. And a kitchen.* I know I can't stop the rain or divert the water by myself so I called the town to see if they could bring some sandbags. No answer. No voicemail.

Fantastic.

I finished eating and began the work of putting all the chairs in my house upside down on tables; rolling up carpets and moving all my belongings that were on, or close to, the floor out of harm's way. I rearranged everything with the same precision and speed I mustered the day I decided my ex's things needed to be, henceforth, separate from mine. My house is on a slab, so there's no basement to worry about but if the water comes—it's coming right in the front door. I didn't want to lose everything. Let's be real, I didn't want to lose anything. These are my things. I had risked my financial security and sanity to hold on to this place; I finally had my own fucking couch; I couldn't watch it all just float downstream without a fight. It was now almost six and still pouring. The dawn had broken so there was misty, albeit ominous, light coming in through the big windows; I'm still in my pajamas with no clear plan: it's time to call in the Marines.

"Howard, look outside."

"Raining, yeah. It's also six a.m. You okay?" responded a groggy Kim.

"I am but Green Acres is under siege."

"What...*Oh, shit, the river!*"

"It's high, Kim; it's raging—like whitewater in my yard—and coming down the driveway; the pond is overflowing and meadow is flooding. I'm doomed."

"I bet you're getting all the snow melt runoff, too. Jeez, what are you gonna do?"

"I think I need to get the town to answer the goddamned phone and bring me some sandbags. If I can divert the water to keep it flowing down the road instead of down my driveway, the rest of it might be okay. It's supposed to stop raining by noon."

"A lot can happen by noon, Bootie. I'm comin' over."

"You won't get down the street, Kim; it's under a foot of water..."

"Big Blue will make it."

"Get here fast and be careful; it's not very safe."

Kim arrived in her trusty old, rusted, enormous blue SUV, parked just before the flooded bridge and walked, in her jammies, about forty yards in the rising water to the driveway. Sophie and I were drenched, waiting and watching her carefully traverse the path, sloshing along holding a coffee go-cup. I was now beginning to get scared. Not because I am currently starring in "Waterworld" but because Kim looks quietly freaked out. Considering all we've been through together, this is a not a good sign.

"Oh, my god, you weren't kidding. This is intense."

There is a long silent pause between us as we take it all in and consider that this could truly be a complete catastrophe and we may have finally hit the crisis-management wall doing eighty. "Thanks for coming," I said with the same intonation one would use at a funeral.

"Yeah. Wasn't expecting this...this is like...Holy shit, what if it keeps raining?"

"Then I'm truly fucked."

"In every way possible. Except the good way." She finally manages a smile and changes course. "Okay, Typhoid Mary, what's the plan?"

"Keep the water from coming down the driveway."

"Yep. We'll need sandbags."

"Tried that. Called the town and they weren't home. Then the fire department came by just before you got here and stopped just short of laughing at me when I asked them for some. They also suggested that I just get out while I can so I don't get stranded here. The last time this river surged like this people drowned. As in *died*."

"Not an option. Plan B?"

"Working on it; but I keep thinking if we move some of these smaller rocks from the stone wall, we can *maybe*..."

"You're in your pajamas. How about some clothes before you start moving rocks?"

"So are you!"

"These are *yoga pants*."

"Is my life ever going to stop being a non-stop drama?"

"Someday. Probably not today, but someday."

"I mean, really, what the fuck else can happen to me?"

"I think you need to stop asking that question because the universe always seems to have an answer for you." And with that she handed me her coffee and walked away trudging into the street which is now knee high with water and when she reached the other side which is an uninhabited and heavily wooded area, she rummaged around in the thicket and started back across dragging a long and heavy branch.

"*Howard, what are you doing?!*" I yelled over the sound of rushing water.

When she reached me at the driveway again, she said very matter-of-factly and slightly out of breath, "We're going to build a dam."

"With a stick?"

"With a lot of sticks. And rocks from your wall and logs from your pile of firewood."

"You sound very sure of yourself."

"I sail, Jude. I know water. We just need to convince it to go somewhere else. C'mon, help me get a few more long ones so we can get this thing started. Nobody's drowning today."

So we set about to carting firewood from the pond in the wheelbarrow, hauling sticks across the road through raging water, and taking the stone wall apart, rock by rock, in the rain, until we built a rather impressive, beaver-worthy dam. The water was still coming through in places but the majority of it was now moving down the road instead of toward my house. Sophie stands guard over the entire operation. Neighbors from down the road, none of whom had the same danger posed to their homes from the river as Green Acres did, stopped by lending moral support and dragging the occasional log. In just a few hours, we had it licked. The fire department finally came back with sandbags because they had some left over and remembered me standing alone and pathetic this morning. But by the time they arrived, we didn't need them. They were amazed at our ingenuity.

"Kimberly, I think we just saved my house."

"Damn straight, we did."

"Who needs boys, anyway?"

"Well, I wouldn't go that far..."

"Listen, we're both going to be out of jobs soon, so maybe we should start thinking about something we can do together, no?"

"The market for dam-building isn't what it used to be, kid."

"Then we need our own TV show or something."

"Something."

We surveyed our creation one more time, linked arms and walked back down to the house with Sophie, laughing, soaking wet, exhausted, and relieved beyond measure. The rain mercifully stopped. Another crisis is wrestled into submission. What a fucking team.

APRIL 25

Reconstruction finale pre-op appointment in New York: blood work, heart monitor, consent forms, yadda yadda. I was back in McDreamy's office for final instructions, but I didn't get to see him or his beautiful Middle Eastern smile. Instead, a new nurse, with a bag of stick-on fake nips that look like small, thin suction cups with rounded points on them, walked in without introducing herself and, in just under seven minutes, scared the living shit out of me.

"I want you to take two of these home and practice with them so you're sure of where you want your nipples to be before surgery next week. Bring them with you and the doctor will ask you to place them as markers. Do it with a bra on and off to see which you like better; symmetry with or without the bra. You can't have both."

"Um, okay. But why do I need two?"

"Didn't you have a bilateral?"

"No! It's only one."

"Oh, my mistake."

"Yes, and it's an absolutely ridiculous mistake to make! How many times have I been to this office? I do not care if you're new. Did you not read my chart before you came in here waving suction cups at me? It's not bad enough I'm having an actual conversation about where to put my nipple on my fake boob, but I have to endure your incompetence as well? You with your two perfectly good breasts staring me in the face, all high and mighty. Dear god, it's a simple thing: read the fucking chart."

This was my imaginary response. In reality, I just quietly stewed.

"You know you can't exercise for a few months after this, right?"

"Well, not heavy exercise, no, but the doctor said I could still do yoga after a few weeks and walking was perfectly okay. You know I'm training for a..."

"Well, no, actually, that's not correct. You'll have a big bandage and sore area on your thigh that you cannot get wet for days, and it will be moderately painful until it heals completely, so walking isn't recommended for some time. And you should not be doing yoga at all. Ever. Not with an implant."

"Excuse me?"

"You are potentially changing the shape of your muscle and can damage the implant and then it will need to be replaced," and then she looked over the top of her glasses with a withering I know-better-than-you glare, "no exercise that affects your pectorals, ever again. I'm surprised you didn't know that."

"*What?*! Wait a minute; the doctor said very clearly that yoga is great for me. What is this about not exercising my pecs? And why in heaven's name didn't anyone warn me about the pain and healing of the skin graft? I'm in training for a sixty-mile walk, for Christ's sake..."

"You can talk to him about it when you come back for your surgery, but I can assure you, it's what we tell all our patients. I can't understand why..."

"I'm not waiting. I want to speak with him now."

She was tired of my impertinence and looked away, shaking her head without answering me. There was a ball of self-pity swelling in my throat preventing me from speaking or even breathing properly for a few seconds, but I refused to let her see me cry. I managed to leak out the following words on tiny sips of air, "I will speak with the doctor...*now.*"

How can it be that the one thing I do for myself—the practice of yoga which heals my head and my body—is off limits forever? I am finally starting to feel well! Why the hell is this the first time I am hearing about not exercising my pectorals? How am I supposed to get strength back in this arm? What, I don't deserve to look good and feel good ...I have to choose?! How many more things to I have to give up for this fucking disease?! I have already made room for so many limitations. My breast is gone. My health is in question for the rest of my life. I still can't use my arm to lift anything. I am struggling to get my life and my body back, every goddamned day. When do I get some respite from this tragic obstacle course I'm on?

She reluctantly walked out and a few minutes later, McDreamy came in and found me sobbing. Large, hot elephant tears were searing raw channels into my cheeks and my nose was cranberry red; completely clogged. When the pitiful tears start, they don't simply acknowledge the personal crisis at hand and move on—they reach back deep into a well of hideous memories and gush like a fire hose.

"Oh, boy. What's wrong, Jude?"

I was positively out of control, having careened right off the personal dignity cliff and am actually spitting. "I can't believe it! Your nurse just told me I won't be able to walk...I am training for my...I *have* to walk! I promised so many people I will do it. I've raised like over $10,000.00! I promised my sisters, why didn't you ever tell me I can't do yoga anymore? I can't walk sixty miles without doing yoga. She said I can never exercise my pecs *again* or I have to replace my boob! I mean, do you just expect me to keep coming back every few years for a new one? How am I supposed to get use of my arm again? What is going on here?!"

"Hold on, hold on...Jude, wait a minute." He comes over to me and warmly puts the flat of his hand on my back and rubs lightly right between my shoulders. "Which nurse was this?"

"I don't know...*The old one!*" said the petulant child.

"One thing at a time." He pulls up his doctor stool so he's right below me looking up and trying to get a lock on my eyes, which are almost swollen shut. "Let's talk about the surgery first. I honestly don't think you should go through the skin graft, Jude. Now that I think about it, I can do something just as nice for you right here in the office—and quite frankly I'd rather not give you a scar on your leg on top of what you've already got. You're a young woman. A little tweak of the skin and a tattoo will look just fine."

"Really?"

"Yeah. No more scars for you. You've been through enough."

"Okay." My racing heart began to downshift.

"And another thing, c'mon, look at me. I don't subscribe to the notion that you should not exercise, or you would have heard that from me by now. I *love* that you do yoga—all my patients who do it swear by it and I don't mess with a good thing. It's your body—you know what works and what doesn't work."

"Oh, thank god. It's so important to me; I am finally starting to feel well, you know?!"

"All the more reason to give your body a break from anesthesia and surgery. We can do the simple procedure or just wait for a few months until after the walk and see how you feel. There's no reason to rush. I know you're in a hurry to get put back together, but you look great, Jude. Honestly."

"Ughh. I must look like a Cabbage Patch doll left out in the rain."

"I've seen you look worse." And there's that amazing smile that should be prescribed to people suffering from deep depression.

"Okay. Let's do it. We'll do the simple tweaky thing. That sounds good."

"I can do that anytime you want, just get on my calendar. Are you okay? Seriously, she had no right to say those things to you. I'll talk to her about it and you go back to yoga. See you in a few weeks."

And I was once again to hell and back, only this time in a matter of few minutes. McDreamy was as kind as could be, I had my exercise lifeline back and a reverse decision on the nipple procedure that I was very comfortable with. Big House surgery cancelled—Tweak and Tat scheduled in a few weeks.

I called Kim and gave her the update. "God I need this to be over!"

"Just let me know and I'll be there."

MAY 5

Linda, one of my HR colleagues who was also working on the acquisition, walked into my office a few weeks ago and informed me that, miraculously, she and her husband, Jeff, had decided to not just donate, but actually walk in the 3-Day with The Sole Sisters. They apparently choose one big charity event a year to participate in together and after they received my fundraising letter they decided it was time to walk sixty miles. I was completely blown away; I didn't really know her that well and honestly couldn't imagine why anyone in their right mind who doesn't have a very personal reason to do this would even consider it. Linda and Jeff were immediately adopted by The Sole Sisters, added to our email chains, and began training in earnest. When I finally asked her what made them choose this as their cause this year, she said, without hesitation, "You. You have been an inspiration to me; if you can do this, so can we. We'd be proud to walk with you and your sisters." This is not some cheesy made-for-TV movie script; these were her actual words. Being said to me.

When she left my office, I cringed with guilt. I am not an inspiration. I am just trying to find a way to increase my odds of living longer. It's completely selfish. The notion that I could inspire people—who don't even know me—to walk sixty miles does not compute in my brain. These people must be saints.

Later that day she came back in to my office with a silly smirk on her face. "Hey Jude, I don't want to get too personal or anything but...um, are you dating?"

"WHAT? No! Dating?!"

"Well..." She looked embarrassed, as if she may have crossed a line with me.

"Wait, why? I mean, why do you ask? I didn't mean to—it's just that the thought really hadn't crossed my mind. Like, not even on a good day."

"We know this guy. He's very sweet and he works with Jeff and I just thought you might enjoy meeting each other. That's all."

"Oh, well, I love meeting new people. I'd be up for that. I just don't know about the whole dating thing. I mean I haven't done it in seventeen years. And last time out, I had two breasts."

Now I'd done it. She looked horrified that I made a joke about it and started backing out of my office and the increasingly uncomfortable conversation.

"Linda, don't *worry* about it! I was just kidding; sorry, it's what I do when I get thrown off balance. I'm an idiot. I am actually flattered you asked. And a little astonished." Then I took a very deep yoga breath as I visualized another cliff drawing closer, and in slow-motion pushed the following words off my lips: "So, what is his name?"

"Philip." Her face lit up again. "Philip Robinson."

"Philip." A long pause as my brain registered the name. *Philip*. I was now mildly panicked and filled with butterflies for no good reason other than hearing a man's name and associating it with the petrifying, humiliating social art that is dating.

"Want to know more?"

I was standing on the precipice; I know it's a long way down. I know the jagged rocks at the bottom are treacherous and the nastiest ones hide just beneath the surface of the shoreline. But I dove in headfirst and prayed that I still had a bungee cord within reach.

"Sure. Tell me about him."

So we talked about this Philip Robinson who sounds painfully normal and is also a devoted father to a fifteen-year-old girl. As I listened to Linda speak I allowed myself the ridiculously wild fantasy that someday I might actually not only *attract* the opposite sex but possibly *have some*. But I don't have real hopes or even desires for a normal sex life anymore. I'm like a female eunuch. I look in the mirror and pretend that it's someone else's body. (Who would want to look at this?) I take pills that chemically thwart the last vestiges of my femaleness. I don't even think anything works anymore. So I put that fantasy away in favor of wanting to expand my social circle and meet some new and interesting people who are not healthcare professionals. Who knows? Philip might turn into a friend with whom I could go see a movie or a Yankees game, or perhaps the theater!

Linda is much too kind to suggest I meet someone that she didn't truly like and respect, right? Apparently he's a very good friend of Jeff's and she knows him quite well. She is starting to wrap up her spiel, her sales pitch about this Mr. Robinson—and sneaks in the magic words as her final punctuation. "...and he's gorgeous."

"*Seriously?*"

"Killer handsome. Blue eyes to die for."

"Oh. Well then..."

"Jude, I'm not kidding. I don't know how he's still single. *Gore-juss*."

"Gay?"

"Dates frequently."

"Player?"

"Couldn't tell you, but he pissed off his last girlfriend because he insisted on going to his daughter's softball games on the weekends, so they broke up."

"You just made that up!"

"Nope."

"Hmm. Okay, maybe...*Jesus*, I don't even know how to do this anymore. Maybe we can all meet for a drink after work some night?" And as the words came out of my mouth I thought about my belly-dancing tarot card with the prince holding the apple and the strange tingly feeling that was still in my stomach long after she left my office. The sound of his name was now irrevocably associated with the mystery prince.

However, weeks went by and Linda never scheduled that casual meet-up. Not another mention of our conversation or his blue eyes. I assumed that Philip heard about the pathetic newly single cancer chick and wasn't at all interested. But each day that passed after Linda told me about him was another day I felt more and more gloomy that an important aspect of my life was over too soon. And there was really nothing I could do about it other than be sad in my own surgically altered skin and pre-existing condition. Nevertheless, it was a pleasant fantasy while it lasted.

But this morning I woke up with a much different goal in mind: this would be my first ten-miler. I'd been training hard since the weather was getting warmer and starting to notice signs of growing muscle tone. I was meeting some other 3-Day walkers including Linda and Jeff at a trail in Hamden, Connecticut. I jumped out of bed at six to start my routine which includes sorting essentials such as moleskin, band-aids, extra socks, anti-bacterial hand wipes, sunglasses, cash, and lip balm for placement in my unstylish fanny pack and slathering on sunscreen head to toe. Next I taped my feet to ward off blisters before plunging them in to my socks filled with baby powder, and sneakers one size bigger than my normal gigantic size to allow for swelling toes. Then came the ferociously unflattering olive-colored, water-resistant hiking pants with the handy zippers above the knees so I can unzip into shorts when the sun comes out; a sleeveless T-shirt; an oversized sweatshirt; my pink "Survivor" baseball cap and zero makeup. Water bottle, energy bars, a full tank of gas.

This is go-time. I am an athlete now! Today is about focus and endurance, pure and simple. Flo-Jude!

I arrived at the rendezvous point completely psyched up to see if my body could withstand a ten mile trek on asphalt. On the inside I felt like a muscle-bound Olympic warrior-chick but in reality I looked like a misshapen man wearing tasteful hoop earrings and pink shoelaces. I didn't care if I looked ridiculous; I was bringing my A-game today. When Linda and Jeff and the others arrived we commenced stretching and introductions and small talk. I was leading the yoga moves and feeling smug. Two of the other walkers are survivors and we tentatively started talking about our hair and reconstruction which I guess comes with the territory.

As we were assembling at the start point to begin our journey, a silver BMW convertible pulled in to the parking lot, fast, driven by a man with dark aviator shades and a large handsome head. I immediately thought, "Damn, I wish *he* was walking with us." Then I remembered that distractions are for losers and I need to stay focused. Eyes on the prize: *Get through ten miles and live to tell about it. Snap out of it, Jude.*

Back to warm-ups at the starting gate when suddenly, the tall, broad-shouldered man began walking purposefully in our direction and I panicked that I might have actually said my stupid wish out loud. Linda spun around cheerfully and greeted him, introducing Large Handsome Man to the other walkers as I bent down to idiotically fiddle with my pink shoelaces because I needed to do something other than stand there looking frightful. I put my sunglasses on to hide my naked, unadorned eyes and give myself the ability to stealthily observe. He was laughing. He had a full head of shaggy brown hair. He was wearing sneakers and holding a water bottle. *He is walking with us!* Jeff walked over to me and said, "Hey Jude, let me introduce you to a friend of mine, Philip Robinson. Phil, this is Jude."

HOLY, HOLY CRAP. I have no hope. I may have my A-game with me but I left my A-face on the bathroom counter and I am about to meet the guy that I thought didn't want to meet me but apparently does, or maybe he just decided to come on the walk to check me out and is now grossly disappointed; or maybe this isn't about me at all but just a weird coincidence and maybe his hot new girlfriend is going to join us driving her convertible and looking like Malibu Barbie—but I am now a complete freak show of nerves and the sum total of confidence I had to start this day is now taking up space in my too-big sneakers, as I reach out my now-clammy hand to shake his and give myself away entirely. I smile and mutter something barely intelligible and go back to rearranging my fanny pack as if the exact placement of the lip balm and moleskin were crucial elements to the success of this walk. Kill me now, please. Or just get back in the Beemer and run me over with it.

As if the stress of meeting this guy and walking ten miles is not enough, today is Cinco de Mayo, so Linda and Jeff announce they have arranged for us all to meet at a Mexican place at the end of our walk, cleverly called Aunt Chiladas. If this is the casual meet-up Linda was planning it would have been nice if someone told ME about it.

We began the walk at a simple three-mile per hour pace. The trail is a clearly marked ten-mile paved path that is a haven for rollerbladers, power-walkers, bicyclists, and the occasional strolling couple. I was walking alone. I was making efforts to get involved in passing conversations with the group but I wasn't doing a great job of mingling. My head was on fire with embarrassment until someone in our group shouts to me, "Jude—how long have you been training?" It's Jeff and he's trying to pull me in.

"Since February." And thud. I couldn't come up with anything more interesting to say to extend my answer into a clever anecdote or an invitation for witty banter. In fact my mouth was still open because even it knew better than to put a period on that sentence, but nothing was forthcoming. Large Handsome Phil was now in my peripheral view to the left and gaining ground. C'mon, chemo-brain, engage! Wake up, social skills!

"February? Do you belong to a gym?" he asked from behind his sunglasses as he settled in to a gait that perfectly matched mine, letting me know he was trying to chat. I think. Or possibly get a closer look at my sporty zipper pants that look like an army parachute with an elastic waist band.

"Uh, no, I um. I walk outside. I hate gyms. I think they're smelly." *What am I, twelve?*

He laughed and took off his shades and looked me square in the eyes with two romance novel-worthy blue eyes, "Well, yeah. They're *gyms*. I think they're supposed to be. How often do you walk?" His accent was Bostonian and charming. He didn't run away repelled by my visage and slowly began doing something wildly exotic and exciting: he listened to me. And somehow we seamlessly moved from my training rituals, to the story about the flood at Green Acres, to Kim, to his daughter, to questions about family and jobs and life. Philip and I walked the remaining nine miles either talking to each other or stealing glances from behind our sunglasses trying to appear utterly nonchalant about the fact that we were *meeting each other.* After our ten-mile challenge was conquered, we triumphantly limped en masse to Aunt Chilada's and ordered pitchers of margaritas, piles of spicy food, and huge glasses of water to hydrate. We all sat at a long picnic table outside soaking up the sun and talking about the upcoming 3-Day in August.

Philip sat diagonally across from me and I found myself staring at his hands. They were the closest thing to perfect I have ever seen. I couldn't tell if it's just the whole Cinco de Mayo vibe or my raging endorphins, but I was feeling very good about myself for having completed this challenge. And for getting through the day without throwing up, falling down, making a scene, or quitting. And for meeting a nice man who didn't seem to mind that I have no eyebrows or discernible shape under my clothes; knew full well I am a recent cancer survivor—and allowed me to make him laugh; one of life's greatest joys.

"Hey, Phil," said Jeff, "why don't you do the walk with us in August? You did great today."

"No, I am pretty sure I can't take the time to train for sixty miles. Besides, you guys are in much better shape than me."

"Dude. You just did ten miles without training a day. We all hate you."

"Nah, I've got my daughter's games most weekends — it would be hard to squeeze in."

Linda hadn't lied. *Oh, my god, not even once.*

"Really?" I asked. "That's too bad; The Sole Sisters could use some more testosterone. Right now Jeff is the only one so we're calling him Sole Man." The Cinco de Mayo revelers broke in to enthusiastic choruses of "I'm a Sole Man," Blues Brothers style.

"I will do my best to get up to Boston, though," he said without looking up from his plate, "to see all you brave people at the finish line." The invisible cartoon bubble above my head read: *I sincerely hope so, Mr. Robinson, because you are the bomb.*

MAY 26

Linda and Jeff are holding their annual Memorial Day party which falls one day before mine. This year, my event is entitled "Fiesta Del Sol" in honor of the now legendary trip to Mexico. Julie is flying in to be a special guest tomorrow morning and I cannot wait to see her. I am expecting a pretty big crowd tomorrow and the weather is looking like it will cooperate. Monica's brother has a catering company and has come up with a fantastic South-of-the-Border menu including a salsa bar. I've been working on the garden for weeks and just opened the pool.

I am busy with final preparations and just as excited about going to the Kings', hoping that I might see Philip. I'm trying not to be too obvious with anyone other than Kim but she knows I'm nervous about seeing him again. This time, I put on makeup, a skirt, a top that shows some skin, a sparkly barrette in my short curly hair and dangly earrings. There will be no mistaking me for a shapeless man tonight. I pick up Kim on the way.

"Well now, you're looking mighty purty there, Miss Judy."

"Too much?"

"No, you look awesome. He'll be putty in your hands."

"Not too obvious?"

"Who gives a shit? Let's meet this Mr. Wonderful."

"I didn't say he was—I just said he's interesting. And I'm interested."

We arrive at the Kings', walk into the backyard and it's a mob scene; people everywhere. I scan the crowd and finally spot the tall, unmistakable Mr. Robinson. My butterflies become full-sized sparrows as I traverse the tight groupings of guests. Once inside the house to say hello to Linda and Jeff, I glance out the kitchen window and my heart skips a beat. There is Philip facing away from me with a tall, curvy brunette in a short denim mini-skirt and perfectly tanned, athletic legs, hugging his waist. Her pretty head is gently resting on his shoulder and crushing all the air out of my lungs. I stay upbeat while talking to the host and hostess then grab Kim for an aside.

"Oh honey, don't worry about it. There are a million other boys out there."

"Whatever. Does she have to be so tall and young? And have such long hair? I bet she has perfect boobs, too."

"C'mon, let's get some food and sangria. We don't need to stay long."

I am standing at the appetizer table, swigging down my drink and making small talk with strangers. I realize I have absolutely no reason to feel the way I do because I obviously mistook his good manners and kind attention for something else, but I am instantly catapulted back in time to my eighth-grade ugly-phase and despite my obvious efforts, feel as unattractive as a garden gnome. I mean, I looked a fright the day of the walk and I am forty-seven years old. I'm not going to ever attract a man like him. I am making a mess of the hummus dip with my pita bread, when Philip's date spots me and comes bounding to say a cheerful hello. God knows why.

"Hey, hi," she says in a breathy, high-pitched voice. Not much of a conversationalist.

"Hello." I manage with a polite smile. She has quite a bit of eye-makeup on and gorgeous eyes, but still looks way too young for him. What is it with men?

"I, um, I'm Julia. Nice to meet you."

"You as well. I'm Jude."
"I know, my Dad told me."

MAY 27

Fiesta del Sol went down in Green Acres history as one of the best parties ever. Over sixty people meandered in during the perfectly sunny, 75° day to walk the gardens, take a swim, or just hang out on the stone patio with a cold beverage. I had a big tent for the shade dwellers; an eclectic mix of music blared from the outdoor speakers and everyone commented on the fantastic selection of Mexican food. It was my first really big party since I got sick and everyone, to a person, said something wonderful and encouraging to me. My dad was looking around in wonderment at all the familiar faces and smiling from somewhere very deep inside; especially when he was with my brother, Victor. The connection between those two is indestructible. The family was here en masse; Julie and Kim were taking pictures; my Inner Circle and Priceline posse were here; Jay and Michelle, Lynn, Monica, Sonnie; friends old and new. I surveyed the crowd more than once and thought, "Lucky, lucky girl."

I wish I could bottle this day.

JUNE 11

How Jude Got Her Boob Back was almost over. Kim and I were in New York for my "office procedure" which was now taking on new dimensions since I met Mr. Robinson. I've been having reckless fantasies that our burgeoning friendship might take a turn into the bedroom someday, which is not to say I was doing this for him, particularly because that possibility was a total long-shot from the free-throw line, but he has completely reaffirmed my desire to want to feel whole and confident and rank somewhere on the sexy-meter someday, if that was still possible.

At McDreamy's office, a familiar young intern came in with the suction cups and said with a giggle, "Okay. Let's do this, Jude. Get down to your bra and let's see where this sucker looks good." I had worn a very sheer bra as instructed so we could see what it would look like and establish symmetry with the right breast before official tweaking commenced.

She peeled back my bra and after a long deliberation, stuck the suction cup right in the middle of the fake breast, flipped my bra back on to my shoulder and said, "Look in the mirror. What do you think?" I paused and slowly realized I was ill-equipped to make this momentous decision by myself.

"Howard?"

"Hmm. Hard to tell. A teeny bit to the left. OK. Now down a bit. That's better."

Kelly came barging in to witness the tableau facing the mirror and said, "Jude! We're finally doing this, huh? It's nipple time, girlfriend!"

"Yeah, can you believe it? Almost there." Now there are three women staring at my breasts and moving the cup around trying to find the sweet spot where it will reside for all eternity.

"Jude," said Kim, "I can't really tell because your real nip isn't hard. "

"Well, what do you want me to do, stand in front of the air conditioner?"

"Get her going, girl, we haven't got all day!"

All three women were good-naturedly laughing and I was trying to act as if this was completely normal and not become utterly humiliated. "Now take your bra off so we can see what it looks like without it, too. Cool, so how does that look, everyone?"

As if on cue in some twisted porno-parody of a sitcom, McDreamy walked in on the four of us and said, "Hey, I get a vote, too, don't I?" But after ten minutes of manipulations and me posing from every angle, no one could agree on where to put my new nipple and to be honest, I was not happy with how any of my options looked so far. Bra or no bra.

Then McDreamy said, "Did you lose even more weight? What happened to this one over here?" He cupped my good breast as if it were a leaking water balloon.

"I guess so. I mean, I wasn't going to say anything, but the fake one is really much bigger than my real one. I don't think I lost any more weight but it's possible, since I'm in training...."

"Jesus, why did I go so big with you?" he said, almost to himself.

"You didn't. It used to match. I was a 36C when I first met you, remember?"

"Well, with two breasts so different in size, we are not going to find symmetry today, ladies. We could stand here all day and Jude's not going to be happy. Let me make a suggestion: why don't you come back after the walk and let me fix this?"

"Fix what?"

"Jude, your left breast is a size bigger than your right one, now. Why don't you let me do a small implant on the right to even you out; take a little belly fat with liposuction and drop it in here to smooth this out" he was running his hands into my cleavage, "it will look so much prettier. This line is too harsh here. Then we'll know where to put the nipple. I can even fix this scar under here that's not healing as nicely as we'd like. But the way it is now, you'll just be unhappy. I know how particular you are."

"Kim, what do you think?" I was hesitating because I loved the sound of his words the last time I was here: *no more scars for you; you've been through enough.*

Without blinking or hesitating, she emphatically said, "Do it."

"*Really?*"

"Jude, it's not right; it's too big and you're uneven. Do the surgery, get it fixed and then we'll worry about where the nipple goes." And that was the first time she didn't try to gloss over the obvious disproportion and say things to make me feel better about it. Then of course it went to a vote to Kelly and the intern who replied in unison, "*Go for it!!*"

"Omigod, yes. Get rid of that Tori Spelling cleavage you've got going on there and smooth it out with some lipo! Excellent idea."

"You're young, Jude, do it right."

"Don't you want to be a hottie again?"

I was pretty sure more surgery wasn't going to move me into the "hottie" category, but I fell prey to plastic surgery peer pressure and caved. McDreamy assured me he would get me in on a cancellation and handle it as soon as the walk was over.

So, another setback and eventual leap forward in the reconstruction saga. I left New York without my new nipple, sadly enlightened that I looked worse than I thought I did and now required further surgical adjustment, but hopeful that McDreamy could make me look *"prettier"* which knocked *"very nice"* from its perch as my new goal towards wholeness and hopefully, someday, if there is a god, *sex.*

JUNE 12

I am doing the Loop on a training walk in the late afternoon and my mobile phone rings.

"Hi, this is Phil. Robinson. "

"Hi there. " OH MY GOD.

"Linda gave me your number, I hope you don't mind. "

"No, no, I am just, out for a training walk, actually. Only doing about three miles this afternoon. "

"Well, listen, I wanted to know if you'd be interested…there's an outdoor Shakespeare festival going on in Rowayton the next few weeks and I would love if you could join me. I have two tickets for June twenty-third. But I can easily exchange them if that date doesn't work for you. "

I stop walking and sit down on the curb. Did he just ask me out on a date?

"Oh, well that sounds great. I'm pretty sure I'm free that evening. I love Shakespeare. "

"I know. I remember you mentioning it at the Kings'. " Is this for real?

"That sounds wonderful. I'd love to. "

"I'll call you next week so we can firm up plans, okay?"

"Sure… "

"I also thought we'd go to dinner first at the River Cat. Have you ever been there?"

"No, I… "

"Good. I think you'll like it. They have a lot of vegetarian options. "

At this point I am so dumbfounded I just stop talking and he stalls for a moment as well. We are both still breathing, which is a good sign.

"So" he continues, "I guess I'll talk to you soon."

"Okay, yes, yes, we'll talk next week. Bye now."

I have a date with the prince holding the apple.

JUNE 21

Lynn and I were walking towards Radio City Music Hall to see k.d. lang and Lyle Lovett and his Large Band in concert together; an impromptu invitation that I was tickled to receive. As we got closer to our destination, the swell of T-shirt-buying tourist traffic began to intensify and nearly suffocated us as we tried to walk two abreast without getting shoved or trampled. It wasn't working so we began taking turns in the brave lead position, resorting to intermittent yelling or lip-reading when we could make eye contact. There is a skill to this. Eventually we gave up and just walked in silence until we found a more peaceful alternate route to the theater.

"So how is Big Syl?"

"It's so hard for her. I mean, physically, she is a rock, but I'm not quite sure how she manages the day-to-day with Dad. I worry about her not taking care of herself but we've been having regular Sibling Summits, as we call them, to try and provide support; particularly to Jodi and Glenn who are on the front lines with them every day. I don't think it will be long before she can't take care of him alone and he'll need to be in a facility of some kind. Shit, I can't believe I just said that out loud."

"So sad. It was nice to see him at your party though. Such a frail man, but so sweet and kind; you can tell."

Dad has entered a truly ghostly realm. People talk about him as if he is already gone because he is so obviously on the path to leaving us, disappearing before our eyes, but can still be seen and felt and spoken to. The worst is yet to come for him and for everyone who loves him, but the faint light that flickered in him from time to time at the party was clearly advising us to forge ahead with our lives. So we do.

"Did your cousin Julie like the wine I brought her? She said she liked Cabs."

"You totally made her day, Lynn! I was so relieved to have her back at Green Acres for a few days without having to visit a hospital! I'm so glad the two of you hit it off."

We discussed the upcoming 3-Day, and all the people in my life who attended the Fiesta del Sol; some of whom were also becoming people in Lynn's life. The Inner Circle was getting fuzzy around the edges, expanding, intersecting, and casually re-forming with other concentric rings of relationships in such unexpected ways. It's gratifying. And I stupidly gave myself credit for bringing these wonderful people together when in fact they'd been holding *me* together and all I did was get sick and throw a big party for us.

Then she resumed her careful yet precise interview, which is typical for Lynn. I've come to appreciate her skill, like Kim's, to gently persuade me to talk about things that in other company would be better left unsaid. She asked me to reach back to the hardest days and explain to her what motivated me to keep going. I expect she feared to hear such news about her own health someday and was inquiring about the reality of facing it all down. When the odds are that one in seven women will be diagnosed, this is not morbid curiosity on her part; it's research.

After the concert, she and I headed to B.B. King's to listen to some jazz. During a late night decaf conversation, Lynn accidentally and quite innocently aggravated a raw nerve and I exploded into a self-defeating, idiotic monologue that pushed her back in her chair and left her staring at me, astonished by my reaction.

"So, you're excited about your big date, Jude?"

"Okay, Lynn, put yourself in his shoes. The guy can date anyone he wants. *Anyone.* Do you have even a remote idea of what I look like under this blouse?"

"Well, I..."

"I mean, let's be real. It's just us girls here. This is not going to end well for me."

"Hmm. Aren't you perhaps jumping the gun a bit? How can you possibly predict how he'll react? He might already know...or *presume.* And it's just a date, you're not expected to..." Anyone listening closely might have actually heard the snap.

"No! I'm *a freak!* It's disgusting, Lynn. I look nothing like what a real, normal woman should look like. Go on line and Google 'breast reconstruction' and then try to picture yourself *looking like that,* naked with someone else, and tell me that is not a horrifying prospect for both parties. Not to mention the scars all over my chest and armpit. I can't even look at myself. And did I mention I still can't feel a goddamned thing? I don't even know when I've bumped into something unless I look down. You have no idea what this feels like until you're standing in front of the mirror trying to decide what to wear that will de-emphasize your unevenness, when in reality it won't really matter because once the charade is over—if I don't first scare him away with the fucked-up story of the last few years of my life—he'll speed off in his fancy car at the speed of light. I'm not sure why I even said yes to him. I'm just not that special, okay?!!"

"Oh, dear, I've upset you. I'm so sorry, Jude. I just think...well. It doesn't matter what I think. But I hope you're pleasantly surprised."

This lovely woman had invited me to a concert and doted on me the entire evening, and this was how I paid her back. What a self-absorbed asshole I can be sometimes. But as Lynn discovered, I can obviously talk about the excruciating *past* if probed with the right questions, but the immediate future is forbidding and hopeless for a whole new set of reasons.

> *Resuming a normal life, whatever that means anymore, means circumventing roadblocks that were non-existent when I was sick. I want to detour around this first date and see it in the rearview mirror. I want it to be over so I can say I did it and go back to being a hermit with nice shoes. I am finally beginning to understand what a humiliating event this could turn out to be. Dammit.*

JUNE 23

Jay and Michelle's seventeen-year-old daughter Jessica offered to help me clean the pool this summer for spending money and to be a nice neighbor. I still didn't have enough upper body strength to even skim the pool, much less vacuum it. Lucky for me, she showed up once a week like clockwork. I walked out to the pool area where she was working.

"Okay Jessica, I need your help."

"Shoot, Jude." Jessica has the same upbeat and highly energized persona of her mother.

"I have a date tonight."

"Shut *up*. You do NOT."

"Well, yes, as ridiculous as that sounds...."

"No, it's *totally awesome!*" She drops the vacuum and comes charging over to me like a happy puppy. "Soooo?"

"I don't know what to wear."

"HA! Easy one. First date: tight jeans—no "mom jeans"—and feminine top. Not too much skin. Dangly earrings. Some sparkle if you've got it. Next?"

"Where did you just pull that from?"

"C'mon, it's common knowledge. Every girl knows that. What else do you need, shoes? Sandals with small heels. No flats unless you're doing a lot of walking. Makeup? Basic and nothing flashy. Lip *gloss*, not lipstick. Oh, and if it's super-hot, never, never wear shorts. Opt for a denim skirt."

"You ought to have your own call-in show."

"Happy to help, Jude! So exciting. You *must* let me know how it goes."

I took Jessica's advice and managed to dress myself and leave the house on time. I met Philip at our rendezvous point, his house, and we drove together in his car with the top down on a perfectly balmy summer night, to the River Cat Grille and a thoroughly enchanting evening of theater. The Bard's *The Comedy of Errors* was colorful and well-played by local actors, but the dating theater is superb. The costumes and dialog; the lighting and props, the tone and the pacing all seemed to work. When we got back to his house he very gently asked some of the hard questions. I answered by dancing around most of them but was astonished when the Big One landed as softly as it did.

"Yes, I've had... a few surgeries; it goes with the territory." And I waited for the inevitable *it's-getting-late* cue, and a prompt escort to the door while holding my breath and staring into my water glass.

"I thought so. I'm just so sorry you've had to go through all that. I can't imagine…"

"Yes, well. *It saved my life*," I said more than a little defensively.

"Good thing, too."

Hold the presses: he's absolutely right. It was a good thing; and the right and only thing to do under the circumstances. There was no viable door #2 for me. I made the decision to have the surgeries and go through agonizing treatment, and I needed to stop blaming everything around me for the results. Just like my divorce, it was my choice. And it beats the pants off the alternative. If I'm going to shout, then my defensive and negative energy needs to go to shouting at the medical research community, or our healthcare system, or stupid politicians, or raising money for a cure so women after me have easier choices to make — not toward the nice people orbiting my Shiny New, Post-Cancer Land World.

"Philip, just so I'm clear; you don't seem to mind…about all this."

"Mind that there was a medical option to save your life? I should say not. Besides, I'll let you in on a little secret."

"Uh-oh."

"I'm a leg man."

"Amen to that."

JUNE 24

"Oh good, you're up."

"Yes, ringing phones will do that. It's two in the morning, Bootie."

"Oh my *god*, Kim."

"That good, huh?"

"Better. Go back to sleep. Coffee tomorrow?"

"Wouldn't miss it."

JUNE 28

Kim and I were packing up our offices a few days ago getting ready to walk away from our jobs at Hyperion and reminiscing about the highlights of the last few years, when I received an email from Alex, copying Tony, Ravi, and Arjun. It was an invitation. He and his wife and son rented a six-bedroom villa in his hometown for the month of July and wondered if any of us would like to come spend some time with them. *In Marbella, Spain.*

"Thelma!!!"

"Oh no, what now?" Kim tore into my office.

"Read this."

"Holy shit! Is he kidding? A villa in Spain?!"

"No, he is not kidding. This is real, Kimberly. Should we do it? *Can* we do it?"

"Let's think about this, Louise; in two days, we'll be unemployed with sizable severance packages. Our biggest logistical hurdles will be finding seats next to each other on a plane, cute sandals, and dog sitters. I vote for HELL YES." After screaming and hugging and making adolescent fools of ourselves, we informed the Rodas that we would happily accept their kind offer and started making reservations. I had absolutely no plans for the summer other than to find a new job and live through the 3-Day. And a glimmer of hope that maybe there will be more date nights with Philip. Kim was leaving HR behind and starting an interior design business, which is her true passion, but all of that could certainly wait a few weeks until we returned.

But now that the last day of work was finally here, I felt bewildered and sad. How could I permanently detach from a job that has been such a solid anchor—truly one of the only dependable constants in my life these past few tumultuous years?

Most of the other employees who were laid off due to the acquisition had already left. Hideaki and Beth both accepted new jobs elsewhere and had been gone for weeks; it was like a ghost town, with empty offices and desks on every floor. I sat down at my computer and wrote embarrassingly heartfelt emails to Steve and

Dean. I did not have the courage to say out loud how much they meant to me. Thankfully, they were both in California so I didn't have to face them after they read it. I crafted and sent thank you notes to every person from work who contributed to the 3-Day, for their generosity and friendship. (My total was now up around $14,000.00 and I was on the leader board on the Komen site.)

I walked across the hall to David's old office which sat empty again, sat in his old chair, and took a long, slow, bittersweet breath. I told him I was leaving behind another piece of our history today but would carry him in my heart wherever I go. I said this to him, to the stale office air, as if I had a choice in the matter. I let myself drift back to the day I dutifully and carefully packed up his belongings to bring to his wife as if I was folding the flag of a dead soldier; the day I told Kim I was filing for divorce and listened to her expert and empathetic counsel realizing I had found a true friend; the night I got that fateful call from the hospital and wrecked my office like a five-year-old; the nonstop barrage of heartbreaking news I absorbed while working here. I will be perpetually grateful for colleagues who became so much more than friends when they could have kept their safe distance. And finally, I allowed myself some justifiable sorrow that I will not see them every day, all in one place, ever again.

I sent out emails to remind my dynamic, evolving circles that I can't be found at this work email after today: Monica, Priscilla and Kyle, Lynn, Jay and Michelle, and Sonnie; I called everyone in my family personally to let them know I'm packing it in at Hyperion and leaving for Marbella in a few days with Kim. I was worried about being out of the country for ten days but Jodi assured me if anything happened she'd find me. She also reminded me to keep training and to pack my sneakers. Jayne asked if I was trying to slip out of the country to avoid walking sixty miles next month, and Victor sent hilarious and supportive emails *in Spanish*. It was troubling that I wouldn't get to see my parents before I flew but Julie assured me, "Nothing will happen—*just go!*"

I vividly recall an eleventh hour visualization on the operating table just before my mastectomy when I dreamed of someday going to Spain—instinctively believing that it would heal my very soul.

Now I can't help but wonder if there isn't some larger force out there in the vast and complicated universe, that finally acknowledged I've had enough madness in my life and it's time to turn this thing around.

I leave David's office without turning back, walk down the hall to Kim's and see that she has already left and moved everything out. Then back to my office taking one last look at the bare walls, empty file cabinets and vacant space as if I was never there.

As if none of it ever happened.

JULY 6

Kim is sound asleep on the train from Madrid to Malaga. We're planning to rent a car to drive to the villa on the hill in Marbella, and into the waiting arms of our generous friends and our magically appearing Spanish holiday. We have one guide book, two phrase books, twelve pairs of shoes between us and absolutely no itinerary or agenda. We have no expectations or to-do lists. We are ready for anything and prepared for nothing. I don't have a husband or a job waiting for me. I am limitless. For the first time in my adult life, I am on a journey entirely of my choosing. I am *free*. My best friend is at my side and family and friends are just a phone call or text away. A wonderful man took me to dinner the night before we left and in his own way, let me know he would be there for me when I get back if I want him to be.

In my heart I know I am the most honest version of myself I have ever been. So I dig out my laptop and begin to write. On my hard drive are segments of a diary, two calendars, a chemo journal, research documents, and pages upon pages of essays and angry rants in various stages of completion. I don't try to make sense out of any of it. I simply can't. Not yet.

So I start at the end and decide to work my way backwards. *Kim is sound asleep on the train from Madrid...*

"What are you doing with your laptop? We don't have jobs anymore, remember?"

"I think I am writing a book."

"What about?"

"The last year and a half of my life."

"No one will ever believe it."

BREAST LEFT UNSAID

I wrote *Breast Left Unsaid* to thank my family and friends who had the courage and heart to show up for the hard stuff. They know who they are. And now, so do you.

It was also meant to celebrate that they are still in my life and that I value every day with them, particularly my sisters, Jayne Callirgos McMurdy and Jodi Lussier, my brother Victor C. Callirgos, Daryl Kenny Callirgos, Glenn Lussier, Maggie and Mac McMurdy, Victor Philip Callirgos, The Kevins (Kenny and Callirgos), Kenny Callirgos, Geoff Lussier and of course, my mother, Sylvia M. Callirgos, a/k/a "Big Syl." I quite simply don't know how I got so lucky.

To my dearest Kimberly Howard, who still lives around the corner, and my cousin Julie Brootkowski, who still lives across the country: for their unfailing hopefulness and resilience, I am embarrassingly grateful. I am also bursting with pride to acknowledge Philip Robinson, my amazing husband (yes, husband), and my step-daughter Julia Grace, who gave me the mental and physical space (i.e., I hogged the home office for the better part of a year) to focus on this book.

And to each of the many honorary Sole Sisters—whether you walked, donated, or just prayed for our sneakers to hold out—you will always be in my heart.

This being my first book, I confess to having learned that it can only take shape when there is some objective someone standing over you letting you know when you are coloring outside the lines or your grammar sucks, or your punctuation is off, or whether you've nailed something on the head with a sledgehammer or a deft touch—or missed an important point entirely. This is the work of an editor and mine was superb. Victoria Wright of Bookmark Services helped on all these fronts, but most importantly by encouraging me to keep going; even when I didn't want to write a section and revisit something particularly difficult. I would not have completed this book without her fine work, counsel, and friendship.

To Lynn Woodhall and Jeff Dahlberg for their caring spirit and attention to detail when it came time to proofread; to Sheila J. Levine, Esq., of Levine Samuel, LLP, for her above and beyondness on the legal front; and to Barbara Fisher of Levan Fisher Design for bringing the book design to life.

I would also like to thank all the unnamed healthcare professionals who did their jobs superbly at places like Greenwich Hospital, the Bendheim Cancer Center, Danbury Hospital, and Memorial Sloan-Kettering, especially Drs. Merlin Sung Lee (Bones) and Babek J. Mehrara (McDreamy). I thank all of you for your patience with me. And to organizations such as breastcancer.org, Komen for the Cure, Hip Hats with Hair, Chemo Angels, and so many other non-profits that understand the tragic and absurd world of Cancer Land and selflessly provide hope to patients and loved ones on a daily basis.

Finally, I dedicate this book in its entirety to my father, Victor Albert Callirgos, who passed away on December 13, 2008, sadly and remarkably on the five-year anniversary of David's death. I like to think of the two of them together, lounging around in togas, or heavenly bathrobes, enjoying the peace and perfection of a place where none of this stuff matters anymore.

To my father, I send all the love put into these pages.

Made in the USA
Charleston, SC
29 November 2012